PSI SUCCESSFUL BUSINESS LIBRARY

THE LEADER'S GUIDE

15 ESSENTIAL SKILLS

Randall D. Ponder

The Oasis Press® / PSI Research
Central Point, Oregon

Published by The Oasis Press
© 1998 by Randall D. Ponder

This publication is designed to provide accurate and authoritative information in regard
to the subject matter covered. It is sold with the understanding that the publisher is not
engaged in rendering legal, accounting, or other professional service. If legal advice or
other expert assistance is required, the services of a competent professional person
should be sought.

> — *from a declaration of principles jointly adopted by a committee of*
> *the American Bar Association and a committee of publishers.*

Editor: Janelle Davidson

Book Designer: Constance C. Dickinson

Compositor: Jan Olsson

Cover and Illustration Designer: Steven Burns

Please direct any comments, questions, or suggestions regarding this book to
The Oasis Press®/PSI Research:

> Editorial Department
> P.O. Box 3727
> Central Point, OR 97502
> (541) 479-9464
> info@psi-research.com *email*

The Oasis Press® is a Registered Trademark of Publishing Services, Inc.,
an Oregon corporation doing business as PSI Research.

Ponder, Randall D., 1959–
    The leader's guide : 15 essential skills / Randall D. Ponder.
       p.   cm. -- (PSI successful business library)
    Includes index.
    ISBN 1-55571-434-X (pbk.)
    1. Leadership.   I. Title.   II. Series.
HD57.7.P66 1998
658.4'092--dc21   98-18539

Printed in the United States of America
First Edition 10 9 8 7 6 5 4 3 2 1

♻ Printed on recycled paper when available.

This book is dedicated to the members of my family who gave me the encouragement and love that helped motivate me to create it. I give special thanks to Linda, forever my wife and best friend, and to Josette, my mother, who has been my number one supporter throughout my life.

TABLE OF
CONTENTS

FOREWORD

When visiting with clients all over the world, I am continually astonished by how many people are overmanaged and under-led. Instead of focusing on the basics, most managers spend inordinate amounts of time, energy, and money following the latest management fad. If you are tired of fads — which at best provide only short-term results — you are ready for *The Leader's Guide: 15 Essential Skills*.

The topic of leadership has been discussed and debated for years, and many books are available to introduce you to this vital subject. However, *The Leader's Guide: 15 Essential Skills* goes beyond the basics to explore the fifteen areas that all great leaders must understand and implement to be successful.

The overriding point of this leader's guide is that leadership can be learned. All one needs to do is practice the fail-safe strategies outlined by Randall Ponder. These are some of the analytical and technical skills that you must master if you want to be an effective manager. However, Randall does not stop there. He takes you beyond management and shows you step-by-step how to master the fundamentals needed to initiate and sustain healthy relationships with your team members, colleagues, and customers. He provides you with a guide for achieving dramatic and strategic improvements in performance, productivity, and profitability.

The everyday challenges of commercial, nonprofit, and community organizations — challenges such as global competition, change, downsizing, restructuring, and employee retention — will become increasingly acute throughout the world as we move into the twenty-first century. Organizations of all sizes can realize competitive, economic, and financial advantages in the proper leadership of their team members. When people are properly led, there are no insurmountable challenges because their creativity, loyalty, job satisfaction, and commitment increase dramatically.

Throughout *The Leader's Guide*, there is a strong differentiation between the successful activities and roles of effective managers and leaders. Randall builds on these distinctions and offers you comprehensive skill-oriented solutions. Hence, *The Leader's Guide* accomplishes a unique task of teaching the manager how to be a more effective leader and teaching the leader how to be a more effective manager. Mastering the skills described in *The Leader's Guide* will enable you to function as a winning manager with knowledge that will transform the way you think about management and leadership.

The Leader's Guide will teach you leadership in easy-to-understand language and motivate you to apply this knowledge because of the dramatic results you will achieve. This book outlines new roles for supervisors and managers, roles that managers and supervisors must master in today's super lean, and often mean, corporate, nonprofit, and community organizations. Mastering these new roles and responsibilities is particularly important since most traditional managers, who often have little knowledge about leadership, will continue to be asked to assume more of the duties and responsibilities once solely reserved for executives.

Regardless of how long you have been a supervisor, manager, or leader, *The Leader's Guide* will show you how to master the fifteen core essentials of leading people. So what are you waiting for? Don't just read this book, devour it, and I am sure that you will thrive in this highly competitive and rapidly changing global economy.

WOLF J. RINKE, PH.D., C.S.P.

Author
Winning Management:
Six Fail-Safe Strategies for Building High-Performance Organizations

PREFACE

Congratulations on taking a major step toward becoming a more effective leader. This book is for those of you who have leadership responsibilities in many walks of life: work, community, social, religious, and family. It is a comprehensive and quick way for you to understand the significant issues involved in getting the right things accomplished when you are in charge of the results. You may have already studied many of the individual subjects discussed in this book, and you may be quite knowledgeable in some areas. This book will provide you with the opportunity and framework to consolidate your knowledge with time-proven principles of leadership, while focusing on your use of common sense, sound judgment, and a blending of managerial and leadership skills. The techniques and principles in this book are fundamental concepts that are presented in the context of leadership; you can put them to use immediately. Later, you can study specific areas in more detail by using other available resources that will help you gain as much expertise as you desire.

When using this book as a guide, no situation, challenge, or task will be too great for you to face. You can benefit from using this book whether you are a newly appointed supervisor, the owner of a small business, a manager in a community nonprofit organization, the head of a club, or the chief executive of a global organization.

This book will help you:

► Increase your knowledge of leadership principles and how they apply to your specific responsibilities;

► Intensify your leadership presence by helping you become more effective, proactive, and results-oriented;

► Learn specific skills and techniques to utilize change, to resolve conflict, and to increase the productivity and morale of your subordinates and coworkers;

► Gain support and commitment from subordinates by inspiring them to achieve results and be more self-directing, and by guiding them to seek more leadership responsibility; and

► Enjoy being a leader.

PART I

UNDERSTANDING
LEADERSHIP

CHAPTER 1

IMPORTANCE OF A LEADER

L eadership is the ability to get the right things accomplished at the right time with the assistance of other people. Several words in this definition will be explained as you proceed through this book. For example, how do you get this ability? How do you determine the right things, and when are they considered accomplished? Finally, who are the people that will help you, and how do you get them to assist you?

Leaders are ordinary people who usually have an official position of responsibility. Organizations, subordinates, superiors, and peers depend upon leaders to do the best job that they can. Since so many people rely upon them, leaders have an obligation to do everything within their power to accomplish their job. An exciting aspect of leadership is that anyone who chooses to can become a leader. There has been much debate over the years as to whether people are born as leaders or if they can be developed into leaders through experiences and education. The consensus is that a willing person can learn specific skills and knowledge and emerge as a leader or a better leader than they are now. Becoming a leader can occur if you are shy or extroverted, educated or not, organized or disorganized, charismatic or dull. The only requirements are a desire to become a leader and a willingness to develop the skills.

Everyday Leadership

A central point of this book is to show how much more effective you will become if you practice being a leader in your everyday life, at work, leisure, and home. This does not mean that you must always seek to be the person who takes charge and plans everything. Everyday leadership means that you use simple principles and concepts to approach all leadership situations with a sense of purpose, the right attitude, and a commitment to get your goals accomplished with the able and committed assistance of other people.

Although people often think of leaders as being at the top rungs of an organization, this belief is not realistic because leaders exist at all levels in an organization. Most of the leaders at the pinnacle of any organization got there by learning and honing their skills at lower levels. If you have an entry level job in a restaurant, for example, you can be a leader simply by practicing the skills required of leaders, increasing your participation in the company's decision-making process and assuming as much responsibility as you want. As a leader in low hierarchical organizations, such as in small businesses or in the high technology industry, you may work in teams with other leaders and non-leaders and find your roles changing as teams regroup from project to project.

In addition to applying to the work environment, everyday leadership helps you become more successful at home and during after-hours activities. You will find that by practicing leadership skills, your family will function more cohesively, with fewer conflicts between parents and children and among the siblings. Leadership knowledge is particularly helpful in your group activities such as school associations, neighborhood meetings, sports teams, and clubs. Often in these settings, several people may feel either that they have the right answers to getting the job done or that they just simply want to be the leader, whether they have the skills or not. By effectively applying leadership principles in these situations, you can assume the leadership role yourself or help others become better leaders.

Leadership Versus Management

Most people use the terms leader and manager interchangeably. A closer look, however, shows that a leader may or may not excel at management, and a manager may or may not be a good leader. What are the distinctions between the two roles?

Leaders focus on areas such as identifying problems, managing changes in the internal and external work environments, structuring the organization, and motivating groups to achieve their goals. Their mission is to ensure that the organization achieves specific objectives by subordinates who are energized and excited about their vision and direction. Leaders and their team of motivated subordinates implement their strategy by using specific managerial techniques, such as planning, organizing, problem solving, and communicating. Leaders feel comfortable about challenging the status quo methods of running an organization, motivating their subordinates and departments to get moving in support of organizational objectives, and dealing with the changing business environment. Leaders must do more than identify opportunities, establish vision, and set broad goals. They must have the means to implement their goals, otherwise their organization will stagnate. This is where the management component of leadership is important.

Managers concern themselves with getting the job done in the most efficient and effective manner. They know there are problems, identified by their leader, and they want to find solutions, so that projects and operations stay within budget and on schedule. Although concerned with the broad leadership issues identified above, managers focus more on the short-term, day-to-day, and week-to-week goals of how to implement the leader's vision without taking a lot of risk. A traditional listing of a manager's general functions includes planning, organizing, communicating, and monitoring.

A leader can put to good use many of the specific managerial skills shown above, and the manager can be more effective when thinking as a leader thinks. A wide overlapping area exists where a leader routinely performs several managerial functions and the manager assumes leadership roles. It is exciting, therefore, to envision what the leader and manager can accomplish if they focus on the specific skills necessary for them to do their jobs better. This set of skills will broaden their abilities by helping them become better managers if they are already a leader or to become better leaders if they are a manager. The best overall situation for an organization, whether it is a business, nonprofit, or family unit, is to have a sufficient number of people who can function both as strong leaders and strong managers. Otherwise, major organizational needs will go unfulfilled, which you will read about later in the book.

Many managers do not desire to become leaders and are more interested in simply doing their job well. However, by beginning to think and act like a leader, they automatically will become better managers. With the huge amount of complex change that will continue to occur into the next century — such as competitive domestic and global pressures, speed of technological innovation, restructuring, and constant economic uncertainty — traditional ways of managing organizations will not work well or at all in the future. Organizations of all types need more people at every level thinking like leaders, not managers. Leaders with vision, persistence, and skill will be the primary driving force that will enable organizations to succeed.

This book's goal is to help you understand that to succeed at leadership you must learn certain skills and apply them to your specific duties at work, home, and in the community. You will perform best as a leader if you concentrate on doing certain skills well. It is not necessary to do each one perfectly, and it is reasonable to believe that you may have some reluctance or difficulty in sharpening some of these skills. Nevertheless, successful leaders are aware that, since they must attend to many areas in their organization, it is wise to gain some knowledge about those areas and apply that knowledge on the job. You can, one step at a time, master simple techniques that will help you lead others in all walks of life.

Leadership Skills

Leadership skills are classified into three categories: technical and analytical, relationship, and strategic. The technical and analytical skills, which are discussed in chapters 4 through 9, are the primary skills traditionally thought of as the management of things. These six skills include mastering job specific skills, solving problems and making decisions, managing priorities, managing a project, monitoring progress, and promoting training and development.

Relationship skills, discussed in chapters 10 through 15, form an intermediate level of people skills. These skills include communication, teamwork, motivation, diversity, conflict resolution, and coaching.

Finally, strategic skills, in chapters 16 through 18, comprise the upper level of leadership skills at which the leader provides long-term focus and direction for the organization through vision, strategy, and change.

CHAPTER 2

YOUR LEADERSHIP STYLE

An important point in this chapter is that effective leaders can be true to their own nature and not have to assume radically different personae when in a leadership position. A person's mannerisms and personality typically do not have to change when assuming a leadership role. This does not mean that great leaders do not make some changes in their leadership presence and style, especially when changes are needed. These changes occur primarily after self study, evaluation sessions with superiors or subordinates, or on-the-job experience. Develop your own leadership style, therefore, based upon your own set of beliefs and personality traits, as well as what you learn from studying leadership.

Theories of Leadership

There are scores of leadership theories, models, and studies available for you to examine, if you choose. Although developed primarily in the 20th century by scholars, leadership ideas have existed at least since A.D. 100. Thanks to these great men and women, the curious have been able to analyze leaders on the basis of personality, situations, interaction with others, psychology, politics, humanism, and perception, to name a few. In addition to the theories, there are countless leadership surveys, tests, and aptitude indicators that are available to determine a leader's style and interests.

What can you do when faced with this complexity of leadership information? Most leaders do not study the many theories of leadership in detail. Some general knowledge is helpful, however, to know what the relevant major issues are so that you can apply them to your specific situation. These issues will be explained in this chapter. Then you can choose to study in more detail those areas that are of most interest to you.

Leadership Orientations

To help prepare you for your leadership role, you will briefly examine five categories of leadership orientations in this chapter. Since every leader has a distinct style made up of combinations of these orientations, it is impossible to accurately predict your style without a thorough analysis. As with most leaders, you will tend to use different styles when faced with different situations. The orientations in each category present two extremes between which leaders have to determine the right balance for themselves, based upon their personality and specific leadership challenges. For example, there are effective leaders who have high orientation scores in both relationship and task; others score high in relationship and low in task. By understanding these five leadership orientations, you will be better able to understand the framework within which most leaders operate.

- ▶ Democracy or autocracy.
- ▶ Participation or direction.
- ▶ Relationship or task.
- ▶ Consideration or initiation.
- ▶ Action or inaction.

Democracy or Autocracy Orientation

These two orientations are the first classification because they encompass attributes of the other four orientations. It makes sense that leaders tend to lean naturally toward one or the other because followers will do either one of two things. They will do what they are asked to do, thus requiring the supervision of a teaching and facilitating type of democratic leader, or what they are made to do, which requires a more punishing and coercing autocrat. There is no conclusive proof as to which type of orientation is more effective at getting bottom-line results. One may be more effective in different organizations or situations than the other. A person's style of leadership, however, does affect employee job satisfaction, although the effects vary from person to person. A higher degree of satisfaction in an organization will encourage loyalty, teamwork, and sharing of the leader's goals; each of these can lead to higher levels of personal and organizational productivity.

Democratic leaders focus on their followers because they feel the welfare of their team is of great importance. They tend to be easily approachable, relationship oriented, and considerate of others' feelings. They prefer to lead their teammates by collaboration and empowerment. They are convinced that tasks will be better accomplished if their subordinates' needs are tended to. These teammates tend to have high job satisfaction.

Autocrats primarily are concerned with tasks for which they are responsible. They believe the key is to focus less on subordinates and their needs and more on the work-related issues. In doing so, they use their position to prescribe solutions and direct others to comply. This type of leader usually has more subordinates with low levels of job satisfaction than does the democratic leader.

Participation or Direction Orientation

Leadership also can be analyzed in terms of how much contribution the leader obtains from subordinates before solving a problem or making a decision. As previously discussed, most leaders are situational, and they use both styles on different occasions.

A popular leadership trend since the 1980s has been to encourage employee participation in problem solving and decision making. By obtaining and considering the suggestions of subordinates, a leader has access to more data, experience, and opinions. Participation can occur when the leader either delegates total responsibility for tasks or allows subordinates to participate in a task's problem-solving and decision-making processes. A more restrictive form of participation is used when a leader discusses the task with subordinates but ultimately makes the decision as to what will be done. By using a participative style of leadership, a leader does not relinquish the responsibility to get the job done, but gives subordinates the authority to help arrive at the right decision to get the job done correctly. Participation is particularly effective in less structured or rapidly changing work environments.

Leaders who have a direction orientation decide what needs to be done and communicate it to subordinates. They may or may not explain why a course of action was chosen, and they may use persuasion techniques to bolster their directives. These leaders autocratically assume that, since they know the right answer, seeking input from subordinates is unnecessary. They may rationalize the use of a directive style by citing organizational problems, such as low employee educational levels and competence, even though they may not be applicable. The degree to which a leader may be directive depends upon a number of factors. For example, leaders tend to be more directive when there is high uncertainty in the situation, little time is available, their experience level is low, a short-term increase in productivity is needed, or they exercise a high degree of positional or organizational power. Directive leadership tends to be used more than participative leadership in slow-changing situations or where less employee input is needed.

Relationship or Task Orientation

The best leaders concern themselves both with people relationships and the tasks for which they are responsible because tasks usually are accomplished more effectively when human factors are considered. The degree of integration of task and relationship varies considerably with each leader; the exact mix partly depends upon task urgency, subordinates' work performance and ability, organizational climate, and the leader's natural inclination towards one orientation or the other.

Leaders who set relationships as a priority recognize the synergistic effects of attending to the human side of work. This does not mean they are less concerned with task accomplishment but that they know the best way to achieve high quality success is to make sure subordinates' needs are considered. They do this by maintaining warm, close, and friendly relations with their followers and by openly trusting and supporting them.

A complete task orientation means that a leader has the job that must get done foremost in mind. Without seeking input from subordinates, they structure the work, define the goals, allocate resources, and focus on achieving production quotas or delivery of services. People are of concern, but only because they are necessary to get the work done. This leader uses an inflexible, no-nonsense approach with subordinates.

Consideration or Initiation Orientation

Considerate leaders do what any considerate person would do, but in the context of leadership. Since they concern themselves with subordinates' interests and well-being, they are sensitive towards their feelings, needs, and goals. Before making decisions, they seek suggestions from subordinates and consider what effects these decisions will have on the team. By openly praising and privately correcting subordinates, they establish a working environment in which people trust, respect, and follow them.

Initiation refers to a leader's ability to start activities and organize work. Strong initiators prefer not to let the group completely structure its work or make all of the on-the-job decisions. They prefer not only to determine what must be done but also who does it and how it is to be done.

Consequently, they focuses on tasks, and most of their daily initiatives occur simply to facilitate achievement of work-related goals.

Since there can be overlap in these two orientations, a leader could be both highly considerate and initiating and still be effective. A good example is a leader who is quite particular about structuring the work, but considers what effect the structure will have on subordinates. People appreciate a thoughtful boss, but they also are thankful if he or she is organized, structured, and mission-oriented. Their positive reaction to an initiating leader could lead to increased consideration by the leader — a winning situation for all.

Action or Inaction Orientation

Action-oriented leaders involve themselves with accomplishing work responsibilities. They take charge of these responsibilities by using the leadership and management principles discussed in this book and by realizing that subordinates perform better when their leaders are aware of work-related issues, interested in seeing goals accomplished, and actively monitoring performance. Active leaders establish and communicate their subordinates' authority, responsibilities, and work parameters. Having this knowledge of what is expected of them and the encouragement to perform well, employees will gain the autonomy that most of them crave. There are sharp distinctions between action and inaction. By asking a subordinate to complete a task, for example, the leader is actively delegating an assignment, not avoiding taking action.

Leaders who are inactive are much less engaged in their work than the active leader. On a spectrum of reasons for such inactivity, you will find leaders who consciously shirk their responsibilities and those who do not realize that they are less active than they need to be. Inactive leaders tend to react to a daily work challenge after someone tells them about it, whereas the active leader proactively seeks out impending obstacles. In addition to the risk that inactive leaders pose to their organization's ability to accomplish goals, the leaders themselves risk being perceived as irrelevant or ineffective in the eyes of their subordinates.

Personality, Psychology, and Leadership

The previous discussion of leadership orientations shows you there is much room for leaders who have various combinations of leadership styles. Most leaders take a situational approach and use different styles under different conditions depending upon the urgency and nature of the task, experience and expectations of subordinates, and the degree of trust and rapport that has been established in the work relationship. A central concept in leadership study is that to better understand the behaviors of leaders and subordinates, it is useful to have an understanding of the psychological nature of the people involved.

Dozens of questionnaires, tests, studies, and other resources are available to help you assess your leadership personality. Developed primarily by psychologists and management consultants, these tools quickly allow you to group yourself into various categories, predict how you prefer reacting to different leadership scenarios, and provide you with feedback on areas upon which you can improve. Most of them are alike in that they classify leaders into similar categories that have catchy descriptions. Although there is much research available in this area, it is not necessary for you to get too involved in all this resource material. It is useful, however, to look over the commercial products that are available and integrate one or more into your leadership duties.

One popular and extensively used resource is the Myers-Briggs Type Indicator. After individuals respond to several questions based upon how they usually would feel or act in several situations, this survey classifies them into one of four major categories: extroversion or introversion, sensing or intuition, thinking or feeling, and judging or perceiving. Then they are further typed into one of sixteen subcategories that will provide insight into their work preferences and decision-making patterns. A leader can use this as a tool to gain insight into their subordinates' preferences. It can be a useful way to increase understanding between them.

Although these resources will give you a quick profile of yourself or your subordinates, it is important to be careful when using them and never completely rely upon them. They should be used only in conjunction with skill development tools and other resources. There are several reasons for this. First, though many companies use the tests, the experts disagree considerably as to their reliability. Unfortunately, there is no magic formula for what test is best. It is up to you to examine those that are available and make the best choice for you and your organization. Second, these resources are sometimes misunderstood, with people often making major style changes based upon the results of one survey. A change may not be warranted, for example, due to bad testing conditions or the person's mood at the time of the survey. Third, some people are skeptical of tests or resentful of being arbitrarily typecast. You can avoid this reaction if you take the time to explain the process and results to them.

Qualities of a Leader

As scholars have studied leaders over the years, they have attempted numerous times to document identifiable leadership qualities. There are certain recurring qualities that seem to surface in the best leaders. To give you an idea of what makes a great leader, here are some of their best qualities.

Adaptable	Confident	Creative	Discerning	Fair	Persistent
Ambitious	Convincing	Curious	Empathetic	Honest	Responsible
Caring	Courageous	Decisive	Ethical	Innovative	Self-directing

It has been difficult to conclude the degree to which these qualities help people become great leaders; therefore, it is important to understand three points about leadership qualities. First, very few, if any, leaders have all the qualities on any given list. It is not necessary nor is it possible for a successful leader to completely fit a leadership mold that someone suggests is best for them or their organization. Leaders, like their subordinates, are individuals who are alike and different in many respects and can be successful without radically altering their inherent qualities. Second, there is no complete list of leadership qualities. If you attempted to list every possible quality of a leader using published studies since the early 1900s, you will have hundreds of qualities. Third, a person can possess many leadership qualities and still not be a leader.

Nevertheless, these qualities provide great insight into leadership behavior and help provide you with clues as to why some leaders are more effective than others. As you read this book, you will see how you can integrate these qualities into your daily leadership challenges. You will reach your leadership potential when you use these qualities and think and act daily as a leader at work, home, and in the community.

CHAPTER 3

DEVELOP A LEADER'S ATTITUDE

Attitude usually refers to a feeling or state of mind toward something. You probably agree that you have different feelings and emotions when faced with various circumstances and events. While having some reaction to your leadership challenges is guaranteed, one of the decisions that you do control is choosing how you react to these daily situations. Fortunately, attitude can be adjusted at will and made positive or negative, or additionally, more positive or more negative.

By habitually focusing on the positive aspects of any situation and de-emphasizing or ignoring the negative, you will reap several important rewards. First, you will begin to perceive daily challenges as opportunities that you expect to seize, not as intrusions that distract you from your work. This positive attitude provides you with a sense of calmness, resolve, and courage that will give you an edge in getting things accomplished. Second, when inevitably something does not go the way you had intended, your positive frame of mind will allow you to quickly accept it and move on to your next challenge. Third, with a positive attitude, you will become gradually less dependent upon external sources of satisfaction such as wealth or social status and more interested in developing solid relationships with others. Friends and coworkers will soon see you as someone who is fun and interesting.

Finally, the overwhelming positive effects of a great attitude will neutralize any self-imposed barriers to success, such as unhappiness with your physical appearance or lack of self-confidence.

Importance of a Leader's Attitude

As a leader, it is crucial that you are aware and take advantage of these concepts because your attitude has a tremendous effect on your subordinates' work performances and attitudes. Since you are responsible for setting the tone of the work relationship with your subordinates, imagine the positive impact you can have by being known as the leader who has a great attitude.

Ten attitude characteristics a truly great leader will display are: 1) loyalty to the organization, 2) appreciation of subordinates, 3) focus on solutions, 4) we-can-do-it approach, 5) authority with responsibility and accountability, 6) enthusiasm, 7) curiosity, 8) a leadership image, 9) a balance of professional and personal life, and 10) integrity.

Loyalty to the Organization

One key reason you are in a leadership position is that your organization's leaders depend upon you and your good judgment to help them achieve their goals. By being openly supportive of your organization, you will be part of the solution, not the problem. Loyal leaders, regardless of their level in an organization, are not complacent when they see threats to their organization, better ways of doing things, or opportunities to question previously made decisions, policies, and procedures. Because of organizational loyalty and commitment, they will raise questions and seek answers to the issues that puzzle or inspire them. They respond to the call of leadership and fill the position with purpose.

Appreciation of Subordinates

Great leaders recognize that they need the best efforts of their subordinates if they intend to succeed at their job. Some leaders go as far as saying that employees are their most important asset, a declaration that is true in most if not all organizations. As a leader, you will have numerous opportunities to show your subordinates just how much you value them and want to act in their best interests. You can do this by being accessible, rewarding, and fair. You also can demonstrate how much you value them by training them, listening to them, coaching them, and creating a great work environment for them. Subsequent chapters in this book will show you how you can lead your organization to greater successes and gain the commitment of your staff. No one assumes that you can do it by yourself. You need your subordinates as much as they need you.

Focus on Solutions

By focusing on solving a challenge or making something work better, you will reap more and quicker success than if you concentrate on why you have a problem. This is not to say that you should ignore the causes but instead that you do not use them as a reason to blame, avoid taking action, or paralyze yourself into a state of fear. You and your subordinates will think more creatively and work more proactively if you are boldly pointed towards the future, not lamenting the past.

We-can-do-it Approach

Your positive and competitive winning attitude will go a long way in motivating your subordinates to achieve goals. It is important to realize that since your subordinates often depend upon you to provide them hope, direction, persistence, and resources to get their jobs done, you can increase the likelihood of success simply by demonstrating to them that you know anything can be done and that you are determined to do it in the best possible way. Let them know, however, that the team needs them to work hard and smart in order to reap success. Lead the way by setting and enforcing high standards of performance. Imagine the possibilities with them, and minimize dwelling on limitations or possibilities of failure.

Authority with Responsibility and Accountability

Authority is the right that your superiors give you to lead your organization and accomplish certain responsibilities, or expectations of performance. The chief executive of a company has the ultimate authority to complete all possible responsibilities, but due to time constraints, he or she assigns to you and other leaders many of these responsibilities and, hopefully, the authority to go along with them. However, the chief executive cannot delegate accountability because he or she alone is accountable to the organization and its shareholders. This concept applies to leaders at any organizational level, and therefore, you as a leader cannot evade accountability for your responsibilities by blaming others or using excuses. Accept credit for how much or how little you accomplish and then, if necessary, be sure to do a better job next time.

Enthusiasm

Most subordinates naturally admire and respect their leaders. Why not take advantage of this and reward your subordinates by being a leader who is fun to be around, enjoys leading, and has a high energy level? Not only is this attitude great for your well-being and successful leadership performance, it will catch on with your subordinates who will begin copying your actions. An important part of a leader's enthusiasm is their ability to act on a great idea. This ability to take risks is not reckless but is calculating and well conceptualized.

Curiosity

Leaders envision possibilities and avoid the contentment of the status quo. A central component of this attitude is a natural curiosity of the work environment, including people, industry processes and products, and customers. Leaders question subordinates about their job, suggestions, and daily challenges. When difficulties occur during the day, leaders attempt to isolate the origins and resolve them with an open-minded approach. Their intellectual curiosity is further evidenced by reading books, attending personal development seminars, and taking university classes.

Leadership Image

The image, or impression, that you portray to subordinates, superiors, and peers is vital to your success as a leader. The image is affected by several factors, including your ability to understand and accomplish job requirements, solve problems, get along well in relationships, react to stressful situations, and communicate. In addition to giving you an increased ability to lead, the right image will do wonders for your career advancement, either within your company or outside it. The skills you learn in this book, therefore, will go far in boosting your image to where it should be.

Balance of Professional and Personal Life

Do you ever notice people who completely absorb themselves in their work and neglect their families or personal lives? They tend to associate happiness or satisfaction with achievements on the job. Eventually they suffer from these choices because instead of attaining happiness and fulfillment, they make themselves miserable due to increased family or health problems.

To counter this trend, it is helpful to develop an idea of what you value most in life. Researchers have shown over the years that people do not find true happiness at the workplace; it resides elsewhere such as in family, religion, or community. Once you decide what is really important to you, then you will make better choices between work and home, and your overall contentment and attitude at both places will improve.

Integrity

A strong sense of personal integrity is one of the most frequently listed attributes of outstanding leaders. Your organization and subordinates depend upon you to get the right results while the details of how you accomplish this often are left up to you. Although you could achieve a short-term gain by cutting corners, stealing, not keeping your word, or lying, you will certainly suffer some negative consequences in the long-term. Other examples of possible integrity violations include accepting or giving bribes, ignoring a conflict-of-interest policy, and avoiding potentially damaging organizational problems. Because one of the most important components of your integrity is honesty, your ability to survive as an effective leader will be reduced to nothing if you are perceived to be dishonest. An act of dishonesty or a pattern of such behavior will suggest to others that you are untrustworthy.

Does this mean that successful leaders never slip up and make mistakes? No, they deal with these decisions and temptations every day. The more successful ones, however, continually develop and adhere to a set of values that evolve from what they believe is right or wrong. Consistent statements of truth, objective and impartial interpretation of facts, and honesty with others and yourself will go far in anchoring your belief system. Thereafter, your daily actions of unwavering integrity will demonstrate to everyone that you are serious about matters of integrity and that you expect them to be equally serious. In the long-term, your integrity becomes a compass that will help you consistently make the right decisions in leading your organization.

Importance of Maintaining Your Leader's Attitude

Congratulations on now knowing how a leader must think and act. By truly believing these powerful concepts and applying them in your daily life, you are on the way to being a successful leader. Experience tells you that your leader's attitude will be challenged several times a day by people, events, and you yourself. Your reaction to such inevitable occurrences determines how quickly you will bounce back and continue on with your leadership responsibilities. The skills that you learn in this book will help you tremendously in maintaining your attitude by making you more confident in your ability to handle leadership challenges. In addition, these daily attitudinal challenges give you the opportunity to use a series of steps to periodically adjust and retain your leader's attitude.

Three simple steps to help you maintain your leader's attitude each day are:

- ► Eliminate the challenge to your attitude,
- ► Adjust your attitude, and
- ► Replenish your attitude.

STEP

◄◈► 1 ◄◈►

Eliminate the Challenge to Your Attitude

Identify what conflict is causing you to lose your positivity, such as a subordinate's performance or a meeting that did not conclude in your favor. Recognize that you must first deal with that situation by deciding what your reaction will be, then quickly react. After eliminating the challenge, your attitude will bounce back and you will reap two benefits. You will be able to move on to your next task and not be continually burdened by what just happened, plus you will not get involved in plotting useless strategies to get even or win the next round of conflict.

What are some typical responses you may use? Sometimes it is your behavior at issue. If you are responsible for or involved in causing the conflict, it is helpful to bring up the issue with the person involved and explore why the situation turned out as it did. Simply by talking about what happened, or explaining why you made a certain decision, you will go a long way in eliminating the conflict. If appropriate to the situation, apologize sincerely.

Another person's infrequent behavior may be the issue. When someone's upsetting behavior affects your positive attitude, consider whether their behavior is a one-time occurrence or a pattern that may repeat itself. It is best to forget isolated actions, such as a subordinate's first tardiness in two years, or your normally supportive supervisor's decision against your proposal. If you constantly think about these events, your attitude will suffer and your subordinate and supervisor will notice the negativity — whether you believe they notice it or not. Since you are not able to change the subordinate's tardiness or the supervisor's decision, why not pleasantly accept their behavior and concentrate on things that you can influence? You will feel better and the people who work with you will perceive you positively.

Another's frequent behavior may be the problem. Often, you face attitude challenges that are repetitive in nature; sometimes they are related to your daily leadership responsibilities, sometimes not. For example, if you have a subordinate who consistently underperforms in his or her job, it is essential for you as a leader that you improve the employee's performance. By determining how best to solve the situation and then implementing your decision, you will help the productivity of your organization and the employee's performance as well as retain your positive attitude.

You will learn specific techniques later in this book to resolve such situations. The important point now is that by resolving a situation, your positive attitude will be protected. In another example, you may encounter consistently negative or hostile people at the corporate headquarters. Decide if your involvement with these negative people is necessary. If so, be as positive as you can be when you conduct business with them, but minimize your contact with them. In time, your consistent positive attitude may be the impetus for their behavioral change. However, if the negative people are unrelated to your completion of duties, avoid them as much as possible. You will find that by withdrawing from selected negative work-related or personal relationships, you will better guard your positive attitude.

STEP

◆ 2 ◆

Adjust Your Attitude

You can use specific techniques during the day to help you retain your positive attitude. Some may be more effective for you than others, so choose what works best.

One technique is to focus on your successes. You have numerous reasons to be happy and thankful. Why not think of them when you need an emotional lift? Although one subordinate is having problems, be thankful for the others who are doing a great job. If your flight just got delayed, be grateful for some additional quiet time to think or read. By focusing on your successes, you will crowd out the negative thoughts, fears of failure, and other doubts.

Another technique is to improve your self-image. People notice fewer physical characteristics of others than is widely suggested by advertisements. When you project a positive confidence to others, they notice this attitude more than any flaws that you might have. You can develop a great self-image by taking more pride in how you look and feel to yourself, not others. You will then find that others will compliment you more frequently, thus making you feel all the more confident.

Keeping a humorous perspective is always a good technique. The adage that laughter is the best medicine is a great principle to use. When you look at the funny side of unpleasant or unexpected events, you disarm their potential negativity. By lightening your mood, you are in a better mental state to either resolve the challenge or move on to other things.

It is important to remember your purpose. Knowing why you choose to do what you do will give you the energy and focus to maintain a great attitude every day. Your goal may be to move up the corporate ladder, retire early, or provide for your family. Regardless of your reasons, you will find it easier to cope with leadership challenges because you realize that these hurdles are just one step along the way in your achievement of personal and professional goals.

STEP

◆ 3 ◆

Replenish Your Attitude

You are faced daily with threats to your attitude. Even with the techniques described above, sometimes it is helpful to pause and give yourself time to recover from work, family, and personal challenges. As a leader, this is especially crucial because you are constantly making important decisions, supervising people, and handling quickly occurring situations. It sometimes seems as if you have no time to yourself because so many people are demanding that you help them with their needs. Although you will explore stress management in more detail in Chapter 6, the key to replenishing your attitude is to realize that you must regularly practice techniques to restore it.

For daily replenishment, establish certain routines that will allow time for you to relax, think, and reinvigorate. Possibilities include closing the office door, reading from a positive book, listening to an inspirational tape, exercising, praying, confiding with a close friend, or thinking about your pets; the possibilities are endless.

Unless you work seven days a week, you probably will have one or two days that you can use at will. Do whatever you can to make yourself feel better and to recharge your batteries for Monday morning. Great attitude adjusters include trips, movies, or religious activities.

Take personal holidays several times during the year to help you revitalize your attitude, focus your goals, and simply relax. This personal time can take many forms, such as three-day weekend trips, extended vacations, job-related conferences, or family retreats.

Have you ever thought that a person whom you had casually met had a bad attitude or that a fellow worker would be easier to work with if he had a better attitude? As an extra benefit to you, the concepts discussed in this chapter not only improve your own attitude but will help you make substantial progress in changing the attitudes of people you encounter: subordinates, peers, superiors, and family members. By helping them adjust their attitude, you will become a more effective leader because they will improve their work behavior and, consequently, you will more efficiently and effectively achieve your goals. In the long term, you will be viewed by others as a great leader, simply because of your infectious positive attitude.

As subordinates replicate your attitude, you will dramatically see an increase in worker morale and output, team productivity, and work environment harmony. Additionally, you will find that your good reputation will spread across your organization and into others. This, in turn, will help you as you develop important relationships within and outside your organization. As you change your attitude and use the other skills you learn in this book, you will be on your way to success as a leader.

PART II

TECHNICAL AND ANALYTICAL SKILLS

Primary-level Leadership Skills

CHAPTER 4

MASTER JOB SPECIFIC SKILLS

Job specific skills include those that are specifically related to your job position and must be learned in order for you to work according to standards. Examples include using a computer, operating a machine, administering payroll, assembling a vehicle, or preparing a production schedule.

To help you determine exactly what is expected of you in your job, several published resources are usually available from the human resources department or your organization's files. These include the job description, job analysis, and job specifications. It would help you to get copies of all three and study them thoroughly because they are the official word on what you are supposed to do in your job. Not only do they address your specific technical duties, but they could indicate additional responsibilities in the areas of relationship and strategic leadership skills.

The job description contains a summarized listing of the most important aspects of the job, including tasks and specifications. The job analysis is a detailed mass of data that explores all aspects of the job such as its required skills and responsibilities. It is developed by observing people in the job, examining all data available in the company, and studying external research. Finally, job specifications give a summary of the job analysis but provide more detail than the job description.

Importance of a Strong Skills Foundation

Before you progress to more advanced leadership skills, it is helpful to realize that the first set of building blocks relates to the nature of your job. You will succeed more quickly as a leader if you fully understand the technical aspects of your job and those of your subordinates. With the leadership training available in this book, you soon will be performing and supervising these functions in the context of great leadership. This, in turn, will be the impetus for an overall increase in skills knowledge for both you and your subordinates. The intent of this chapter is not to teach you these job specific skills; it is to show their importance to you as a leader and to demonstrate a framework that you can use to increase your skills inventory.

It is the successful daily completion of these primary level job skills that enables you and your organization to function smoothly. For example, if your intention is to become a great marketing manager, it is imperative that you know as much as you can about marketing. A corporate logistician needs to know the nitty-gritty details of transportation, such as those related to shipping, trucking, and railroads. A controller is concerned about the language of finance, including cash forecasting, capital expenditure controls, budgeting, and automation. If you are in charge of a diverse crew of experts such as in a software development team, a knowledge of programming and coding will help you lead the team to success.

Though knowing the many skills of your job is crucial to your success, it is not necessary or realistic to know all the minute details of every job position under your realm of responsibility. Many of your subordinates will perform their jobs much better than you could since they usually have more experience, expertise, and training in their specific skills than you have, unless you have previously mastered those skills. It is extremely helpful, however, to learn as much as possible about their jobs because when you are armed with such valuable information, you will make better decisions, understand your organization more fully, and monitor what occurs more precisely. This large base of knowledge will help you develop your leadership intuition, which will permit you to make quality decisions when working with limited time or facts. Additionally, your subordinates will better appreciate you and accept your leadership authority more if you demonstrate that you understand the many aspects of their jobs or at least show that you are willing to learn.

Job Specific Skills

Most business organizations have training programs that will take you through a skills development process. They are known as management training programs or apprenticeships and typically vary in terms of length, training location, and degree of supervisory control. The programs may even be part of a probationary period in which you have to meet established training standards in a variety of tasks or face dismissal from the program. Although your supervisor will coach you during this program, it is your responsibility to manage the process proactively. This includes thoroughly learning the skills within the established time frame, ensuring your supervisor evaluates you when required, and completing the paperwork required by your training office.

Skills in Other Areas

Once you master the skills involved in your own job, it is time to make yourself more helpful to other leaders in the organization. By personally making the effort to branch out into unfamiliar departments in your organization and to learn new skills, procedures, and ways of doing business, you will benefit both yourself and your organization. You will broaden your skills inventory and make yourself more valuable to your department by developing an expansive picture of the organization's and industry's business issues.

The knowledge you obtain from seeing business done in other ways gives you a fresh perspective and will help you better lead your department. In addition, you will meet new and interesting leaders throughout your organization. This can serve you well later as you develop cross-functional working relationships and a power base within the company. Finally, by being cross-trained in and knowledgeable of other areas, you will become more valuable to the company, which can help you later if other leadership positions become available. It is in your interest, therefore, to broaden your network by seeking opportunities to help a fellow leader, serve on a committee, or socialize with your counterparts in other departments. This exposure will earn you the reputation of being supportive of the overall organizational effort.

It is important to note that, in helping others, you should not have as your primary goal to get credit; if so, others will soon perceive you as hungry for power. Credit will naturally arrive as others realize you are a caring leader and loyal to your co-workers.

Formal Education

There is little debate as to whether a person needs a high school diploma. Most employers expect it, and for those workers who do not have one, employers often encourage them to get one by offering on-site classes or time off to attend classes. You will probably agree that you prefer working with high school graduates because they possess a knowledge base that allows them to be trained more easily than those without diplomas.

What are the implications of formal education for a leader? Depending on which industry you are in, a college education may or may not be required. There are some employers who would prefer a great leader with strong technical skills and no bachelor's degree to one who has a degree and no skills base. However, the consensus is that leaders on the way up the corporate ladder require a bachelor's degree; a master's degree would be an advantage after the candidate gets some actual work experience. Moreover, most executives concur that having a degree from a school that has high standards is valued over a degree obtained through minimal standards. Even so, there is substantial disagreement over the value of a master's degree, in particular the master's of business administration (MBA), since most employers tend to promote based upon performance, not educational credentials. Some employers would rather train the leader through their in-house training programs, which provide heavy doses of on-the-job skills training as well as development of common sense.

The mere possession of a college degree does not necessarily make you any better or more intelligent than someone who does not have one. It does, however, give you several advantages that will help you develop as a leader. First, the experience of taking 40 to 50 college courses will give you a wealth of knowledge to draw upon as you progress in your career. Not only will you learn specific skills in math, science, communications, and English, but the humanities and other elective courses will also make you a much more culturally diverse leader, which is useful in today's global environment. Additionally, this wide exposure to knowledge will develop your overall creative intelligence level, which will be advantageous as you assume increasingly more challenging assignments in higher-level leadership. Second, a college degree is a discriminator that can help you get a promotion. If there are two equally qualified and motivated leaders, the one with the degree probably would advance more quickly than the high school graduate. Third, getting a college degree proves to you and others that you can start a major project and see it to its end.

There are several routes to continuing your education. If you are already in the workplace and your employer permits it, you can attend school part-time and take classes in the evening or occasionally during the day. This low-cost option takes more time to get a degree, but you will not starve in the process. If your finances permit, you could quit work and attend school full-time. In both cases, employers may help you with the costs if you make a commitment to remain employed with them.

Maintain and Improve Your Skills

To help you continuously seek improvement in your job area, consider using two resources. First, consult with those experts within and outside your organization who have developed considerable job or institutional knowledge.

Often they are quite helpful in passing along tips about the details of jobs. Second, stay up-to-date in your functional area by reading industry magazines and publications, attending professional development seminars, and networking at local professional organizations.

You and your subordinates must develop an attitude that learning does not end when you complete a training program or obtain a college degree. It should be no surprise to you that in the early years of the 21st century, the world will continue to change at a rapidly increasing pace. As a leader, your best way to cope with this change is to build upon your existing knowledge base by continually seeking to update that knowledge. This in turn will give you the foundation to improve your skills and to better solve challenging situations.

CHAPTER 5

SOLVE PROBLEMS AND MAKE DECISIONS

Of all skills, problem solving and decision making are those used most often by leaders throughout the course of the day at work, home, or in the community. Like communicating, they relate in some way to practically everything you do, and they are components of all the other leadership skills that you use. Your ability as a leader to solve problems and make decisions is crucial to how your effectiveness is perceived by you, your subordinates, and your superiors.

Problem solving and decision making are closely related in that they are both action processes and frequently overlap each other. Solving a problem initially involves determining possible solutions to remedy a discrepancy that should not exist. For example, you may be concerned about a low level of customer satisfaction, and you determine that several solutions would fix the problem, such as hiring more customer service representatives or increasing the frequency of training. Your final step, however, is to decide which of the alternatives to accept and implement. Once you determine possible solutions to the problem, you must use decision-making techniques to choose the best solution and eliminate the problem.

The purpose of this chapter is to show you how you can approach any problem in a logical manner, resolve it without spending a huge amount of time, and then decide what is the best way to implement the solution. The approaches are simple and effective and can be routinely used as your sole problem-solving and decision-making tools or supplemented with the more complex procedures that you currently use in your leadership position. You will first examine problem solving and then address the slightly different issue of decision making.

Problem-solving Process

It is not necessary or possible to examine every fact and analyze every possible scenario when involved with problems or decisions. Your job is to take the initiative to think through the situation, use good judgment, and act decisively. The best way to do this is to use an eight-step process for problem solving that can be used in all situations you encounter.

1. Identify symptoms.

2. Collect information.

3. Compare desired results with actual results.

4. State the problem and its effects.

5. List, analyze, and eliminate possible causes.

6. Choose probable causes.

7. Identify and examine possible courses of action.

8. Choose and implement the best course of action, then evaluate.

As you get more familiar with its use, you will find yourself mentally going through this process every time you encounter a problem. Use it even if you only have seconds or minutes, because a proper diagnosis of the problem now will later save you much further effort and time. If you think about your problem in terms of the structured process shown here, you will be less likely to ignore potential causes of the problem and will generate better solutions. You will arrive at solutions more quickly because you are dividing the problem into manageable bits and pieces that can be examined more easily. To better explain the details of this problem-solving process, an example of a retail clothing store will be used.

Identify Symptoms

Determine what is happening that indicates something could be wrong.

*A clothing store manager, Mr. Fergus, notices that sales are down
15 percent from the same period last year.*

STEP

❖ 1 ❖

STEP

◈ 2 ◈

Collect Information

Get any information that you believe could be related to the symptoms, including input from your subordinates, peers, superiors, and customers. This information can include human observations, organizational performance, studies, or industry data. Feel free to tap the wisdom and knowledge of subject-matter experts within and outside your organization.

Mr. Fergus questions his sales staff and finds out that customers seem to be buying the same number of items per visit. He queries a nearby clothing store manager who says that her sales are up from last year. Finally, after speaking with a few valued customers, he hears that his personalized sales service recently has been deteriorating.

STEP

◈ 3 ◈

Compare Desired Results with Actual Results

The objective here is to clearly show what is expected in an ideal situation and what is actually happening with performance or behavior.

Mr. Fergus examines projected versus actual sales for each of the ten salespersons and notices that four of the ten have not met their monthly goals for the past three months. One of these missed the objective only slightly each month; the others were off by 20 percent or more. In addition, because of recent negative customer comments, Mr. Fergus knows that he is not performing up to his expectations since the store's policy is total satisfaction with the shopping experience.

STEP

◈ 4 ◈

State the Problem and Its Effects

The problem is the difference between the desired results and the actual results you identified in step three. Clearly and concisely state the problem and examine its effects upon you, the work environment, goal accomplishment, or customers. Notice that you do not actually identify the problem until step four. This allows you sufficient opportunity in steps one through three to correctly identify the problem by asking the right questions and probing for facts.

Mr. Fergus concludes that his two problems are: 1) three of his sales staff are not consistently meeting their monthly goals, causing him not to achieve store sales projections; and 2) customer service is deteriorating and is causing alienation with his loyal customers.

List, Analyze, and Eliminate Possible Causes

By examining possible reasons for your problem, you will begin to isolate the actual causes. Avoid prematurely eliminating possible causes before you adequately consider them or consult with others about them. You will soon develop a list of possible causes for your problem. To properly identify a cause, ask whether its absence would eliminate the problem.

STEP

◆ 5 ◆

> *Mr. Fergus considers several possibilities, but concludes there are three likely causes: 1) the three underperforming salespersons could have a sales training problem; 2) the three could be experiencing personal problems that are affecting their customer relationships and ability to sell; and 3) the three's underperformance could be affecting the performance of all the sales staff, thus contributing to customer alienation.*

Choose Probable Causes

By using methods such as logical reasoning, investigation, tests, or a group consensus, pick the most likely cause of the problem. Many problems have multiple causes so do not be surprised if you find this is true in your case.

STEP

◆ 6 ◆

> *After questioning the sales staff again in more detail, Mr. Fergus determined that seven of the ten salespersons were extremely motivated when everyone showed up for work. However, when a full crew was not available to properly service the customers, salespeople had to come in on their day off on short notice or had to work more quickly to take up the slack and risk offending customers who were used to personalized and lengthy attention. After examining work records for the past three months, Mr. Fergus found that the three underperforming salespersons were five times more likely than the others not to show up for work on any given day; their performance when they did show up was excellent. He concluded that the underlying cause of his two problems was the three salespersons' inability to consistently work five days per week.*

Identify and Examine Possible Courses of Action

The objective is to find solutions that could eliminate the cause of the problem. Determine some possible solutions, either by yourself or with the help of others through brainstorming and creative thinking. After listing and examining the possibilities, keep those that are acceptable and realistic to you. If required or desirable, consult with staff or other leaders whose comments are

STEP

◆ 7 ◆

needed. In the interest of time, tell them what information you need and when you need it.

> *Mr. Fergus decided to speak with the three salespersons, and he found that all three were having significant family problems that sometimes required them to stay at home on short notice. He listed some possible courses of action: 1) a pay system revision that would focus more on commissions and less on base pay to motivate them to show up more frequently; 2) intense coaching focused on their inconsistent work performance to improve their behavior; 3) a contingency plan that better predicted employee absences to give others more notice if they had to work for someone else; and 4) the hiring of new salespersons if the three did not change their behavior.*

STEP

❖ 8 ❖

Choose and Implement the Best Course of Action, Then Evaluate

Choose the best solution after examining each possible solution's effects, costs, and practicality. List any obstacles that may prevent you from implementing that solution and generate ideas to overcome these obstacles. After communicating the solution to others, direct the implementation of your plan. Evaluate it later for its effectiveness, and modify it if necessary. The how-to-choose part of this step will be further explained below in the decision-making process while the implementation and evaluation steps will be explored more thoroughly throughout the book.

> *Mr. Fergus chose to immediately implement courses of action numbers two and three and later implement number four if necessary.*

The Nature of Decisions

As you just saw, minor decisions are made constantly in the problem-solving process. For example, as you collect data and interpret information, decisions have to made about what data to collect and how to interpret it. Those kinds of routine decisions typically are easily learned and eventually become instinctive through experience. As you move along in the problem-solving process to steps seven and eight, you make increasingly complicated decisions, such as evaluating options and choosing the best alternative. In steps seven and eight, you temporarily overlooked the details and considerations involved in making these choices. The following sections address these decisions that have important implications to you in terms of long-term consequences, riskiness, unpredictability, and accomplishment of your goals.

The Decision-making Process

Identifying courses of action does you little good unless you determine their pros and cons, which one is the best, and the consequences of implementation. Such consequences could include likelihood of success or potential implementation problems. A logical path for you to take after determining the cause of a problem, therefore, is to think in detail about how best to eliminate the cause and successfully implement the solution, given an environment of challenges, barriers, and uncertainty. This is decision making.

The problem-solving process described above will provide you the structure to thoroughly explore and analyze problems. Ultimately, it is up to you to construct your own decision-making process for each decision that you encounter by using techniques that are most appropriate for the specific decision. You can best do this by exploring and understanding some of the major issues involved in making decisions, by asking yourself these questions.

- ▶ What are the time constraints for making a decision?
- ▶ Who will participate in the decision making?
- ▶ Will this be a recurring or a one-time decision?
- ▶ What are the components of the decision?
- ▶ What techniques will be used to make the decision?

What Are the Time Constraints for Making a Decision?

QUESTION ◈ 1 ◈

After you identify when you will make the decision, you then can outline a decision-making process based upon a realistic schedule. Assuming that you have plenty of available time and that you start the process immediately, you will be able to choose from more resources such as group assistance, advanced decision-making tools, and extensive research. You can use several methods to assist you in decision making; some are simple and easy to apply to all facets of work, while others are much more complicated, time-consuming, and math intensive. This chapter will concentrate on using simple processes of decision making that conserve time. You can then explore more advanced methods as you choose.

Who Will Participate in the Decision Making?

QUESTION ◈ 2 ◈

Since several individuals usually are involved in the decision-making process, coordinate your actions with theirs in order to better manage the process. This will help you eliminate duplication of effort, minimize frustration, and ensure that you make the best decision. Seek the input of those individuals whose contributions are obvious in helping you evaluate courses of action. These individuals include the technical staff specialists, such as in the marketing, human resources, legal, customer service, or accounting departments. Contact those people who will be affected by your decision or who must be committed to it for it to be successfully implemented; these include your superiors, subordinates, and customers. You are not consulting with these individuals to get their approval, necessarily, but to obtain information, experience, and guidance to help you structure your decision-making process, pinpoint the decision's long-term implications, and identify any competing interests that may affect your decision or its implementation. In addition to the immediate benefits of involving others in your decision making, you likely will notice more long-term acceptance of your decision by the participants.

QUESTION
❧ 3 ❧

Will This Be a Recurring or a One-time Decision?

Decisions are either programmed or nonprogrammed. Most of your decisions are programmed if they routinely occur, are mostly predictable in nature, and can be scheduled. These include decisions such as inventory reorders or customer service inquiries. Responses to these situations are predictable and can, therefore, be standardized wherever possible by using written procedures or rules that clearly show how to make the decision. This will allow quicker decision making in your organization and will permit you to delegate more decision-making authority to your subordinates.

The rest of your decision-making time will be spent with nonprogrammed decisions, which are those that occur less frequently and can have enormous consequences for you or your organization. Examples include opening a new manufacturing plant or retail store, restructuring the organization, or revising the incentives program. Because these decisions are nonroutine and possibly unprecedented, can involve a high degree of uncertainty, and are usually vitally important to your organization, it is helpful to have as much knowledge about them as possible to guide you through the decision-making process.

QUESTION
❧ 4 ❧

What Are the Components of the Decision?

Decisions have three elements: conditions, courses of action, and consequences. Conditions refer to the uncertainty and risk that always exist in your business or personal environment. Since very few of your future actions have completely certain results due to these usually uncontrollable factors and circumstances, you must isolate and estimate the uncertainty and risk during your decision making. Courses of action are simply potential solutions to the causes of a problem. Consequences are the implications resulting from each course of action.

Mr. Fergus' clothing store's sales revenue on a given day could be conditional in part upon whether all, most, some, or none of the sales staff show up for work. Before the store opens for business, the manager will evaluate the actual conditions to see how many salespeople showed up for work. If the expected number did not

*arrive, then he has a staffing decision to make. He must imple-
ment one of several possible courses of action, such as calling in
another salesperson, sending one home if too many showed up, or
not calling one in. Each of these alternatives has different consequences on total sales for the day. Ideally, the manager would
have determined in advance some courses of action by predicting
the workplace conditions, their probability of occurrence, and the
consequences of each course of action.*

What Techniques Will Be Used to Make the Decision?

QUESTION
◆ 5 ◆

Several techniques are available to help you structure decisions and guide
you to your best decision. Use them individually or in combination with each
other. Discussed are some of the most popular techniques.

Prioritization

By establishing a ranking system of available courses of action, you can
easily make a decision when confronted with choices. For example, if
you need to decide who among several volunteers gets the opportunity
to work overtime, you could prioritize them according to the amount of
overtime worked thus far in the month. Your choice could be the person who has worked the least amount so far. Prioritization works best
for recurring decisions such as allocation of resources or customer service procedures; it is not as handy with one-time decisions.

Checklists

In simple decision making involving a low number of alternatives such
as to accept or not accept, to buy or not buy, it can be helpful to list significant factors that affect the decision, such as cost, dependability, and
servicing. You can then simply check off the factors as acceptable or
not, decide the impact of any unacceptable factors, and make an overall decision as to which alternative is best — to accept the proposal or
reject it, to buy the new computer system or not buy it. This process is
helpful in that before you check off a factor, you examine the factor in
detail and thoroughly understand its implication. The main drawback
to this technique is that typically it does not allow you to weight the
factors unless you modify the technique to fit your needs.

Brainstorming

Brainstorming encourages members of a group to let their minds wan-
der in an uncritical environment free from judgment to find creative,
nontraditional ways to solve problems and develop alternative courses
of action. As the group leader, you designate someone to record the
ideas while you facilitate the session. Because this technique will help

you generate ideas and alternative solutions, it is, therefore, not solely a tool for making decisions but also one for helping you generate options that will lead eventually to your decision.

Intuition

You develop your intuition after gaining experience on the job, solving problems, and making decisions. This databank of knowledge hones your intuitive skills sometimes to the point of allowing you to trust your feelings completely. As you will see during the discussion of payoff charts, intuition can be helpful in providing you with some basis to start the decision-making process. Although some leaders are quite successful in primarily using their intuition for decision making, most leaders do not rely totally on their hunches without having some other objective techniques to provide balance.

Payoff Charts

When one main decision is needed, you can use a payoff chart to help you structure your options in a clear, concise manner. A payoff chart consists of a simple diagram that shows each of your various courses of action and their consequences. Constructing a payoff chart forces you to think through all the details of your decision. A complete example of how to use a payoff chart is given in the next section.

Decision Trees

This popular tool is used when multiple decisions are made at different points in time, a situation that cannot be managed by the payoff chart. A decision tree allows you to graphically chart decisions, consequences, and conditions in an easy-to-read diagram that branches out like a tree. It is indispensable for tracking complicated decisions and their effects on subsequent decisions. It is best to consult a detailed guide that will explain the many nuances in constructing decision trees to help you integrate their use into your decision making.

Advanced Techniques

There are dozens of advanced decision-making techniques to choose from. These include synectics, a problem-solving process that focuses on group creativity; morphological analysis, searching for connections and linkages among concepts; and operations research and decision theory, both of which seek the best solution using math- and statistics-intensive processes. No one technique is best because each has its own limitations, applicability to certain situations, and ideal conditions of use. If any of these interests you, consult the many instructional texts that are available.

The Payoff Chart

Conditions, courses of action, and consequences, the three elements of decision analysis, are shown in more detail in a payoff chart. A payoff chart lists all practical courses of action, which are distinct and exclusive of each other. A close look at a fully detailed example of a payoff chart can help you use this technique in your own situation.

In the example of the clothing store, Mr. Fergus expects eight salespersons to arrive for work. The actual number of arrivals results in different consequences, or net sales revenue, which is total revenue less sales salaries. Assume that:

- ► Each salesperson is paid $50 per day in base salary, plus $20 if they have to come in on short notice or as a replacement for an absent worker;
- ► The largest possible revenue for the store is $8,000 per day when a normal staff of eight works — $1,000 per salesperson — and if fewer than eight work then the revenue for the store is $1,000 per salesperson; and
- ► The total available sales staff is eleven.

The Staffing Decision Payoff Chart indicates which course of action (CA) is best for each condition (C), and it clearly shows that when a salesperson does not show for work, it is always best to call for a replacement or sometimes two. This may appear obvious, but by constructing a simple chart, you can actually see in detail what your options and their anticipated consequences are under multiple conditions.

Staffing Decision Payoff Chart

Condition (C)	Course of Action (CA)			
	CA 1: Do nothing	CA 2: Add 1 salesperson	CA 3: Add 2 salespeople	CA 4: Add 3 salespeople
C1: 8 people arrive for work	$7,600 Best CA	$7,530	$7,460	$7,390
C2: 7 people arrive for work	$6,650	$7,580 Best CA	$7,510	$7,440
C3: 6 people arrive for work	$5,700	$6,630	$7,560 Best CA	$7,490
Totals	$19,950	$21,740	$22,530	$22,320

In this example, the manager must ensure that not too many salespersons are working on any given day or potential income will be lost. The example used was a simple one. Most store managers, in other words, would intuitively recognize that it is a good idea to have eight salespersons working per day because this would maximize the store's revenue and that it would be a good idea to telephone for a replacement if someone does not show for work.

The payoff chart has a number of limitations. First, it can be used when only one decision is needed, not multiple ones over a period of time. Although you could construct a chart for each phase of a multiple decision, it is more practical to use more advanced tools such as a decision tree. Second, the pay-off chart does not completely show all possible conditions for the store manager. It is possible, for example, that no worker will show up for work, or that a busload of customers could arrive, which would require the use all eleven salespersons. Third, the payoff chart does not account for the uncertainty inherent in any decision situation. In the example, the manager was certain how many employees were at work on any given morning because they were counted after they arrived. But there may be times when the store manager can not call for his replacement workers during the morning and must decide by the previous evening how many workers will probably show up for work.

Uncertainty like this exists in most decisions. Rarely does a leader make a decision under absolute certainty. You can address this concern through two options, by using intuition or probabilities.

Estimate Uncertainty by Using Your Intuition

You have the ability in a payoff chart to make a quick estimate as to what course of action you would choose, given your feelings of optimism, pessimism, or neutrality as to what conditions will actually prevail. These feelings are important because in a quick moment of decision making, you may be forced to rely upon them. Additionally, as you become more experienced as a leader, you will increasingly begin to trust your intuition. This can become valuable to you as you assess which conditions are most likely to occur in different situations.

Return to the Staffing Decision Payoff Chart. If you are optimistic, for example, that all eight employees will arrive, you could quickly decide that CA 1 is the best option since it has the highest payoff of all the three courses of action when eight employees arrive. If you are pessimistic and believe that only six will show, simply pick the lowest or most pessimistic payoffs in each CA, which are $5,700, $6,630, $7,460, and $7,390. Then select the highest of these values, $7,460 in CA 3, as your best option. Finally, if you are neither optimistic nor pessimistic as to which condition will actually occur and believe that each is as likely to occur as the others, you could choose the CA that has the highest total for its three expected conditions, or consequences. In the example, CA 3 with its $22,530 total is the best choice.

Estimate Uncertainty by Using Probabilities

It is best if most decisions are not left completely to chance and inner feelings. More formal methods are available to assess the likelihood, or probability, that one condition will prevail over the others. These methods provide needed structure to the intuition, experience, and available information used by the decision maker. This chapter examines only one simple method, and it avoids the details of probability, which you can eventually learn as time permits. Many fine guides are available to teach you these fundamentals and help you develop the important skills of assessing your decision's inherent uncertainty and choosing the right course of action. The purpose here, however, is to give you a method that you can put to use immediately.

In the next chart, probabilities, or best estimates, as to the likelihood of each condition occurring have been added. It shows that the store manager, based upon his past experiences and personal knowledge of his sales force, believes that there is a 60 percent probability of all eight workers arriving, a 30 percent probability for seven workers, and a 10 percent probability for only six workers. These probabilities are more specific than the optimistic and pessimistic intuitive predictions made in the previous section. In this example, simply multiply each probability with the resulting revenues for each course of action in each condition; you will get an expected revenue (ER). This is a weighted revenue that accounts for the uncertainty of not knowing what will happen, but predicts the likelihood of conditions one, two, or three occurring. In this example, after totaling the individual ERs in each course of action, choose CA 3 because it has the highest expected payoff, $7,485, of all four courses of action.

Staffing Decision Payoff Chart – Probabilities and Expected Revenues (ER)

Condition (C)	Proba-bility	Course of Action (CA)			
		CA 1: Do nothing	CA 2: Add 1 salesperson	CA 3: Add 2 salespeople	CA: 4: Add 3 salespeople
C1: 8 people arrive for work	0.6	$7,600	$7,530	$7,460	$7,390
		ER = $4,560	ER = $4,518	ER = $4,476	ER = $4,434
C2: 7 people arrive for work	0.3	$6,650	$7,580	$7,510	$7,440
		ER = $1,995	ER = $2,274	ER = $2,253	ER = $2,232
C3: 6 people arrive for work	0.1	$5,700	$6,630	$7,560	$7,490
		ER = $570	ER = $663	ER = $756	ER = $749
Totals	1.0	$19,950	$21,740	$22,530	$22,320
		ER = $7,125	ER = $7,455	ER = $7,485	ER = $7,415

The main point of this exercise is that, to be an effective decision maker, you must make a judgment about the uncertainty in your environment and then predict the likelihood of your potential decision-making conditions. The best way to do this is to use the concepts of probabilities and apply them to your decision making. Since this chapter barely scratched the surface of probability theory, read more about it when you get some spare time because it is essential to your development as a great decision maker.

Creative and Critical Thinking

Some say that leaders get paid to solve problems and make decisions. A better statement would be that they get paid to correctly solve problems and make the right decisions. In this chapter, you have seen several methods and techniques to help you correctly solve problems and make the right decisions. This final section will put these in broad perspective by showing you how your problem-solving and decision-making abilities can improve simply by the way you think about your challenges.

Think About Your Style

People tend to think in one of two ways, in an adaptive or innovative style. Neither of these is right nor wrong. What is right is what is natural for the person. Adaptive thinkers are characterized by goal orientation; adherence to policies, procedures, and structure; and great organizational abilities. Their brain's left hemisphere, which is the logical, analytical, and detail-oriented side, dominates over the emotional and creative right side. Innovative thinkers, on the other hand, tend to be more free spirited, less organized, and open to new methods of solving problems.

No matter what your orientation is, you can practice using the opposite orientation to strengthen those characteristics and become an overall better thinker. For example, if you are not too innovative, try using unconventional ideas to help you get your work accomplished, such as meeting new customers, changing your daily work routine, or trying new problem-solving techniques. If you want to ground yourself more in adaptive thinking, try progressively implementing time management principles or referring more often to your own or your department's goals.

Think Thoroughly by Questioning Others

As you noticed in this chapter, problem solving and decision making involve a considerable amount of involvement with others. As you proceed through the process, remember that you cannot do all the work yourself. Question your customers, subordinates, peers, and superiors about their thoughts on the problem by asking them leading questions that will pinpoint both the problem and potential solutions. You will soon find out what their concerns are and will be better able to devise winning and long-term solutions that will benefit everyone.

Think About Other Things

Giving your mind a break from the problem will invigorate your creativity. Listening to soothing music, watching fish in an aquarium, or exercising will give you a chance to look at the problem from a new perspective. Additionally, by focusing on the attributes of the music or fish, you may be able to associate what you see with potential solutions to your problem. For example, a fish in your aquarium may be swimming slowly and competing with other quickly moving fish. This could prompt you to wonder whether your proposed product line will gain market share quickly enough compared to your competitor's products.

Think About Your Objective

If you periodically remind yourself why you are solving problems and making decisions — to achieve a specific objective — then you are more likely to remain on the path of critical thinking, use relevant tools and techniques, and minimize distractions.

Decide With Confidence

Sometimes you make decisions several times per minute; more complex decisions can take you days or weeks. You solve some problems completely by yourself and others with team members or committees.

You already use a wealth of experience and intuitive ability to help you solve your problems and make your decisions. By combining this knowledge with the techniques in this chapter, you will make better decisions regardless of the volume of information, deadlines, or uncertainty that confront you. By having methods that you can readily use in your business and non-work challenges, you will be able to approach problems confidently and know that you can be proud of the results.

CHAPTER 6

MANAGE YOUR PRIORITIES

How you manage your priorities as a leader is irrefutably linked with how successful you are at achieving your objectives. This chapter will discuss how to manage priorities well, given the constraints of time and the inevitability of stress. You will soon be able to get more accomplished in less time, and you will gain more valuable time to spend wisely on the crucial job of leading your organization.

Control Your Time

Time, one of the few commonalities among people, is a resource you use to put your life in order at work, home, and leisure. Although everyone has the same number of hours a week to accomplish a multitude of tasks and obligations, some people are more effective than others at managing their time. Fortunately, it is not difficult to observe successful time managers to see how they achieve their priorities. They use simple techniques and principles to help them proactively choose what they want and need to do.

Since most leaders have a considerable amount of personal contact with others, they sometimes erroneously believe that they have little control over how that time is spent. This is simply not true. The key to effective time management is gaining control of your time, then taking steps to retain control. No matter how busy you are or what your work circumstances are, you can learn how to control your time and to free up time for more important work. For example, you may feel that because your subordinates constantly interrupt you during the day you are not getting important work accomplished. There are many solutions to this situation such as limiting the amount of time you spend talking with the subordinate, asking someone else to speak with the employee, or reserving specific time periods during the day exclusively for you.

You can use the following time-management process not only to gain control of your time but also to maintain control by periodically reviewing the process.

1. Analyze your current use of time.
2. Eliminate nonessential and inappropriate tasks.
3. Delegate tasks.
4. Improve performance of essential tasks.
5. Maintain control of your time.

Analyze Your Current Use of Time

STEP

◆ 1 ◆

Your objective in this step is to clearly show what you do during a typical day and when you do it. You can accomplish this by using a time journal, which will give you an accurate record of your daily activities in specific three-hour time periods throughout the course of a week. It will take you several minutes each day to document your activities, but the reward is substantial, as you will see. Get a 20-page spiral notebook and organize it so that each page is devoted to a three-hour time segment for a specific day of the week. The three-hour time segments are grouped together to make it easier for you to compare them later.

▶ Pages 1–5: for time periods 7–10 A.M., Monday through Friday.
▶ Pages 6–10: for time periods 10 A.M. to 1 P.M., Monday through Friday.
▶ Pages 11–15: for time periods 1–4 P.M., Monday through Friday.
▶ Pages 16–20: for time periods 4–7 P.M., Monday through Friday.

Keeping the notebook with you at all times, document accurately every few minutes what you did during the previous few minutes. Be specific and honestly note 1) the names of people you spoke with and the topics or specific project you were working on, 2) the time span of the task such as 9:45–9:55 A.M., for example, and 3) major occurrences if any, such as whether you accomplished what you had intended or if you had any interruptions. Do this for each of the four time periods during all five days. At the end of each three-hour time period, take a moment to add up the time you spent in major activities such as in-office visits, planning, telephone conversations, reading correspondence, and meetings.

After five days of documenting your activities, you will make some major conclusions about what you do daily. Most notable will be startling observations such as, for example, that reading mail took 45 minutes, incoming telephone calls covered two hours, or personal business occupied one hour. You probably will find several hours during a typical day that could be characterized as wasted time, waiting time, or time not spent in support of your primary functions. In addition, you will realize that there is a certain time period during the day when you seem to get more work done, think more creatively, or are more alert. This is your most productive time, and it will be further discussed in step four.

STEP

◄► 2 ◄►

Eliminate Nonessential and Inappropriate Tasks

By taking a critical look at your time journal, you can locate tasks that you should not be doing, either because they are not essential to your personal goals or your organization's mission or they are irrelevant to your primary leadership responsibilities and thus should be delegated. Some typical examples of nonessential tasks are compiling data that you rarely need or use, attending a meeting that does not concern your responsibilities, and reading magazines that have no relevance to your professional responsibilities.

Some typical examples of inappropriate tasks are compiling necessary data that another department already regularly collects, approving routine requests that a subordinate could handle instead, and opening and reading your mail when you have a capable assistant.

Stop doing the nonessential tasks and transfer the inappropriate ones to their rightful owners in other departments or else delegate the inappropriate ones to subordinates. These actions will recoup a significant portion of your time. Stopping a nonessential task can be done quickly if you have the authority. Otherwise, you will have to persuade your subordinates or superiors as to why you want the task eliminated. If you explain the task's lack of pertinence to your responsibilities, this persuasion should be simple.

STEP

◄► 3 ◄►

Delegate Tasks

Without question, delegation is one of the best time-tested methods of helping you accomplish your responsibilities. This process involves giving subordinates the responsibility and its accompanying authority to autonomously accomplish tasks. If you follow a few simple guidelines, delegation will 1) dramatically increase your available time to spend on priority tasks; 2) train your subordinates to accomplish more without your close supervision; 3) increase subordinate performance, morale, and job satisfaction; and 4) improve the overall performance, creativity, and reputation of your organization.

There are six basic guidelines to an effective delegation process.

▶ Decide what to delegate.
▶ Choose the right person.
▶ Communicate the task.
▶ Give responsibility and authority for the entire task.
▶ Check progress.
▶ Evaluate results.

Decide What to Delegate

A general principle to use is to delegate whenever someone else can effectively do the task for you. This allows you to concentrate on your more important leadership duties or on special tasks related to your personal strengths, skills, or enjoyments. A task that can be delegated is normally routine and of average risk and importance. These criteria are not absolute, however, because you may want to delegate an extremely difficult and risky task with the intention of developing the capabilities of a key subordinate, for example. Moreover, by frequently delegating ordinary, unpleasant, or unrewarding tasks and keeping the exciting ones for yourself, you will damage your leadership effectiveness in the long run.

One of your main goals should be that both you and your subordinates grow professionally to be the best leaders that you can possibly be. In this context, consider initially delegating important tasks associated with the primary level of leadership's technical and analytical skills, such as implementing solutions or overseeing individual projects. As your subordinates prove to you their ability to accept increased responsibility, delegate more to them. Remember to stay deeply involved in the crucial relationship and strategic areas, such as dealing with the needs and concerns of your subordinates, structuring your organization, and implementing major changes.

Choose the Right Person

Consider several factors when choosing the person to delegate to. Ask yourself who is the most junior individual with work experience or interest in the task, who needs the task in terms of career development, and who has the availability to finish the assignment. By correctly matching a person's abilities with the task's requirements, you dramatically increase the likelihood of success.

The most helpful way to choose the right person is to completely understand your subordinates' personal and professional goals and motivation. Once you know your subordinates, use this knowledge to guide you toward the right choices when delegating.

Communicate the Task

Explain your concept of the task to your subordinates, including the expected final results, pertinent details but not every detail, priorities, constraints, available resources, milestones and deadlines, expectations, and any other important guidance. To secure their commitment, explain why the task must be done, its history, and its importance to you and the organization. Ask your subordinates to repeat in their words the details of the assignment; this will ensure that they receive and understand your communication and will be less likely to deviate from your intentions. Specify that since you trust them with the assignment, you will not constantly check their progress but that you expect them to freely approach you with any questions or unresolvable problems.

Keep a record of this conversation's details so you can later refer to it when checking your subordinates' progress.

Give Responsibility and Authority for the Entire Task

Tell your subordinates that this task is completely their project to accomplish using the guidance that you gave them. They must understand that you are committed to supporting their authority for the task's completion and that you will back them up with the required resources and any assistance or intervention needed. By assigning the entire multifaceted task, your subordinates will gain much more experience than if they only had responsibility for a component of the task.

If your subordinates find they cannot accomplish certain aspects of the task alone, they in turn can choose to delegate a component of the responsibilities and learn delegation skills at the same time. In this instance, carefully monitor their decisions to ensure they retain sufficient control over the task. If you decide, however, that the complete assignment of a task to a subordinate is impractical, make sure they understand the importance of their responsibilities to you and the organization. As a result, you will inspire your subordinates to commit to the assignment and see it through to its end.

Check Progress

Monitor the progress and guide the efforts of your subordinates by periodically meeting or speaking together to discuss details and provide feedback. If they are having difficulties, resist all attempts by them to delegate the assignment back to you, which sometimes occurs when subordinates face challenging tasks. Instead of eagerly agreeing to resolve a small problem for them, get them to resolve it by asking them leading questions such as, "What do you think?" or "Is that a viable option?" This valuable coaching, encouragement, and assistance will help ensure not only that your project remains on track but also that your subordinates develop new skills and additional leadership experience.

Evaluate Results

Notice what caused the project to be successful or to encounter difficulties. Discuss these lessons with the subordinates involved and integrate what you learn into your next opportunity for delegation. Praise their accomplishments in front of their peers and to your supervisor.

Improve Performance of Essential Tasks

Now that you have freed yourself of nonessential and inappropriate tasks, look closely at the remaining ones. Determine your goals and link them to your most important tasks. Your success at performing job-related tasks and your overall success as a leader depend upon you establishing short-, medium-, and long-term goals that are realistic, achievable, measurable, and time-specific.

Goals are one of the most powerful motivators that are available to you because with them you can overcome challenges that would have normally been unachievable. Numerous studies have shown that the most successful people, despite obstacles or disabilities, are those who have clearly identified and committed themselves to their personal and professional goals. Take time to think specifically about what you want to accomplish on the job, at home, during leisure, and in the community over the next few weeks, months, and years. These could include a job promotion, a certain level of income, a healthy relationship, or a family. Keep these written goals nearby and review them daily to help you prioritize your activities. Once you determine why you are working every day, that is, to achieve specific goals, then you will have gone far in preparing yourself to do what is necessary to accomplish them.

Plan and prioritize your daily, weekly, quarterly, and annual tasks. Prioritization consists of ranking your tasks in terms of their value to you and

STEP

◆ 4 ◆

your organization. Think of each task's value in terms of importance and urgency. Your objective is to spend most of your time on important/nonurgent tasks such as planning, solving long-term problems, or accomplishing goals. Since these high-payoff tasks are where you make the most contribution to the organization, it makes sense to spend a significant amount of time in this vital area. Throughout the day, you will encounter planned and unplanned important/urgent tasks such as personnel or customer crises. You must attend to these, but your objective is to minimize them from occurring because they distract you from other important priorities. Spend less time on unimportant/urgent tasks such as reading the mail or certain administrative duties because they do not significantly help you to accomplish your most important priorities, although accomplishing them often deceptively makes you feel as if you are getting important work done. Avoid the remaining tasks, which are unimportant/nonurgent tasks such as gossiping or computer games.

If you write your tasks on some type of planning document, you are more likely to accomplish them. These tasks reflect daily and weekly short-term planning, medium-term quarterly planning, and long-term annual planning. Before you leave work or, alternatively, before you start work the following day, develop your daily plan by listing your required tasks in order of priority. Simply taking a few minutes to plan your activities and tasks will help you stay focused on the most important. Remember, you have the time to plan and planning is crucial to keeping you focused on your important goals. Keep the plan nearby so you can easily refer to it throughout the day and coordinate it with your weekly plan, which is what you want to accomplish during a five-day period. Your weekly short-term plans are achieved by accomplishing the detailed tasks included in the daily plans. Your quarterly plan reflects your goals and activities for the upcoming three months; it is achieved through accomplishing your weekly plans. Likewise, the annual plan shows your major goals for the upcoming 12 months and the following two to five years.

Use your most productive time for the most important tasks. When developing your time journal several pages ago, you identified a time period when you got more work done and seemed to be more alert. For most people, this is sometime before lunch, but it can vary for anyone. Since your energy level is highest during this period, use this time wisely by working on your most important tasks.

Schedule specific time for no interruptions, specific activities, and routine events. Let daily planning liberate you to schedule what you need to schedule. First, block off time during each day when you will not allow anyone to interrupt you, either in person or by telephone. You then can better concentrate on your high priority tasks. For this to be successfully implemented, first coordinate it with your assistant or subordinates. Second, always schedule sufficient time for any planned event that requires your presence, such as meetings, ceremonies, coaching sessions, or interviews. Third, allow for time during the day when you can group routine activities together, such as returning telephone calls, signing documents, or reading.

Avoid overscheduling. When tempted to schedule every hour of the day with some activity, do not forget to build in some slack time so that when a crisis or unplanned event occurs, you will not get behind schedule.

Eliminate time wasters. Whenever you do something that is unrelated to accomplishing your most important priorities, then you are wasting time. Examples of personal time wasters include gossiping, office clutter, and procrastination.

Other time wasters originate from external events such as unscheduled visitors and telephone calls, crises, and periods of waiting. Your time journal no doubt has several of these listed and vividly shows you how they creep into your daily schedule and distract you from your most important tasks. You can reclaim a significant amount of time if you simply focus on eliminating the time wasters. The best way to detect if you are wasting time and to prompt you quickly back to your important work is to ask yourself a simple question several times a day: "Is what I am doing right now helping me achieve today's priority tasks?"

Here are seven tips to help you eliminate time wasters.

Avoid Office Clutter

When you cannot access a document or file within two minutes, or if you have missed deadlines because paperwork has gotten lost on your desk, it is time to reorganize your office. There are many books available about paperwork control, filing systems, and office layout, but here are some key points that can immediately help you.

► Use documents until you no longer immediately need them, then file them in your personal filing system near your desk if you will need access to them for a specific project, in a tickler system that reminds you on a certain date of a required action, or permanently in the central files so others can find them if you are away. Never leave loose documents lying on your desk overnight. With the help of your assistant, periodically purge the files and discard documents that no longer have value to you or your organization. Keep only critical items that are legally required to be retained, one-of-a-kind documents, or key information that likely will be referred to again.

▸ Identify infrequently used desktop items and put them inside the desk or give them to someone who can use them.

▸ Routinely screen paperwork or mail with the goal of handling it only once. If that is impractical, each handling must move the task one step closer to completion. If you are the action officer for an item, place the document in an action folder along with related documents. Act on these items according to their priority and limit the number of times you handle the correspondence. Place anything else, including mail, in folders for reading later, pass it along with comments to the proper action officer or your assistant, or discard if of no use. Coordinate any deadlines with your planning system so that you do not lose track of them. Instead of keeping magazines after skimming them, clip out those articles that are pertinent to your work and toss out the magazine.

Reduce People Interruptions

Remember that when people visit your office or workspace, you are in control because it is your domain. When you invite them to your office, have a clear goal of what you want to accomplish and how long it will take. When you finish your agenda with them, simply stand up to indicate the visit is over. Your visitors should get the hint. If not, thank them for coming, and let them know that you intend to move on to other work. You can discourage unwanted interruptions by facing your desk away from the door, closing the door, or instructing your assistant to screen visitors. When unexpected visitors arrive, your three choices are to chat with a purpose, chat briefly and get back to work, or not chat at all.

▸ If your visitor is an infrequent but important unannounced visitor — your supervisor, a vice president, a key subordinate, or client, for example — take the necessary time and chat with them, trying to keep the focus on constructive topics related to work. Even though these people are an interruption, you can insert slack time into your schedule to cover unplanned events such as these. Take advantage of the situation and resolve important issues or get to know the visitor a little better.

▸ Some unexpected but regular visitors may warrant a brief conversation, such as a quick update on a project. Stand up and greet them but do not invite them to sit down unless you have plenty of time. Get to the reason quickly of why they need to talk with you. When finished with the conversation, indicate to the visitor that you have other work in progress.

▶ Get in the habit of firmly, but politely, telling unwanted visitors that you simply do not have time to talk. If they have business to conduct, tell them to call you at a certain time later in the day, or schedule an appointment with them. Eventually, these visitors will learn to play by your rules.

Keep Your Focus

After eliminating an office time waster, immediately refocus on your priority tasks. You can gain several minutes simply by quickly getting back to what you were doing before the interruption.

Avoid Procrastination

When tempted to delay taking action on a task for whatever reason, dullness, complexity, or nonurgency, for example, remind yourself that delay will only make your overall work much more complicated. Not only will the task not get done but you will also constantly think about it, which will affect how well you accomplish other tasks. Your best solution is to commit to finishing the task, tell someone about your commitment, set a completion deadline, think about how good you will feel when you finish the task or what you will do as a self-reward for finishing it, and start work on the task immediately. Other anti-procrastination tips include delegating and breaking the task into simpler steps.

Manage Telephone Calls

Although almost everyone seems to complain about telephone calls, phone conversations are useful ways to get your work done if you learn how to control them. When on the phone, be brief, to the point, and focused on work-related topics. Your assistant, if you have one, is integral in helping you screen out routine and inapplicable calls. Return routine calls during specific time periods; handle urgent ones immediately.

If you leave someone a message through an assistant or voice-mail, state four items: your name, the subject of the call, when you can and cannot be reached to eliminate phone tag, and telephone number repeated twice for accuracy. Your own voice mail message for incoming callers should state that you would like these same four pieces of information. When you or the recipient have knowledge of a telephone call's subject, it enables you to have any pertinent information readily available when you return the call. As a matter of courtesy, if you tell someone you will return their call, do it or have someone else return it for you.

Manage for Crisis

When an unexpected emergency occurs, your schedule gets pre-empted and anything you had planned to do is delayed or canceled. Your mission then is to get the crisis resolved so you can return to your important/nonurgent duties. The key to eliminating this time waster is preventing it from even occurring whenever possible. You can prevent some crises by analyzing the details of previously similar crises and thoroughly planning to prevent them from recurring, or at least knowing what actions to take when they do recur. Keeping certain truck parts on the premises, for example, might prevent another delay of several hours if your only delivery truck broke down again. This, in turn, would save you the time you would have spent locating the parts in a crisis situation.

Avoid Waiting for Events or Answers

Waiting steals your time primarily in two ways, when you are temporarily stalled waiting for some activity to begin or when you are waiting for answers so that you can continue your work. In the first situation, the key is to always have something productive to do when confronted with the inevitable waiting situation; this will minimize your wasted time. Some leaders welcome periods of waiting because they can use that time productively to think or read without interruption. Those people with long commutes often listen to professional development tapes in their automobiles. To avoid wasting your time in the second situation, go and dig out the answers instead of waiting for them to come to you. If someone is late in providing you with information, go to him or her and stress the importance of your getting this information as soon as possible. When you politely explain how you need this information to assist you with one of your priority tasks, he or she will likely increase the urgency.

STEP

◆ 5 ◆

Maintain Control of Your Time

There are dozens of time management systems that you or your organization can purchase or devise. The most used systems for time management include calendars, to-do lists, master planning documents, and planners and organizers. If you have a choice in which one you can use, take the time to explore what is available and choose one you feel comfortable using as your sole organizing tool. Even though time management has evolved considerably over the years from handwritten lists to elaborate systems that keep track of your personal and professional goals and values, you may initially only require a simple system, depending upon the range and complexity of your responsibilities.

The minimum considerations for a time management system are to have one that is simple to refer to, updatable, and mobile; keeps track of your short-, medium-, and long-term tasks and goals; is expandable to note telephone numbers, expenses, and other key information; and helps you effectively control your time. Most systems will be comprehensive enough to allow you to permanently stop using scraps of paper or notes to keep track of appointments, telephone calls, or routine information. In light of this, you will probably want a system more advanced than a to-do list but possibly not one as elaborate as an electronic organizer. Some leaders may require a computer-based system if they oversee difficult projects, manage multiple customer or supplier relationships, or need to receive frequent reminders.

Calendars and to-do lists permit you to easily note appointments, a variety of tasks, or long-range plans. Used alone, however, they typically do not allow you to effectively consolidate everything that you might do during the day, such as jotting down notes, tracking complicated tasks or projects that you have delegated to others, or managing frequent and recurring deadlines.

A master planning document does these things by listing your significant tasks and activities over the upcoming weeks and months. It groups all these activities by priority, or alternatively prioritizes them during specific days or weeks. Having such a broad overview of your responsibilities will show you your activities at a glance and will make it easier to do detailed daily planning. You can list simple activities together on one sheet, while more complicated projects and tasks can each have their own sheet. Most people who use master planning documents devise a format with which they are comfortable, or they use one of the many commercially available products.

Planners and organizers are great for people who frequently travel or quickly need access to a broad range of information. They consolidate the features of the previously discussed tools and improve upon them by integrating time and goal management. With the intent of making you much more productive, some of them encourage you to explore your values and align them with your daily actions.

Traveling is a traditional and useful means to visit customers or employees, inspect operations, or attend conferences. It is not a reason, however, for you to lose control of your time. Determine first if the trip is necessary and if the work can be done through alternative means such as telephone or video conferencing, if available. If the trip is needed, could someone go in your place or could someone travel to your location? If you choose to travel, consider the trip an extension of your workplace and continue using your priority and time management skills. A well-prepared travel checklist will quickly remind you or your assistant what personal and work-related items you need to take with you so that the trip will go smoothly.

Since you will be leading your organization from a distance, there are four points to note. First, take special care to inform your subordinates in advance that you are departing so that they can properly plan for your absence and avoid inundating you with last minute questions. Second, your superior and key subordinates must be able to contact you at any time. A good idea would be to give them a copy of your itinerary that has your hotel and pager numbers listed. Third, because traveling creates more uncertainty than working at the office, double check all appointments and meetings to make sure they are still scheduled. Finally, to help you keep your sanity and ability to react to on-the-road crises, allow yourself plenty of time between appointments and flight connections and for hotel checkouts. If you are a frequent traveler, consider joining airline, hotel, and rental car clubs because they provide extra amenities and savings that can make your trip more enjoyable and productive.

As a final suggestion to maintain control of your time, consider taking a reading comprehension course. Although traditionally known as speed reading courses, these seminars accomplish much more by helping you achieve greater levels of productivity and performance. In addition to reading faster, you will learn how to increase recall and comprehension of what you have just read. As a leader, this will help you in several ways. First, you will efficiently process the mountains of paperwork that flow across your desk and free up time to spend on previously neglected reading or to act on what you have just read. Second, you will learn proven techniques of abbreviated note-taking and will soon use them during meetings, traveling, or on-site supervision. Finally, you will learn how to better comprehend difficult and lengthy material, such as technical, financial, or legal documents.

Manage Stress

Along with the enormity of your job comes unavoidable stress, which affects you differently than other challenges. It is useful, therefore, to develop your knowledge about stress so that you can recognize it and manage it. This will allow you and your subordinates to cope more effectively with the inevitable stressful situations that occur in the workplace and, in turn, allow you to better focus on your daily priorities.

What is stress? Stress is the internal response you have to everything that happens to you. Higher stress levels usually manifest themselves in two ways: in your inherent circumstances, such as in your family problems, work challenges, or time constraints; and in your unique reaction to circumstances, such as in headaches, anxiety, denial, or serious physical problems. Stress intensity can range from a low level, such as when reading a document, to a high level, when making a presentation to the organization's board of directors. Temporary surges in your stress levels are not harmful and are difficult to prevent. When your system is routinely under moderate to high levels of stress, however, you will experience hormonal imbalances that could eventually lead to serious health problems.

One of your responsibilities as a leader is to proactively identify and ultimately reduce the stress in your organization. This is important for two reasons. First, by identifying stressed individuals and then committing to helping them, you will not only make them more productive, you often will identify major organizational problems and get them resolved too. Second, by becoming more aware of other people's stress, you can be more attentive to your own symptoms and then take actions to help yourself. You experience the same types of stress as your subordinates, but since you carry the additional responsibilities of leadership, your stress levels can be more intense. Your level of stress and your reaction to that stress will affect your subordinates; your objective is to not let it negatively affect them.

By talking with your subordinates and knowing what is happening in the workplace, you can spot some of the most common symptoms of stress, including increase in employee hostility, decrease in positive attitudes, excessive use of overtime, and increase in family conflicts. You can remain alert to other stressful situations by observing specific employee indicators such as lethargy, illnesses, absenteeism, substance abuse, irritability, and a decrease in work performance. There are four specific actions you can take to manage workplace stress.

Create and Maintain a Great Work Environment

As you use the leadership skills presented in this book, you will make tremendous progress in minimizing the stress in your organization. Pay close attention to all areas of your responsibilities and handle challenges as they arise, not later.

Subordinates need you to be realistic, fair, reasonable, honest, appreciative, participative, and caring. They do not need ambiguity, volatility, or indecisiveness. If they are convinced that you are concerned for their personal and professional welfare, they will better cope with workplace stress.

Encourage Open Communication

If your subordinates can easily approach you about workplace issues, such as job deadlines, career development, or any dissatisfaction that they are having, they will continually relieve their stress instead of keeping it inside of themselves. This periodic venting is a simple way for them to gain some control and power in the workplace, and it provides you with an excellent opportunity to offer them the encouragement and coaching they regularly need.

Advocate Healthy Living

Since most people do not sleep enough, exercise regularly, relax sufficiently, or eat properly, think of the opportunity you have to promote a healthy lifestyle for your subordinates. Not only will they appreciate your caring enough to think of them but they will also develop habits that will decrease their stress and help them live longer.

There are experts in just about any city who can speak to your subordinates about healthy living; you also can distribute widely available literature. The advantages of these methods are that they help you avoid forcing people to cooperate and allow people to inform themselves and proceed at their own pace. Remember that your leadership actions speak louder than words, so take your own advice and pursue a healthy lifestyle.

Conduct Stress Management Training

Schedule training for your workers and expose them to these stress management concepts. Your company's insurance plan may provide for it or a local hospital will be able to refer you to a qualified representative to speak on the subject. It is ultimately the responsibility of each subordinate to manage his or her own stress, and since stress transcends all areas of life, including family, social, and work, your subordinates will greatly benefit from formal stress management training.

Maintain Your Lead

A leader encounters a greater variety of challenges and usually has more complex responsibilities in the work day than does the typical nonleader. This chapter has shown you specific techniques to prioritize these tasks in a way that will allow you to accomplish much more than before. The time management process will help you focus on your most important professional and personal objectives, be more efficient with your time, waste less time, and let others assume more of the work. Stress prevention will ensure that your time remains efficiently and effectively used, thus increasing your leadership success.

CHAPTER 7

MANAGE THE PROJECT

A project is a unique undertaking that has a distinct start and finish, its own budget, and an objective of producing a specific product, service, or event according to specific standards. Everyone works with projects, whether the projects are small ones, such as setting up a birthday party, or mammoth ones, such as planning an annual conference or building a manufacturing facility.

Projects differ from your day-to-day responsibilities because projects are a one-time undertaking, not repetitive like your normal duties; require considerably more interdepartmental support, unlike the degree of departmental autonomy that normally exists; and are divided into specific sections that are sequenced and independently evaluated, unlike the unordered tasks that occur daily.

There are similarities, however, between projects and your daily operations. These include the need to use existing resources to get the job done and the necessity for the appropriate functional areas or subject matter experts to take responsibility and ownership of specific technical tasks under their realm of responsibility. This task ownership occurs even though the task may be part of someone else's project.

Regardless of their size, projects all share similar characteristics and processes. This chapter will present a leader's approach to project management that you can apply to all your project challenges at work, home, or in the community. The objective is to provide an easy-to-implement process for project management, help you to organize your projects, and give you the flexibility to use your existing organizational project management procedures. In time through practice on the job or specific training, you will learn many more details, techniques, and styles of project management.

Managing projects involves utilizing your skills, the skills of team members, and established principles and methods to efficiently guide an otherwise unmanageable series of activities to their end. If you analyze your daily tasks, you can relate almost everything to a specific project. A telephone call could be part of your decision to buy a new information management system. Your brainstorming session with key subordinates could be the start of a new product launch. All projects contain similar tasks that must be performed with the cooperation of several individuals from different departments within the organization. The objective of project management is simply to plan, organize, direct, and monitor this process, with the goal of producing the best end product or service that you can.

If you are in an organization that relies upon projects, it is likely you follow a prescribed methodology for managing projects, and you and your subordinates regularly train on the subject. Your company may even be heavily oriented towards project management as a primary method of structuring work, and you may have access to state-of-the-art computer programs to track every detail of a project. The principles you learn in this chapter, however, still apply and are important in providing you with a solid background that you can use no matter how proficient you currently are or what techniques you currently use. There are several steps for successful project management.

- ► Choose the project manager.
- ► Establish objectives and requirements.
- ► Select the team.
- ► Plan the project.
- ► Manage the project.
- ► Monitor the project.
- ► Coordinate follow-up activities.

Choose the Project Manager

As a leader in your organization, you will often work as a project manager and be in charge of all aspects of a project. You will typically have this assignment in addition to your regular responsibilities. At other times, you will choose others to be the project manager and will exercise supervisory responsibility over them. This section will help you to correctly choose those people.

It is important that you designate your project managers as soon as you can; this will enable them to be an integral part of the planning process from the early stages of the project. Due to the importance of getting the project accomplished correctly and on time, you cannot arbitrarily choose project managers. They should have proven leadership abilities, appropriate technical skills, and sufficient cross-functional experience. If you have the luxury of choosing among several candidates, three guidelines that will help you choose the right person to manage your project are to assess their leadership ability, skills, and experience.

Leadership Ability

The project manager should know how to energetically lead a team of individuals to accomplish a multi-faceted project. Examine the potential candidates and judge if they possess a variety of leadership experience that has prepared them for your project. Since they will need their leadership skills during the project, the candidates should have experience in using the skills that are presented in this book, especially the primary- and intermediate-level skills.

The right person will be a confident and decisive leader who is particularly good at planning, implementing, delegating, problem solving, and handling multiple priorities. Since they will be involved in directing the efforts of a diverse team, they should be extremely adept in relationship skills such as communication, teamwork, conflict resolution, and coaching. Some candidates will have had previous experience managing similar projects; others will not, but do not automatically exclude them from consideration.

Technical Skills

It is imperative that project managers understand the technology and processes involved in the project. They do not have to be an experts in the area, but they must have some depth of knowledge to effectively plan, monitor, and complete the project.

Cross-functional Experience

The project manager will lead a team composed of individuals from various departments or functional areas within the organization. Look for someone who has worked in several areas or has the organizational savvy to know how to approach these departments to garner support and resources.

Establish Objectives and Requirements

As the project manager, your initial work will be to clearly identify and define the major aspects of the project. By taking the time to do this correctly and thoroughly, you will save yourself time, expense, and aggravation later on. From the beginning, take detailed notes in a notebook or binder called a project log, which acts as a journal and clearly documents key decisions, comments, and promises made by the many people involved in the project. It serves as institutional knowledge and will easily refresh your memory when needed or update other people if necessary.

Confer with each client so you can thoroughly grasp their intentions and needs. The project's client is an accountable individual, not individuals or departments, who is committed to successfully completing the project and guiding you when necessary. Your client may be the person who tasked you with the project or someone they designate or recommend within the organization. More likely, however, the client will be someone who has the most interest in the project or is funding the project. You may have to meet with the client two or three times to exactly pinpoint the project's objectives and requirements. You will then have sufficient information to develop a tentative plan to discuss later in your meeting with key individuals. Specific points to cover in detail include:

- ▶ What are the objectives of the project? Determine what the client is looking for, how the project will serve a need or solve their problems, if there are any special risks, and whether similar projects were tried previously.
- ▶ What is the anticipated schedule? Create a timeline with start, finish, and milestones.
- ▶ Who are the key people? Determine the final approval authority, other decisionmakers, and community liaisons.
- ▶ Is funding approved for the project? If not, determine when it will be approved and what the targeted cost is.
- ▶ What are the end product's specifications, standards, and constraints? Specify details of quality, performance, reliability, applicable regulations, and any special considerations. Quantify this information whenever feasible.

Get approval to begin the project. Prepare a project proposal for the client that concisely incorporates all the information you have gathered. The key is to succinctly address all the major issues, background information, and assumptions that you and the client have made. The proposal serves as your official record of what you understand the client wants. It also will serve as a key document that you and your project team will use until the completion of the project.

Assemble key individuals to define the project. Schedule a planning meeting that includes the client, line managers who have the relevant expertise, your supervisor if requested, and any staff officers or peers whose input you need. Your client may prefer not to attend this meeting because they may not want to be involved with the details at this point. Encourage them to attend part of the meeting if possible because they will be invaluable in providing immediate clarification of any issues. Let the attendees know in advance the purpose of the meeting and that you expect them to come prepared to discuss the project from their perspective and experience. This meeting will provide you with sufficient answers to update the client with any significant conclusions or challenges, arrive at better estimates, and proceed to the more detailed planning stage.

Soliciting input from all group members, analyze and discuss the project in detail. You already have the answers to some of the key questions, but the purpose of this meeting is to communicate them to your attendees, validate your tentative conclusions, troubleshoot all major areas, and elicit buy-in from the attendees, whose efforts will be crucial to successful project completion. During the meeting, first present the conclusions reached by you and your client, then discuss the project in detail. Seek answers to these questions:

- ► How should the project be organized?
- ► What are the most important tasks and their major subtasks?
- ► What are the resource requirements for each category, such as people, equipment, and money?
- ► How will these resources be estimated, allocated, and controlled?
- ► Is the deadline realistic and achievable?
- ► What are potential problems that could occur?

Select the Team

You alone cannot complete the project; you will require the efforts of a skilled, committed, motivated, responsible, and cohesive group of individuals. By paying particular attention to the team's composition, responsibilities, and leadership, you will complete your project more effectively by generating superior planning and implementation tactics. This section will outline basic points about teamwork within the context of project management. Chapter 11 will further expand on the topic of teamwork.

These are the steps for creating a project team.

- ▸ List major staffing requirements.
- ▸ Identify sources of team members.
- ▸ Select specific team members.
- ▸ Create a skills inventory.
- ▸ Match skills with responsibilities.
- ▸ Assemble, inform, and organize the team.

List Major Staffing Requirements

To identify your major staffing requirements, estimate the numbers of people and kinds of skills that you will need to complete the project. For each required position, write a brief job description that will outline exactly what type of individual you need.

Identify Sources of Team Members

Sources include your staff, permanent staff in other departments, and part-time assistance such as temporary employees or consultants. Usually the human resources department will assist you in analyzing who is employed by the company and if there are part-timers or consultants who routinely assist the company. The human resources department may even centralize the process of staffing projects or could give you suggestions about the etiquette involved in staffing from within the company; if so, this could simplify your task.

Seek out strong performers who have worked with you in the past. Especially note potential team members with critical skills. Avoid excluding otherwise qualified people who lack a certain skill; you later may be able to schedule training for them.

Select Specific Team Members

Once you know the type and departmental location of the team members you need, recruit them. Do this delicately and sensitively with a firm respect of your organization's culture. Although you have the authority to staff your project, you can count on some resistance from the potential team members' supervisors, since they will not have complete use of their employee if you select them for your project. Individually approach each supervisor and explain your needs and how they can help by supplying team members. If your organization routinely has projects or if its culture is supportive of projects, the supervisors will probably easily work with you to get the right staffing. If not, you will have to negotiate to get what you need; this will involve give-and-take from both you and the supervisors. If your efforts fail to satisfy your staffing needs, you can approach other supervisors or your senior leadership for assistance.

It is always wise to interview the selected team members before you officially make them part of your team. You want to ensure that they have a good attitude, team relationship skills, and sufficient availability for the duration of the project. The interview will permit you to explore their job experience, technical skills, and any other special skills they may have. If at the end of the interview you believe that they are the type of person you want working on your project, extend the offer to them.

Create a Skills Inventory

Once you have all the team members identified, itemize their skills by using a simple listing called a skills inventory. This valuable document will clearly record the team's available skills, and it will later ensure that you have both the right mixes of team members and sufficient overlap among the skills in case someone becomes unavailable during the project. Though none of the team members will have the exact skill expertise as the others, you certainly want each of the major skills requirements covered by two or more people, as described next.

Match Skills with Responsibilities

Prepare a responsibilities chart that clearly shows who has primary responsibilities for the tasks and who has supporting responsibilities. The chart officially records the project responsibilities of each team member. You will use it during the project to reassign work and to keep team members' supervisors informed of what their subordinates are doing. List all tasks vertically down the left column, with the team members' names across the top. The goal is to assign the most qualified person to each task's primary position and then support each task with lesser qualified people. Before you permanently assign team members to each of the tasks, use good judgment by seeking their input. This will help you identify any potential conflicts now rather than later, and it will increase the team members' long-term commitment to their project responsibilities.

Assemble, Inform, and Organize the Team

Meet with the team to introduce them to each other and to explain the project's background and details, including objectives, work done so far, strategy, and the responsibilities chart. Then get them excited about the upcoming mission. They need to know the project's importance to the organization, that they are the best team for the project, and how it is crucial for them to accomplish their tasks on-time, as a team, within budget, and according to project standards.

Make it clear to your team that you are their leader. Explain to your team members that, although they may be permanently assigned to another department, you have operational control over them and will provide details of their performance to their supervisor.

Before the first team meeting, arrange for all supervisors to personally express to their subordinates their support of the project and their desire for the subordinates to treat the project as an extension of their normal duties. It would also be a good idea for you to thank the functional supervisors for their support of your project; a solid relationship with each supervisor will help you later when you need to get tasks, decisions, and special favors handled quickly and without conflict.

Now is the time to get to work with your team to begin the detailed planning portion of the project.

Plan the Project

Your objective is to develop a project plan, which is a series of documents that explains all the project's details. It is foremost a communications plan that will let all interested parties know exactly who is on the team, where the team is headed, and how it will get there.

The purpose of project planning is to develop the details of a strategy that links the project's goals and objectives to specific implementing activities. During this process, you examine all your resources and constraints, such as personnel, supplies, time, and budgets, and organize them into a strategy by using planning tools. These tools will be described in detail later in the chapter.

You accomplish the planning process with your team. Since you alone cannot possibly have all the information to create an effective plan, expect to involve as many experienced people in the planning process as necessary.

There are five steps in creating a project plan.

- ▶ Design the project.
- ▶ Estimate the project.
- ▶ Schedule the project.
- ▶ Budget the project.
- ▶ Finalize and approve the plan.

Design the Project

In designing your project, you first specify the actual tasks to be performed during the project. This list of tasks is called a work breakdown structure. The work breakdown structure is one of your most important project tools because it concisely shows what needs to be done and provides a framework for other project documents. To achieve detail and accuracy, develop the work breakdown structure during several meetings with your team and, if necessary, by using questionnaires targeted to functional supervisors.

First, list all the major categories of activities of the project. You can base these classifications of work on any one of several categories such as stages of time, product development cycle, functional work areas, and major components of the product or service.

Next, determine all the second and third levels of activities that must be completed to achieve each first level end product. Once you have identified all the levels, list the tasks that must be completed for each level.

Below is a partially completed chart of a work breakdown structure for an office redesign project. It identifies two of several major activities, along with their subordinate activities and tasks. Its list of specific tasks begins at level three, but there could have easily been another level or two of subactivities before the task listing began.

Work Breakdown Structure Chart (partial)

Project: Office Redesign

Level 1:	*Major Activity*		*Major Activity*	
	Construction		Temporary Office	
Level 2:	*Activity*	*Activity*	*Activity*	*Activity*
	Physical Design	Computer Wiring	Site Location	Relocation
Level 3:	*Tasks*	*Tasks*	*Tasks*	*Tasks*
	Retain architect	Determine needs	Locate realtor	Hire movers
	Review proposal	Examine equipment	Examine sites	Choose day
	Seek employee input	Seek bids	Sign lease	Curtail work

Continue this listing process for each major activity category until you reach a task level where you can dependably estimate the task's completion time and resource costs, and where you are certain that no major task has been left out. Usually this occurs at level four or five, but it could go lower. You and your team now identify all the tasks' owners which are people who are primarily responsible for the tasks, who will support these owners, the tasks' end product, and each product's quality standards. Throughout the process, you can divide the team into subgroups to analyze specific activities and their tasks. However, to prevent faulty conclusions, it is important to have each subgroup defend their conclusions in front of the whole team.

As the project manager, you should know prior to the beginning of your first team meeting what the first and second-level activities will most likely be. You surmised this from your earlier discussions with the client and key individuals. Knowing these sublevels will give both you and your team the right direction to proceed. Include sufficient detail to be able to later quantify the project's cost and duration, but avoid using too much detail at this point. To promote team discussion, it is helpful to chart your work breakdown structure on a chalkboard or flipchart.

The next step in the process is to develop the project's network. The project network shows the associations, or dependencies, among the tasks. The process of constructing the network is called dependency analysis. By sequencing the tasks on a chart, you will see exactly how each task relates to the others.

The first part of this process is to use all the tasks on your work breakdown structure chart to decide their relationship to each other by identifying them with their preceding task. Since the Work Breakdown Structure Chart shown lists just two major activities in a large project, not all task interdependencies are given nor are the task listings complete. In reality, you will need all tasks listed in order for it to completely identify task interdependence. But it does show you how the concept works.

Group the tasks within their major activity and assign them an identification number of your choice. The key point to remember is that tasks are accomplished in three ways: 1) immediately after another task, 2) at the same time as other tasks, or 3) at the beginning or end of a project. Find the first task that can start the project and identify it by a dash in the fourth column in the Project Network Chart on the next page. Tasks 1.1 and 3.1 are the first ones and can begin simultaneously if you choose.

Next find the tasks that can be immediately done after tasks 1.1 and 3.1; identify them with the task numbers of their predecessors. For the remainder of the analysis, always ask which other tasks can be started and ongoing with each new task you analyze. These will be assigned the same predecessor task as the new task. If there are no such parallel tasks, determine what the next task is. This process continues until all the tasks are linked.

After you have determined the dependencies, define what the end products are for each task and then indicate the task duration. The product is the result of completing the task. Unlike the task, which is listed as an action verb, the product is a noun. The final step is to estimate the time it will take to complete each task; place this number in the duration column. The next section will discuss duration estimates in more detail.

Project Network Chart (partial)

Project: Office Redesign

Task ID #	Description	End Product	Preceding Task	Duration
Construction – Physical Design				
1.1	Retain architect	Committed architect	—	2 days
1.2	Review proposal	Proposal knowledge	1.1	3 days
1.3	Seek employee input	Employee collaboration	1.2	2 days
Construction – Wiring				
2.1	Determine needs	Needs document	1.3	4 days
2.2	Examine equipment	Top equipment choices	2.1	2 days
2.3	Seek bids	Bid variety	2.2	3 days
Temporary Office – Site Location				
3.1	Locate realtor	A committed realtor	—	2 days
3.2	Examine sites	Site knowledge	3.1	4 days
3.3	Sign lease	Signed lease	3.2	2 days
Temporary Office – Relocation				
4.1	Hire movers	Moving contract	4.2	2 days
4.2	Choose move day	Company-wide move day	3.3	1 day
4.3	Curtail work	Relocatable work force	4.1	2 days

If you prefer a graphic approach for dependency analysis, there is a popular charting method you can use. A PERT (Program Evaluation and Review Technique) chart is a type of flowchart that depicts sequencing of tasks. Your objective is to list each task on sticky notecards and order them from left to right on a chalkboard or wall, starting with the lowest level task that can naturally start the project. Then search for tasks that can be going on at the same time as this first task. If you find that some tasks have the same predecessor, then these could begin at the same time and should be placed accordingly.

The PERT Chart of the Work Breakdown Structure's Project Network graphically depicts the project network's sequencing of tasks.

PERT Chart of the Work Breakdown Structure's Project Network

Project: Office Redesign

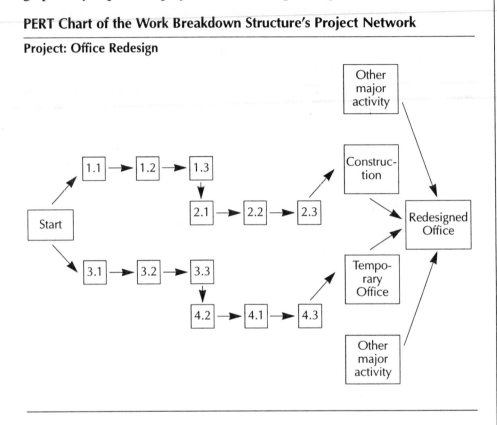

Estimate the Project

STEP
◆ 2 ◆

You can make the process of estimation simple or complex, depending upon your particular project, your level of expertise, and the forecasting techniques used in your organization. Despite the potential complexity, the process is straightforward. You and your team analyze each task and decide how long it will take to realistically complete it. Write the estimates in the duration column of your project network chart. If there is disagreement on the estimate, delay a decision until the task owner can analyze it and make a suggestion to the team. Before approving a final estimate for a task, ask if it is realistic considering the task owner's experience, knowledge, and time available for the task.

Once you determine the duration of each task within the project network chart, you have enough information to compute the anticipated duration of the project or its critical path. This is done simply by determining which sequence of tasks, from the project's start to finish, is the longest. In the abbreviated example, the tasks along the construction activity comprise the critical path because sixteen days are required for construction and only thirteen for the temporary office. As the project manager, one of your major responsibilities is to frequently monitor task activity along the critical path because disruptions in accomplishing these tasks will increase your project's duration. If you complete the tasks sooner than expected, your project's duration will decrease.

Your job as the project's leader is to understand all the nuances of task duration so that you can supervise a valid estimation process. You must know how to speed up completion of the project or what to do when faced with unexpected bottlenecks. It would be helpful before beginning a project to study a manual on project management or consult with an experienced project manager in your organization. You then will have access to detailed knowledge and techniques that only a comprehensive source can give you. As you practice using the many estimation techniques, they will become second nature to you.

STEP

◆ 3 ◆

Schedule the Project

Placing each task on a timeline gives you a broad picture of the project's task sequencing that will be useful in your final planning. There are many ways to schedule a project. At the very least, your scheduling document should have two axes, a vertical sequencing of the tasks and a horizontal listing of time.

Gantt Chart (partial)

Project: Office Redesign

Task ID #	0	1	2	3	4	5	6	7	8	9	10	11	12	13	14	15	16
1.1		██	██														
1.2				██	██												
1.3							██										
2.1									██	██	██	██					
2.2													██	██			
2.3																██	██
3.1		██	██														
3.2				██	██	██											
3.3								██									
4.2										██							
4.1												██					
4.3														██	██		

Your organization may have its own scheduling format, or it may use one of the many computer software programs. These tools will help you better manage your project, but you cannot completely rely upon them to monitor events because it is you who is responsible for the project, not a management tool.

The simple scheduling document on the previous page is patterned after the popular Gantt planning chart. Notice that each task is scheduled for completion during a specific time period. The critical path tasks, numbers 1.1 through 2.3, are listed in the priority position at the top of the table. The remaining tasks, which are on a noncritical path, are shown next. Tasks on noncritical paths have float time, or additional time, in which to get accomplished before the critical path tasks are finished. If necessary, this float time can be used to keep your project on schedule when unplanned events cause you to miss your anticipated timelines.

If your schedule shows that you cannot finish the project by the completion date, make adjustments to the individual tasks in order to compress your timeline. Verify that all critical tasks are crucial to the project, then examine if you can redesign them to be more quickly accomplished.

To speed up their completion, consider redistributing these tasks or assigning additional resources to them. Another alternative is to review the sequencing of tasks and attempt to complete more of them at the same time rather than sequentially. Finally, you could start a task after its predecessor is only partially completed, thus reducing the total time committed to that particular path.

Budget the Project

Your next objective is to assign specific team members to each task and identify other needed resources. The net effect of this step is a firm estimate of the cost of the project. This step is commonly called resource and cost loading and can require several revisions before you develop a viable budget.

The key to task assignment is to equitably balance the workload within the project. Consider details such as team members' expertise, their availability during the project, and whether they have a primary or supporting role for the task. Identify the percentage of time each team member will work on each task during each time period. If after making the assignments you determine that an imbalance exists, there are creative ways to further balance the workload and still keep your project on course, such as using overtime or temporary help to eliminate a labor shortage. After communicating the assignments to your team, ask them to determine what other resources are needed to accomplish their tasks.

STEP

◆ 4 ◆

Once you identify the required resources, coordinate their use with others who need them. This interorganizational balancing may be centrally controlled within your organization but most likely is handled at each functional level. Regardless, this coordination is crucial to your project's success and has to be done before obtaining final project approvals.

After this coordination, accurately determine all the costs related to the project. Using input from the team and the previously identified supporting departments within your organization, identify the costs associated with each individual task. Include costs related to personnel, overhead, training, research, and all other resources, such as material, equipment, and supplies. Most functional departments can easily identify the costs after you give them detailed information on the tasks, such as specifications and standards. Document the costs on an easily revised budget document, such as on a spreadsheet or project management software.

Finalize and Approve the Plan

By now, you have spent considerable time and effort in developing the best plan for your project. Assemble all your planning documents and objectively examine your work to determine if you have planned a feasible project. Check whether you are meeting the client's guidelines and project objectives, effectively and efficiently using the assigned resources, identifying frequent milestones to evaluate progress, and assigning responsibilities for every task.

Since you and your team members already have discussed possible disruptions to your project, now is a good time to formalize contingency plans with them. Develop these plans from an in-depth risk assessment in which you examine all areas of the project and prioritize them for their riskiness and potential for failure or disruption.

Contingency plans specify what you will do when events do not proceed exactly as planned or if resource and cost factors change. Examples of unforeseen events include critical tasks taking longer than expected, loss of a key worker, or a major resource disruption. In addition, identify what preventive measures you can take now to minimize the disruptions from occurring, especially in the high risk tasks, such as assigning a risky critical task to a top team member or more closely estimating a critical task's duration.

Once you have finalized the plan, your objective is to get final concurrence from all key individuals and to proceed with the project. Obtain written approval from departments that are supporting the project and from your supervisor, if necessary. Present the project's final outline to your client and explain the major areas of your plan, specifically noting any changes from your previous meetings. The client now decides if your plan is acceptable, given their knowledge of competing requirements within your organization, such as other projects, funding, and resource constraints. Once the client grants approval, notify your team and everyone else involved in the project.

Manage the Project

By completing the steps thus far in the project management cycle, you have done the most difficult part of the work, even though you have yet to start the project. You have now assembled a project team that understands what to do, how to do it, and when to do it.

This detailed preparatory work will ultimately save you a tremendous amount of time and will allow you to concentrate on completing the project in a timely manner. You will rely on your leadership skills to keep your team enthused, encouraged, and focused on the right path. Because these skills are so important, they are discussed in depth in later chapters of the book.

Start the Project

Communication during the implementation phase is crucial because of the certainty of change, disruptions, and the need for team and interdepartmental coordination. As the leader, it is your responsibility to create and maintain an atmosphere where everyone feels free to raise questions, seek guidance, and make suggestions.

This communication starts at the kickoff meeting during which you will present your team with all the project's details. These details, which should not surprise the team members in light of their recent input into the planning process, will include organizational structure and responsibilities, assignments and timelines, policies and procedures, and reporting and control mechanisms. Tell them you plan to regularly update the team, functional managers, and client, so the team must keep you regularly updated.

Since you are the person on the team who has the most knowledge and broadest overview of the project, it is imperative for you to stay involved in all aspects of the project. This will make it easier to spot trends and identify problems at the early stages, thus giving you more reaction time to solve the problems. Staying involved means daily monitoring of task progress, financial developments, and resource conditions. The best way to do this is to continually utilize the project's control procedures you developed during the planning process. You can count on staying busy, conferring with a multitude of people, and resolving several conflicts each day.

Respond to Change

Plan on encountering many changes to your project because no project is completed without some change to the original plan. These changes will start occurring within hours of obtaining the plan's final approval and will continue to the project's end. The changes typically affect two major areas, the end product and the plan. Your reaction to these changes will determine whether you successfully complete your project. It is your responsibility to identify and study these changes, then to respond with a viable solution that will allow you to continue on with your project management.

Now that you have noted this inevitable onslaught of modifications, a simple solution is to have a well-prepared change management plan that will easily allow you to integrate the changes into your project cycle. The ability to adapt to and implement change as a strategic leadership skill is the topic of Chapter 18; its application in project management is discussed next.

Changing the End Product

These types of changes, which modify in some way your end product, originate either from the internal environment by key individuals involved in the process, such as the client or team members, or they can be traced to the external environment, such as in technology, government, or business. Your client, for example, may decide after the plan's approval that they want to make changes to the end product's specifications. A team member may likewise recommend a major change based upon newly discovered information that they identified while working on the project. Emerging technologies may affect how certain tasks are completed. Finally, new regulatory constraints or the competition's moves may require that you alter aspects of the end product.

Your responses to these concerns must be well-reasoned because a minor change in the end product could involve significant changes to the project's plan, such as in cost, resources, and scheduling. To assist you in choosing a response, involve other people in a change management process. The person who believes that a change is necessary should submit a written request through you to a committee that has responsibility to consider, investigate, and approve the change. The committee is comprised of representatives of the functional areas involved in the project, the individual who has the authority to fund the change, key organizational decisionmakers, and you as the chairperson. The committee has the authority to decide if the change request warrants further action or not, to approve an investigation, if justified, to determine the details of the change and its impact on the project, and to approve or disapprove the change request and its funding.

As the project manager, you will lead the committee and control this process to ensure that it works efficiently without getting bogged down in committee. Do this by keeping track of ongoing actions, keeping committee members informed as to statuses of these actions, and reminding the committee members that since their time and their subordinates' time is valuable, they must make change decisions intelligently and quickly. Once a change has been approved, integrate it into your project by updating your scheduling and control documents, assigning task responsibility, and keeping your team updated.

Changing the Plan

As just shown, a change to the project's end product will most certainly impact your plan by causing you to make some adjustments. The other type of major change concerns that which does not immediately change the end product but which changes the plan that you have developed to produce that product. Whenever any aspect of your plan is altered such as cost, schedule, or resources, the change must be managed. This type of change can originate from the internal environment of client, team members, process, resources, and the organization's hierarchical levels, or from the external environment of government, regulation, economy, competition, and society. Adding complexity to the situation, change may occur on global, national, state, or local levels. Regardless of where the change originates or what the change is, you have to expect threats to your plan and to be prepared to respond to them.

Unlike the change management process suggested in the previous section, use a different approach when dealing with changes to your plan. In most cases, the changes will occur whether you want them to or not. Your best reaction, therefore, is to develop policies and procedures that will allow you to smoothly integrate the changes into your plan. First, ensure that all team members know that you want to be notified of all significant changes immediately while less important changes can wait until a regularly scheduled time, such as a weekly meeting. It is up to you to determine what is significant and communicate this to your team. Second, clearly define those changes you personally want to approve and those that you delegate to leaders on your team, and then enforce this rule. Third, since you will probably make regular changes to your plan, make sure that you communicate the changes to people who need this information, including team members, the client, and other departments. Finally, while realizing that change is inevitable, do not arbitrarily make changes without considering their impact and whether there are other options to try first.

Monitor the Project

Monitoring a project simply means knowing how close you are to achieving the components of your plan and then using this information to take corrective actions that will put you back on course. Monitoring, sometimes referred to as controlling, involves much more than passively watching the events of your project unfold. The leadership skill of monitoring is discussed in more detail in the next chapter, but it is addressed in this chapter as it pertains to project management.

You can best accomplish monitoring by involving yourself daily in the activities of your project and team members and by instituting formalized control procedures. Each day, go where there is project activity. By actually observing team members as they complete their tasks, you will see firsthand your plan in action and instinctively track your progress. As a result, you will quickly know of problems before they become crises, and you will be in a better position to react to them. Not only will you gain a more thorough understanding of individual tasks and their relation to the overall project but you will also be able to talk to team members in their own environment. They will be more likely to speak frankly with you and raise issues that they might have avoided had you met in your office. While conferring with your team members, praise those who are doing a great job or making particularly good suggestions. This will motivate them to greater achievement and prove to them that you are an involved, approachable leader who cares not only about the project but about them as well.

In addition to your daily involvement in the project's implementation, it is essential to have formal monitoring procedures that will supplement your on-site efforts. Some procedures will be mandated to you by the client, regulatory authorities, or your organization; you can develop others. The results, which are usually gathered and examined at least weekly, will help you objectively analyze your project's status, confirm what you discovered during informal monitoring, and give you the detailed information you need to prepare status reports. In a formal monitoring process, you must:

- Collect information and identify variances,
- Analyze the causes and effects of the variances,
- Take corrective action, and
- Communicate the action to your team and others.

Collect Information and Identify Variances

Use the planning documents you developed to analyze your progress in all areas, including cost, task accomplishment, schedule, labor, and resource use. The planning documents will indicate where your project should be while your newly collected information will show you where the project is; the difference between the two is the variance.

Collect information from team members through personal contact, scheduled review meetings, and project-tracking documents. These documents should require only the information you need, and plan on collecting them at a regularly scheduled time. To keep your team concentrating on their project work, avoid seeking information from team members when you can obtain it from your organization's functional departments, such as human resources, payroll, or accounting. Armed with this information, identify the variances from your plan.

Analyze the Causes and Effects of the Variances

Using the problem-solving method described in Chapter 5, determine the causes of the variances and their projected effect upon the project. Possible causes include higher-than-expected resource cost, low team member performance, or unrealistic estimates. Possible effects include increased project cost, duration, or risk. If you determine that the variance has no anticipated effect, do nothing. However, if you anticipate the variances will negatively affect the project, take corrective action.

Take Corrective Action

Modify the plan to eliminate the variance. You often will be able to make changes within the existing plan without significantly altering your budget or timeline, such as shifting resources or compressing the schedule. If you determine you will need additional resources or that new deadlines must be approved in order to deliver a quality end product within the planned timeframe, obtain clearance from the functional department or client, if necessary. If you do not obtain the additional resources that will allow you to complete a quality project as planned, then you are obligated to negotiate a change in the scope of the project.

Communicate the Action to Your Team and Others

Because your decision to correct the variances will alter your plan, this must be communicated to team members, functional departments, and the client. Do this by issuing status reports and revised plans and by conducting regular meetings and formal presentations. You will probably update your team members more frequently than the other parties; tailor the updates to your audience by giving more detailed information to your team than to the functional departments or the client.

It is equally important to keep nonteam members properly updated on the project's status. You will gain more cooperation if you make a special effort to keep them updated, both informally throughout the course of the project and formally at scheduled presentations. The key to effective communication is to clearly explain how the project is doing overall in terms of schedule and cost, what has recently occurred, what corrective action will be taken, and what you need your listeners to do. Remember to use any encounters with your team members as opportunities to seek their input about all aspects of the project. In addition to issuing status reports to your team, periodically update and issue a revised plan whenever the plan changes. Specifically note the changes in order to save everyone reading time.

Coordinate Follow-up Activities

As you reach the end of your project, coordinate the transition of the final product from your team to the client. Typically, this involves arranging for inspections, testing, and installation, if applicable. Redistribute any excess resources to the functional departments or according to your plan. Prepare a summarized project report for the client that details your major project accomplishments, significant events that altered the plan, and any major lessons you learned that could benefit the client. Also prepare a detailed internal report that compiles the main experiences of the team during the project. Feel free to be candid about difficulties, successes, and recommendations.

Your final action will be to reward your team members for a job well done. You probably have been rewarding them throughout the project, but now is the time to make sure that they know how much you, the functional departments, and the client appreciate their efforts. At a minimum, schedule the client to personally recognize your team members and thank them for the hard work. Your team members also will appreciate a letter of thanks from you, an end-of-project party, and recognition from their functional supervisor.

CHAPTER 8

MONITOR YOUR PROGRESS

Monitoring is a continual process that you use to check progress in all your leadership activities. It provides you with a framework to boost your goals into reality, your plans into action, your instructions to subordinates into accomplishments, and your organization's objectives into success.

A crucial aspect of monitoring is a proactive effort not only to observe what is happening but also to do something about it if necessary. This effort involves affecting the potential outcome of events by changing the behavior of people or other resources with which you are involved. It also relieves you of the need to wait until the end of a project, the completion of a task by a subordinate, or the arrival of a crisis to discover that there are significant problems that need correction.

When you monitor during the exercise of your leadership duties, you will reap several benefits. First, you will better understand the challenges, issues, and concerns facing your subordinates and organization. Knowing what is actually happening in your organization, not just what you think is going to happen, will give you the knowledge and conviction to direct subordinates to the proper path. Second, monitoring allows you to quickly identify bottom line trends that signal a threat to you and your organization. These dangers include unexplained declines in profits, revenue, operational performance, or customer satisfaction; unexpected variances from your plans, directives, or intentions; and subordinate-related issues such as discontent and high turnover. Finally, consistent monitoring of your environments, including your business, economic, political, and cultural environments, will help you spot more slowly evolving trends that might impact you, your subordinates, and your organization.

You can easily integrate monitoring into all your duties because almost everyone is aware of the concept and expects monitoring to occur. Despite the obvious need for monitoring, some people resent it as a manipulative process used to keep track of their activities. They may refer to it by its typically used name of controlling, which suggests images of dominance and power. Your challenge is to promote monitoring as a useful, necessary, and positive activity that is crucial to you, your subordinates, and the organization. You do this by communicating the benefits of monitoring to your subordinates, clearly publicizing the methods you use, and consistently using your results to make needed changes quickly and decisively.

Use of Monitoring

Although monitoring is simple to understand and implement, it is helpful to examine how to use it in the context of your leadership responsibilities. Monitoring is either anticipative or reactive and is implemented by either formal or informal systems.

Anticipative and Reactive Monitoring

Leaders are charged with the responsibilities of both anticipating future events and anticipating the consequences of unexpected events. A well-devised monitoring system gives you feedback that will help you accurately predict future outcomes by indicating whether your plan and strategy are proceeding as envisioned, such as in the areas of costs, production quality, employee retention, or accomplishment of goals. Likewise, if an unexpected event occurs such as the absence of key employees or a customer crisis, your consistent monitoring habits will have made you more knowledgeable about the potential consequences of someone not arriving at work or having an unhappy customer. You then will more quickly predict the results of the event and make a better decision about how to respond.

After evaluating reports, conversations, performance, or information about a completed event, a leader responds by using this knowledge to positively influence the outcome of future events and not repeat mistakes. If your monitoring shows you, for example, that your organization gets more telephone inquiries on Mondays, then make plans to have more assistance available on Mondays. If departing customers in your restaurant tell you that the food was great but the service was terrible, respond to this information by eliminating the cause of this poor service.

Formal and Informal Procedures

Several procedures exist that allow you or other leaders to formally monitor your plans and activities. External auditing, performed by certified public accountants, is a routine procedure used to verify the organization's financial records. As a leader, you can extend this concept by using nonorganizational personnel, such as consultants, to examine and comment upon any aspect of your responsibilities. Internal, or operational, auditing is similar to external auditing but is done by you or other organizational personnel, and it addresses all aspects of the organization. Its goals are to check the organizational systems, operations, and procedures to verify that operational plans are being implemented.

As mentioned in Chapter 7, a leader develops situational monitoring procedures, such as a schedule or budget, to assist in assessing specific activities and projects. A leader also uses these formal procedures in numerous instances throughout the day, such as in performance management or other reporting systems. The payroll department, for example, may require you to verify the work attendance of your subordinates. Moreover, the organization may mandate monitoring procedures to be used by everyone. You will examine some of these formal methods later in the chapter.

An informal method to keep track of your responsibilities is an outstanding way to supplement your formal monitoring procedures. There is nothing magical about this process. It involves using all your leadership skills to remain involved with the activities of everyone with whom you work, including your subordinates, peers in all organizational departments, and customers. The next section presents a monitoring process that you can use and tailor to all your duties.

The Monitoring Process

Monitoring is an essential component of everything you do, and you must integrate it into all your leadership activities. It will make your job easier and less frustrating, make your efforts more effective and efficient, and save you an enormous amount of time. Your monitoring often will be simple, occasional, and broad; at other times it will be detailed, intense, and focused. In addition to helping you accomplish your duties, monitoring will encourage your subordinates to do their job well. Since they know you assuredly will check their work performance, an awareness of your potential monitoring activities will give them a goal to work toward, that of performing well according to the expectations that you and they agree upon.

This chapter's monitoring process is derived from many processes that you probably see in your organization. Use it as a format in developing your own unique informal monitoring systems that you can use in all aspects of your professional and personal life.

An effective monitoring process includes these four steps.

- ▶ Establish the monitoring plan.
- ▶ Communicate the plan.
- ▶ Evaluate the performance.
- ▶ Guide the performance.

Establish the Monitoring Plan

Develop separate plans of action to monitor each of your responsibilities, including recurring duties, one-time activities, or delegated tasks. The plans do not all have to be written, exhaustive, or unique; they simply need to persuade you that you have an effective way to check progress on each activity. In developing your plan, define what activity to monitor, how well your subordinates must perform the activity, and how best to monitor the activity. Do this by identifying the objective, standards of performance, and monitoring procedure.

Your task's or activity's objective must be simply stated, clearly identified, time-specific, and measurable so that you and your subordinates understand without doubt what you must do to satisfactorily complete the task. An objective gives both you and your team a target at which to aim. Having no objective will result in indiscriminate aiming. It is not enough to say that you want satisfied customers; you have to clearly express an objective by stating, for example, that you want to achieve 95 percent positive comments each week on customer surveys.

Standards of performance are intermediate checkpoints to keep you on the right path towards accomplishing your objective. Sometimes referred to as mini-objectives, criteria, or expectations, standards break down the main objective into more manageable pieces and provide you with early warning if you are not on track towards accomplishing the main objective. You can state the standards quantitatively or qualitatively, as long as they are clear indicators of performance. Standards can be described in many ways, such as in cost, revenue, investment, or intangible terms. As is the case with your objectives, clearly define your standards so that they are time-specific and measurable. In the previous customer service example, typical standards could include a telephone-on-hold time limit of one minute, total telephone time limit of three minutes, or zero tolerance for employee ambivalence or rudeness. Each of these standards contributes to the overall objective of 95 percent positive comments.

Devise monitoring procedures that you will use for the task; they may be strictly formal, informal, or a combination of both. They could include written or oral reports, meetings, presentations, spot checks of operations, or elaborate procedures. As is true with your leadership style, you cannot use just one type of monitoring procedure for all your activities because the procedure may be inapplicable or ineffective. Tailor the monitoring, therefore, to each of your major responsibilities. Your choice of monitoring procedures depends upon many factors, including the importance and nature of the monitored activity, your level of knowledge and experience with the activity, and the degree of experience and expertise of the activity's participants. The procedures should be simple for your subordinates to understand and implement, easy for you to integrate into your daily duties, and effective in helping you keep track of your responsibilities. They must be flexible enough to still work effectively in the event of a major disruption to your plans. It is important, though, that you regularly review your procedures to ensure that they remain realistic. Finally, use the procedures consistently; otherwise they will not be of great use to you.

There are two key points to remember when designing your monitoring procedures.

- ▶ Make ample use of personal contact between you and those involved in the activity, and closely listen to, observe, and question people. You will learn many more details than you would have by only reviewing a report. You can never ask too many questions about what is happening with your subordinates or the progress of their activities.
- ▶ Integrate your monitoring into your time management system so that you can consistently schedule time to monitor. Use the allotted time for reviewing reports, inspecting processes, and interacting with people.

Communicate the Plan

Your subordinates must know what your monitoring plan is, how you will evaluate their performance, how the monitored activity relates to other people in the organization, and what the potential rewards are for successful performance of the activity. If you do not properly communicate this information to your subordinates, you will dramatically decrease the likelihood of achieving the objective according to standards. You can use several occasions to communicate the monitoring plan, such as in team meetings, personal contact with key subordinates, or written guidance. It is essential, though, that the monitoring plan, like all other information for which you as the leader are responsible, be correctly transmitted to the lowest levels of your organization.

Evaluate the Performance

This step is similar to step three of the problem-solving process of Chapter 5 in comparing the actual results with the desired results. If you have carefully and thoughtfully prepared the standards of performance, then it will be simple to measure the performance and examine the results. If there is an unfavorable difference between the two, you as the leader must take action to guide the performance to where it should be.

Guide the Performance

Using your leadership skills, take any action necessary to correct the performance and ensure that the activity gets back on track according to its plan. This could involve directing your subordinates to take certain actions to correct the problem or devising and implementing a new procedure to solve the problem. Your subordinates must understand that there is a problem and that everyone working as a team is going to correct the problem and keep it from recurring. Remember to praise them for any outstanding work and remind them how important they are to the success of the activity. After guiding the performance, continue the monitoring process by reevaluating performance and providing additional guidance until you have accomplished your objective.

Formal Monitoring Procedures

Much information on formal monitoring procedures is available for you to study when you choose. To guide you, this section will briefly highlight some of the most popular methods in use, many of which you probably already use. By no means exhaustive, this list will give you at least an idea of the variety of monitoring procedures that exist.

Budgets

Budgets are primarily numerical planning documents that you and your organization develop to achieve certain objectives. They traditionally have been, however, a popular form of monitoring because they permit you to easily compare plans with actual events and then to take corrective action. Types of budgets include revenue and expense, cash, or physical budgets pertaining to nonmonetary resources. The use of budgets has evolved into a widely used flexible budget that allows you to better anticipate actual events through the use of predetermined standardized costs.

Financial Information

Financial data helps you to access the past and current financial status of your organization and selected departments, to make better decisions, and to understand financial and operational trends. Although you might not use financial information as frequently as other monitoring tools, it nevertheless will provide you with a wealth of knowledge and insight if you choose to analyze it and use it in conjunction with your other monitoring procedures. You will increasingly rely on these financial monitoring tools as you assume more of a leadership role in your organization. Pay particular attention to the financial documents that pertain to your responsibilities, and ask the originating departments if they can separate the bulk information to provide you with details on your specific areas of responsibility. It also would be helpful to study a brief introductory book on finance and accounting because it will give you a greater understanding of the subjects and show you how they relate to you and your responsibilities. Your knowledge of these areas also will help you as you converse with the senior and interdepartmental leadership within your organization.

Several specific items will be of interest to you. The financial statements, including the balance sheet, income statement, and cash flow statement, show the overall financial picture of the company. When compared to previous statements, you can spot trends that are developing in your organization. Use these statements and other data to determine financial ratios, which give you the statistics to compare your organization with similar ones in your industry, and also to analyze trends. It is beyond the scope of this chapter to discuss them in detail, but understand that these interrelated ratios will help you spot potential problems and fix deficiencies before they become worse.

Quality Assurance

Quality assurance is fundamentally a process of assuring that your organization produces its goods or services the way it intended. It is known by several names, including quality control, quality assurance, and total quality. There is practically universal agreement that most organizations need some form of quality program in order to anticipate and react to inferior production or service efforts. A well devised and implemented quality program that monitors the operations in your organization is a sound business strategy. There are many variations of such programs, but most include a reliance upon statistical processes, monitoring of customer satisfaction, cost control, and a commitment to continuous improvement. As with most programs that you implement as a leader, success with a quality program depends upon you. You must create and sustain the right attitudes throughout your organization and obtain commitments from your subordinates and organizational leaders.

Customer Feedback

Paying attention to what your customers think about your service or product is a proven method of effectively monitoring events in your organization. By actively seeking feedback from your customers, you get the opportunity to analyze detailed comments that could have enormous consequences on your organization's bottom-line and long-term survival. After evaluating this information, you can guide your subordinates back to your strategy of superior customer service.

Performance Management

Monitoring individual performance of your subordinates and communicating to them about their performance are essential components in your leadership efforts. The coaching process discussed in Chapter 15 presents this in greater detail, but several points are pertinent for this chapter. It is essential to clearly identify for each of your subordinates what their major goals are for the upcoming year and beyond, then to agree on specific performance objectives for each of these goals. A written plan for each person ensures that everyone is in agreement on what is to be done, and it provides you with an excellent base document to track your subordinates' performance. Informal performance reviews with each person occur at least quarterly or more frequently if necessary. This review is usually supplemented by a formal appraisal conducted at least annually.

If leaders accomplished everything exactly according to their wishes, there would be no need for monitoring. However, as you well know, it is rare that anything happens exactly according to the plan. Monitoring complements the planning process by helping leaders to stay involved and to take responsible actions over the lifetime of an activity.

CHAPTER 9

PROMOTE TRAINING AND DEVELOPMENT

L eaders have the responsibility to correctly train their subordinates and then to develop them into productive and contributing members of their team. There are usually differences, or gaps, between what your subordinates should know and what they actually know about how to do their job. The purpose of training is to eliminate these gaps by assisting subordinates in acquiring and applying knowledge and skills to their job. The result of this process is an increase in the performance of the individual.

Development, a longer-term process that is related to training, has as its primary objective to prepare the individual for increasingly difficult or responsible jobs within and outside your organization. Both training and development occur foremost as a response to an organization's strategy; they are market-driven programs designed to help you achieve organizational goals and objectives.

Well-trained workers, coupled with effective leadership, are an essential part of what makes an organization successful. You as a leader do not have to personally conduct all the training, nor do you have to personally develop each of your subordinates. Usually you will have assistance from subordinate leaders and those in other organizational departments such as training or human resources. However, you must involve yourself in the process to ensure that training and development programs are designed, implemented, and evaluated with your needs in mind. Make sure they are conducted in a supportive learning environment and they meet your subordinates' needs as well as fulfill the objectives of your organization.

Training and development are not one-time occurrences; they start the day you hire your subordinates and continue until they leave the organization. Training and development take place throughout the day, not just during preplanned, formal training sessions, so you must integrate them into your daily activities. Although you will expend effort and resources and experience a sense of delayed gratification, you will eventually see a huge payoff because of your commitment to training and development. The value of training and development is that it makes your life much easier because your subordinates will learn how to better accomplish their tasks, which means you will have to spend less time assisting and coaching them as they develop their expertise.

A Leader's Four Training Guidelines

As you think about how training contributes to accomplishing your duties, consider how to structure training so that it is most effective. Effective training has three components: presentation of content, application to specific practice sessions, and follow-up to check performance. These components will be developed throughout this chapter. Four guidelines will further assist you in making the right decisions as you lead a powerful training program.

Build Skills to Improve Performance

Many leaders traditionally have viewed training in several limited ways, such as an organizational requirement, an employee reward, or a means to deliver new knowledge. Training is most effective when used as a vehicle to achieve organizational goals by increasing the skill level and performance of subordinates. Training by itself will not eliminate all performance discrepancies because they exist for several reasons, including personal difficulties of employees, the incentive system, and organizational conditions. However, when training is related to the causes of the performance discrepancies, it can be of tremendous benefit as a solution.

Leaders must work closely and collaboratively with the training professionals in their organization to 1) identify the causes of performance deficiencies, 2) develop solutions to overcome deficiencies and increase skills, and 3) create viable training programs. Although you have the primary responsibility to ensure that your subordinates participate in the right kinds of training, the training department can work with you to integrate that training into your departmental operations. If your training department does not yet operate in such a proactive manner, approach its leaders and create this kind of working relationship.

Training programs work best when tailored to a specific group of employees. Office and manufacturing workers, for example, require a different set of skills than middle-level leaders. All groups require a mix of skills from three categories: business skills, such as marketing or finance; leadership and management skills, such as motivation and conflict resolution; and individual skills, such as customer service or writing.

Advocate Continuous Learning and Practice

In your leadership role, promote training as the impetus for a continuous and widespread learning process that can occur informally and formally, in classrooms or on and off the job, and with the guidance of official instructors, leaders, or peers. After spending time learning skills or methods, trainees must practice using them or they will soon lose mastery of them. Subordinates must understand that ongoing learning and practice not only leads to skill improvement in their immediate responsibilities but also will open the door to many opportunities within and outside the organization.

Align Training with the Organizational Mission

Training provides an exceptional opportunity to emphasize to your subordinates the organization's mission, goals, and objectives. By understanding how training and job skills directly relate to the organization's future, your subordinates will have a clearer sense of purpose and direction. An intense focus on strategic objectives also will help you quickly identify the skills your subordinates need to help accomplish these goals.

Measure Training

Your challenge is to make your training accountable in helping you achieve your objectives and your organization's goals. Traditional indicators of productive training, such as the volume of training or number of attendees, are not very useful to you as a leader. You are more concerned with measuring specific results attributable to specific training. Examples of results include an increase in individual performance and output, higher customer satisfaction, or new business generated. Create specific control methods, such as surveys or feedback sessions, to collect information that will help measure training results. These methods need not be elaborate or complex, but they must indicate how effective your training is.

A Leader's Three Training Roles

Training is a pervasive activity that affects almost everything you do as a leader. Because of the enormous benefits training can have in assisting you in accomplishing your duties, it is helpful to understand your role in the training process. Most leaders will agree that they spend a large amount of time teaching, guiding, and informing subordinates on countless issues and skills. At other times, the leaders direct and monitor the efforts of others involved in these activities. Occasionally, leaders assist or are responsible for creating a training program. These routine activities represent the three roles you have in the training process, as trainer, training manager, and training designer.

You As the Trainer

You may often conduct training with your subordinates or act as a guest trainer for other departments. When you train others, it is a tremendous opportunity for you to refine your business, leadership, and individual skills; lead by example through imparting your expertise to others; and involve yourself in guiding your subordinates towards accomplishment of individual and organizational goals. As you prepare for your role as a trainer, your two most important objectives are to develop training expertise and to understand your learners' abilities and preferences.

Your first objective is to develop training expertise. To be an effective and responsible trainer, you must learn how to properly train individuals. The most effective way is to attend a train-the-trainer course that is presented either commercially or within your organization. If this is not possible, ask someone in the training department to teach you the essentials; you then can supplement that instruction by reading a book on training and practicing the skills you learn. Though you later can become extremely proficient as a trainer by developing several specialized training skills, your initial objective must be to learn and practice the minimal skills necessary to lead a training session. These include using teaching aids properly, presenting material effectively, understanding and listening to your audience, creating a learning environment, and knowing your material.

Your second objective is to understand the learner. As a leader, you are obligated to work with subordinates with all types of personal back-grounds, educational levels, motivations, skills, and experience. Similarly, as a trainer you often will have little or no choice in the learning abilities and preferences of those you train. It is possible, however, to better understand your trainees and then make adjustments in your training approaches according to two main learning factors.

People Learn in Different Ways

As discussed in Chapter 5, people usually have a dominant way of thinking. Left-brain thinkers tend to be more analytical and detail-oriented while right-brain thinkers are more creative and open-minded. These facts apply to learners as well.

Left-brain learners enjoy learning at their own solitary pace, receiving as many details as possible, and forming their own conclusions. Right-brain learners, on the other hand, prefer to grasp the big-picture conclusion first, confer with others, then look for the details to support the original conclusion. When you conduct individual training, therefore, you can tailor the delivery method to suit your learner's preferred approach.

It is more difficult in group training sessions to satisfy the needs of all learners all the time. You can, however, vary the delivery methods from lectures, readings, and self-paced instruction to team exercises, games, and simulations.

Motivation Is a Variable

Although you will examine motivation in more detail in Chapter 12, this section will address motivational issues that pertain to learning. One of your tasks as the trainer is to determine your trainees' motives for learning and whether they have any barriers or impediments to learning. It may be necessary to probe because people are not all motivated by the same things.

You then will use this information to create a positive learning experience. Before, or at the beginning of, the training session, poll the attendees individually or collectively to see what value they attach to the training. You could ask them open-ended questions such as why they are attending the training, how they see it benefiting them, or if they have any preconceived ideas about the subject matter. Although you probably will get a range of positive and negative responses, you can use this information to better understand your trainees' motives for learning.

As you continue with the training, make a special effort to overcome their fears and to reinforce their motives for learning. Most people will eventually form their own conclusions about the value of the training. However, you can influence their conclusions by explaining training benefits in light of whatever motivates them, such as promotion or recognition. In addition, you can do your part by making sure the training is solution-oriented, pertinent to realistic job conditions, and readily implemented by the trainee on the job.

You As the Training Manager

Not only will you have the opportunity to personally lead and conduct training, you also will be involved in the management aspects of training. Just like many of your other significant duties, training management includes such activities as directing, monitoring, and influencing the successful implementation of programs and events. As you will see in the next section, there are many details involved in the design of training. After a training program is designed, almost all these details will be reviewed once the training starts. This is where your role as the training manager is most prevalent. You can imagine, therefore, the benefits of becoming involved in the design process from its very beginning.

Even if you are not involved in the design or personal delivery of training, you probably will be involved during its implementation. The training department will need your leadership assistance in overseeing successful training sessions, encouraging your subordinates to attend and benefit from the training, and evaluating the training's impact on job performance. Training management evolves from your primary leadership duties; therefore, it is your responsibility as a training manager to make the training system work for you and not to accept excuses for ineffective training, poorly designed training, or, worse yet, a total absence of training.

You As the Training Designer

It is helpful for you to understand the design process because as the training department develops a course that pertains to your department, it needs your experience and expertise to develop it properly. As a leader who will be affected by an upcoming training program, you should be involved in all stages of the training design process because the information you provide the training department will be important in designing the best possible program that will solve your department's performance problems. Depending upon the complexity of the training program, the design process can be abbreviated for routine programs or can be done in greater detail for challenging or critical programs.

Designing a Training Program

Designing a training program is a thorough undertaking that traditionally has been the responsibility of the training department. It is unlikely, therefore, that you will frequently have the complete responsibility of designing a training program unless you are a leader working primarily in a training capacity. Since most full-time training personnel participate in a formal course on the subject lasting sometimes a week or more, you can appreciate that training design involves many intricacies that cannot be addressed in a few paragraphs. However, this section can highlight the six steps involved in designing a training program.

- ► Determine training needs.
- ► Outline the plan.
- ► Develop the plan.
- ► Write objectives and design the tests.
- ► Develop the course.
- ► Evaluate the course.

STEP

◄ 1 ►

Determine Training Needs

As discussed in the first paragraph of this chapter, training exists to correct performance gaps. If it is absolutely evident why you have performance problems and you know what the training needs are, then this step can be shortened. Otherwise, do a thorough training needs analysis, which is a three-step process that will give you the critical information you need to design the program.

Collect Pertinent Data Related to the Performance Gap

This is done by observing and interviewing the people responsible for completing the tasks. After this, approach their supervisors to resolve and clarify any of the issues.

Identify the Cause of the Performance Gap

Thoroughly probe all areas related to the performance problem, including the conditions under which the problem occurs and recent organizational changes that could have prompted the problem. If the cause is related to knowledge and skills, then training is the answer. If the cause is anything else, such as workplace conditions, communication, or incentives, then training is not the answer, but possibly workplace redesign, coaching, a new incentives program, or other responses may be the answer.

Determine Costs and Benefits of the Training Solution

Estimate as accurately as you can how much it will cost you to design, conduct, and evaluate the necessary training. Compare this to the economic and noneconomic benefits you will receive once you eliminate the performance gap. These benefits might include an increase in production or quality, a decrease in costs, or improved job performance. If the benefits exceed the cost, then you have identified a viable training need.

Outline the Plan

As with any project, start identifying the crucial details. Though you will not know many planning particulars for a while longer, you can make tremendous progress by raising some major concerns with departmental leaders or your client. These include details related to trainees, resources, training location, instructors, subject-matter experts, and others who can assist you. When you finish this step, you will have enough information to know what to do, who the participants are, when and where training will occur, and what constraints may exist.

STEP

◈ 2 ◈

Develop the Plan

Developing a plan involves thoroughly analyzing the two major components of your training program, your trainees and your course content. Use your understanding of the trainees to develop the heart of your training program, which is the task analysis.

In the previous discussion of the characteristics of learners, you saw the importance of understanding your trainees as you prepare to train them; this understanding is just as vital during the design phase of training. If you think of your trainees as customers, you will realize that your product — training — will be much more successful if you know as much as you can about your trainees. Analyze their education and skill levels, job experience and expertise, demographics, and motivation to learn. You then can target the training to the characteristics and needs of your audience, such as by offering multiple training sessions or innovative methods of training.

Next you will develop a task analysis. In a process much like developing the work breakdown structure in Chapter 7, your objective is to organize the training into manageable parts. You do this with the cooperation of the people who know the jobs' duties best, the people who do the jobs. For example, if your training program concerns the job of maintenance technician, first determine the major duties of a technician, such as maintaining equipment and ordering parts.

Separate each of these duties into tasks, or major pieces of work, that must be performed to fully complete the duty. Next, divide each task into subtasks then list all the detailed steps for each subtask. If you follow the above format, you are certain to get the level of detail that you need to complete the task analysis. Here is an abbreviated example for the maintenance technician.

STEP

◈ 3 ◈

Job: Maintenance Technician

Duties: maintain equipment and order parts.

Tasks for maintaining equipment: read manuals, disassemble machines, perform maintenance, diagnose problems, reassemble machine.

Subtasks for disassembling machine: stop the machine, prepare safety mechanisms, remove outer casing, remove fan belt.

Steps for stopping the machine: notify the team members two minutes in advance, press the off switch, unplug electrical cord using gloves.

This may seem like unnecessary work for developing course content, but it is extremely useful for several reasons. In addition to determining the exact makeup of the duties you will be instructing, you and your team members may discover areas of disagreement, such as the subtasks for a particular task. This is a healthy process that ensures that the training you develop will be as pertinent and error-free as it can be. It can also help you create needed procedures that may not have previously existed for certain duties. The task analysis also can be used as a course outline that your trainers will greatly appreciate. The task analysis will also help you write objectives and design tests, which is your focus in the next step in designing a training program.

STEP

❖ 4 ❖

Write Objectives and Design the Tests

Once you have completed the task analysis for each task in the designated training, use it to compose an objective for every task; objectives are not needed for the subtasks and steps. Then develop review and criterion tests to ensure that the trainee has mastered the tasks.

A task objective clearly states what the trainee must do. It consists of three parts: task statement, conditions, and standards. The task statement is a restatement of the task itself. The conditions indicate the circumstances, such as resources and location, under which the task will be performed. Standards show how well, as in time or accuracy, you want the trainee to perform the task. Here is a sample objective for the maintenance technician.

Objective: Given all necessary maintenance tools and equipment on location at the job site, the employee will disassemble the machine. All steps must be completed within 30 minutes according to the performance checklist.

Review tests serve as checkpoints that indicate the trainee's progress during the training session. For every subtask, design a simple review test to ensure that the trainee can accomplish the subtask during a practice session. A review test is given after trainees learn one subtask and before learning the next subtask. Review tests can be either performance tests that are simulations done under realistic conditions or they can be nonperformance tests such as written quizzes that measure the knowledge gained during training.

Nonperformance review tests: List the steps for stopping the machine.

Performance review test: Demonstrate how to prepare the safety mechanism.

A criterion test is a comprehensive final test that shows if the trainee can complete the task's objective. If the trainee completes this successfully, then your training has been successful.

Criterion test: Given all necessary maintenance tools and equipment on location at the job site, the employee will disassemble the machine according to the necessary steps. The trainer will complete a performance checklist during the test. All steps must be completed in order and within 30 minutes according to the performance checklist.

Make sure you follow up all completed training to ensure that the trainee can perform the task on the job. If the results of training are not periodically inspected and enforced by leaders, the training benefits may be lost.

Develop the Course

At this point, you are ready to assemble your course content and decide how you will present the course, how trainees will apply the training, and what resources you will use to conduct the training.

Choose your methods of presentation. There are three general methods, used individually or in combination, to present training: by the trainer in a classroom setting or on the job, by a trainee or group of trainees, or by training material, such as manuals or job aids. Within these categories, there are several methods that have their specific advantages and disadvantages based upon your particular type of training needs and audience. The first guideline is to select the presentation method that most quickly gets you and your trainees to the application phase, which is the practice phase where trainees

STEP

◆ 5 ◆

should spend most of their training time. Second, vary the methods based on your knowledge of the trainees and their learning styles. Include methods that allow you to intersperse realistic and exciting activities, trainee interaction, individual reflection, reading, listening, and seeing. Frequently-used presentation methods include lectures, seminars, job aids, and reading.

Consider various methods of application. Application is the opportunity you give the trainees to practice the skills they have just learned. As a leader, you are concerned that your subordinates not only gain the knowledge but also put it to use during the training session and on the job; otherwise, training is useless. As with presentation methods, there are many applications from which to choose. Remember to consider the different learning styles when choosing. Popular methods include practical exercises, demonstrations, quizzes, simulations, and role playing.

Some training methods combine the presentation and application phases. These progressive techniques can be invaluable in developing a dynamic training atmosphere and promoting successful learning. Typical combination methods include computer-based training, self-paced training, on-the-job training, and workshops.

Assemble your training materials. One of the last steps you take as a training designer is to consolidate your information into a set of training materials. Each individual in the training will need information. The trainee needs a set of course materials that includes all the information pertaining to the training, including training objectives, schedule of events, and evaluation forms. Develop sharp-looking and effective handouts that can be easily written upon and used during training. Distribute any reading material well in advance so that the trainees can adequately prepare. The trainer likewise needs everything that the trainee needs, only further in advance. In addition, you should prepare a lesson plan, which acts as a job aid for the trainer. It contains most of the information related to the training consolidated in one folder. With the lesson plan include copies of all handouts, references, information on trainees, audio-visual materials, resource listings, and any other pertinent information that the trainer needs to teach effectively.

STEP

◆ 6 ◆

Evaluate the Course

Before any official training begins, test your program by training selected individuals. The purpose is to make sure that you have a viable training program that will work well. Look particularly close for logical sequencing, clear links between the objectives and what is actually taught, and dynamic presentation. Go through every aspect of the training. Take good notes, notice everything, and ask these first participants for their evaluation of the course. Make any needed revisions to the program and test it again with another person. If time and resources permit, test again with a trainee group that mirrors the groups you will have during actual training conditions.

As the course designer, you also want to know immediately after the training ends if the course itself was well-presented, organized, and relevant. The best way to determine this is to use course evaluations. Well-designed evaluations, which can be up to several pages in length, ask for written comments on all aspects of the training including the instructor's presentation, training facilities, and subject matter. Evaluation responses from the trainees, trainers, and the supervisors will tell you if the training was effective. The primary information you want is whether your course did what it was intended to do, which is to increase the performance of the trainee on the job. You can determine this by surveying the participants and supervisors before training begins and again several weeks after the instruction. Always ask for any suggested changes or improvements.

Development of Your Subordinates

A development program prepares your subordinates to assume greater positions of responsibility by giving them knowledge and skills applicable to many job positions. It also exposes them to numerous opportunities for career advancement. While development may seem to contradict your leadership goal of keeping your subordinates happy and stable in their current job positions, there are several reasons to prepare your subordinates for new challenges through a development program.

Development gives them the opportunity to move forward with their careers and avoid remaining in a rut. If you challenge employees to make the most of their skills while providing them with the support, hope, and means to get ahead, they will be much more satisfied, productive, and loyal to you and your organization. Your investment in their advancement becomes obvious to them, and they will appreciate your organization and see it as a partner that invests in their professional career needs. The employees will understand that although you may not be able to guarantee lifetime employment, you are offering the best that you can considering the constantly changing economic environment. When you make a pledge to their development, they will reciprocate with loyalty and commitment. A loyal and highly trained workforce, consisting of an organization's vital institutional memory, is crucial to the organization's long-term survival. This is especially important during periods of turmoil and upheaval, as in restructuring, downsizing, or intense competition.

A development program helps you maintain a system to internally replace departing workers whenever job vacancies occur. By knowing the career interests, competencies, and goals of your subordinates, you can more easily align the organization's needs with the needs of its most important resource, its employees. It is a great morale booster for your subordinates to know that the internal promotion and advancement system is viable. In addition, it is usually less expensive in the long run to promote from within the organization.

Even if subordinates eventually leave your department or organization, they will leave more content if they have participated in a development program. They will more likely portray positive feelings about you and the organization in their next positions or while networking among peers. Your organization, as result, will achieve a reputation of being concerned about the welfare of its employees, and it will continually attract superior workers. Moreover, it is unlikely that you would prefer to retain subordinates who are truly unhappy with their position and future in your company; sometimes it is to your advantage to let them go, if they so desire, and to replace them.

Despite its many advantages, a development program involves an issue that frightens many leaders. The company's reward system may not encourage leaders to develop and promote their subordinates. The reward system often acts as a disincentive when the leader is solely evaluated on departmental productivity, training costs, or payroll costs. Yet each of these is negatively affected when you have to recruit and train someone to replace a fully-trained worker who is departing due to lack of developmental opportunities. The ways to overcome this disadvantage will be discussed later.

Types of Development Programs

Once you are convinced that a development program is a great way to improve your company's most valuable resource, its employees, you will have to choose which development program to offer. Three types of development programs will be discussed: career planning, mentoring, and leadership development.

Career Planning Program

This program should address all aspects of a person's potential career within the organization. Even with the employment uncertainty that exists in most organizations, it is imperative that you clearly communicate to each employee the skills and knowledge that they need in order to advance within the organization. A career planning program should serve to 1) help employees assess and promote their career while working at the organization; 2) provide opportunities for employees to assume responsibility for their own career growth; and 3) build up the organization's reserve of qualified employees to meet future manpower requirements.

To accomplish these objectives, the human resources department will work closely with you and other leaders to develop detailed self-assessment documents that will determine the competencies, skill weaknesses, and goals of the employees. These tools will include skill, ability, and knowledge appraisals; interest and aptitude inventories; goal assessment worksheets; and company action plans. Although the human resources department has staff responsibility for the program, leaders at all levels are responsible for implementing the program with their subordinates.

Mentoring Program

Mentors are leaders who advise and encourage their protégé on a variety of issues, including planning a career, dealing with organizational politics and power, and improving performance. You can act as a mentor to your subordinates, or another volunteer can assume the role. Mentoring programs traditionally have been used to benefit an organization's leaders, but they certainly can be applied more inclusively throughout the organization. A well-designed mentoring program should be available to all employees on a volunteer basis, implemented from the top leader through their immediate leaders, and promoted throughout the organization.

Leadership Development Program

A leadership development program is specifically designed to develop more effective leaders. It is a challenging and long-term plan that is linked to your organizational vision and strategy. It supplements traditional sources of training and education, which are on-the-job experience and supervisory guidance. These programs provide needed structure to the often haphazard way that leaders learn how to lead. It is a process of development that can give you as a leader the opportunity to explore leadership issues, develop and cultivate skills, resolve challenges, and learn from the expertise of proven leaders.

This developmental process provides a system for top leaders to identify promising future leaders in the organization. You and your fellow leaders are entrusted with the responsibility of continuing and expanding the successes of the organization. One vital part of your response to this challenge is to find and nurture the next generation of leaders. As the pressures and challenges of competition, innovation, global trade, and society continue to increase, there will be a tremendous need to develop strong leaders who can lead their subordinates as well as acknowledge these external pressures. Leadership development, therefore, is every leader's job and is done in conjunction with your daily duties.

Leadership development programs are shaped differently for each organization. They can be designed internally, created with outside help, or purchased as packages from commercial training organizations and consultants.

Regardless of its source, a leadership development program must have specific objectives that are linked to your particular organization's business goals and strategy. You can derive these objectives from a thorough needs analysis that examines what your leaders currently do in their job positions, what leaders need to do to ensure your organization's growth and success, and what leaders need for their own professional growth. Do not automatically assume that general areas of leadership instruction will suffice for your organization. If you do so, leaders will be under pressure to transfer this generalized knowledge to their very specific job circumstances. This places an unnecessary burden on them. It is better to first conduct an analysis that will help you correctly pinpoint your needs and then to develop the specific content of the development program.

Leadership Development Resources

Many details involved in designing a leadership development program are similar to any training program. However you must be careful so as not to conflict with or overload the crucial day-to-day responsibilities of your leaders. Depending upon your organization's needs, you can design your program to include one or more of the following resources.

Job Rotation

Job rotation allows individuals to work in a succession of different positions in the organization, including supervisory and nonsupervisory, assistant-ships, internships, or trainee positions. The practical experience and challenge of seeing how work is done in other functional areas or different site locations provide leaders with the broad knowledge and skills to move forward in their career. An organization that commits to a program of job rotation will soon develop depth in its leadership ranks, be more able to move leaders to other departments when needs occur, and will ultimately build a more viable organization that can handle growth and competition. To make job rotation a useful learning experience, it is important that the individual provide a needed and useful service to the host department and that they gain experience in leading people and making decisions. The leaders of all hosting departments must remember to explain the purpose of the job rotation program to their subordinates. This is so the subordinates can understand why the rotation is helpful to the organization, department, and the participant, and how their cooperation is needed to help the program succeed.

Internal Education and Training

You will find there are numerous resources for on-site leadership education and training. These include seminars, lectures, simulations, or discussions facilitated by organizational leaders; workshops and training led by consultants or seminar companies; committee assignments, special projects, and formal presentations; or guided reading programs. Your leaders will make significant progress if they relate the reasons for their leadership education to specific on-the-job applications. In-house education can provide this applicability if it is well designed and if it is tailored to the level of leaders involved, such as first-level, middle, and top leadership. You can present and evaluate most leadership skills training on site. The skills presented in this book are examples of those that you can include in your program. Reading programs, consisting of books related to all aspects of leadership or specific technical skills, reinforce the principle that leaders are ultimately responsible for their own career development.

External Education and Training

Many universities, professional associations, and seminar companies are willing to educate your leaders. Depending upon your budget, you may be able to partially or completely fund attendance at programs that offer a wide variety of subjects that range from one day to several weeks. Although it is tempting to assume that these programs can be the answer to some of your leadership development challenges, ask yourself several questions before committing to external education. Will the programs significantly help you reach your development goals? Will the programs improve the leadership performance of the attendee? Is the training specific and realistic enough to be applicable to your organization, or is there too much theory? What are the quality and professionalism of the instruction?

Social Activities

Do not underestimate the effect of informal activities that are designed to bring leaders together. Whether it is a barbecue, dinner, or sports event, these shared experiences provide superb opportunities for leaders at all levels to discuss work-related challenges, career opportunities, and family life. Many leaders fondly remember how personal encounters at these events significantly altered their lives.

Prerequisites for Development Programs

Like any significant organizational undertaking, the process of planning and implementing your development program takes time, effort, and collaboration. Whether you are responsible for creating the program or for providing staff support to their proponents, you can help assure its success by attention to four prerequisites. These involve top leadership support, ready access, fair access, and a reward system.

Obtain Top Leadership Buy-in

It is essential that the senior organizational leadership provide comments during the creation process, approve the programs, announce them to the organization, and enthusiastically support them. To get the programs off to a good start and to understand what their subordinates will be involved in, the top leaders and their immediate subordinate leaders can set a good example by being the first to participate in the programs.

Provide Adequate Resources

Make sure your subordinates are given complete information on the programs' details, adequate time to participate in development, and easy access to seminars, training workshops, and self-help material. Purchase a variety of career development books and manuals to keep available in your departmental or organizational libraries.

Equitably Administer the Programs

Since there is potential for individuals to erroneously perceive that development programs favor one person or group over another, you must carefully plan and administer the programs to minimize inequities and resentment. Areas to watch include the selection process, slotting for choice assignments, effect on organizational operations, and allocation of training expenses.

Require and Reward Development

Encourage your leaders and subordinates to participate in development programs and to develop their subordinates and reward them when they do so. To ensure that this occurs, you can take several actions. First, you can require your leaders to develop their subordinates as part of their official duties. They must know that you believe in this process and, therefore, they should believe. Second, for those leaders who are successful at developing their subordinates, reward them with recognition, special status, merit pay if available, and protection from the departmental costs related to the development process. Finally, organize your own development program if your company has no official one, because you are ultimately responsible for nurturing your subordinates and your current and prospective leaders.

As you have seen in this final chapter for the primary-level leadership skills, training and development provide you with specific opportunities for realizing the potential of your organization, your subordinates, and yourself. Since they are of such importance to your success, vigorously promote training and development by encouraging others to see their benefits as well. No one leadership skill can be the key to your success, but training and development will help others get better and feel better at what they do and provide for the long-term success of your organization.

PART III

RELATIONSHIP SKILLS

Intermediate-level Leadership Skills

CHAPTER 10

COMMUNICATE AS A LEADER

Communication is the most important of all your leadership skills. It is also the first skill learned by human beings. Communication is the bridge that leaders use to successfully transfer their knowledge, plans, and guidance to people who will help them accomplish their duties. Similarly, it is also the means by which leaders receive information from within and outside the organization.

While most leadership skills work in connection with and support of other skills during the day, communication is the one skill that you use the most. Whether you work with a subordinate, peer, supervisor, or customer, virtually all your leadership duties involve the help and contribution of others. Clear communication is pivotal in eliciting their cooperation, retaining their support for future collaboration, and successfully building long-term relationships that will help you, them, and your organization thrive. Quality communication is not the complete solution to your leadership challenges, but it is a crucial factor that permeates all areas of your leadership duties. Communicating clearly involves much more than telling someone what is on your mind. It involves determining the message you want to send, choosing how you will send it, accurately sending it, and then making sure your recipient receives and understands the message as you intended it. Because you are in a position of leadership, you cannot arbitrarily send messages to your subordinates and others. Because subordinates see you as a credible messenger, they expect you to prepare and present a reasoned and unambiguous exchange of communication. If you do anything less, you will lose effectiveness and esteem in the eyes of your subordinates.

Fortunately, there is a three-step process to assist you when you communicate with others. Since you could conceivably communicate hundreds of times a day, this simple process can easily guide you through any communication situation. You can teach this process to subordinates to improve the communication you receive from them. In the communication process, you must:

- ► Determine your message,
- ► Choose the method of delivery and send your message, and
- ► Monitor the receipt and understanding of your message.

Determine Your Message

STEP
❖ 1 ❖

Examining the purpose, recipient, and content of your message will give you the insight to prepare the most effective message for delivery.

Purpose

Knowing why you need to send a message will put you in the proper frame of mind to construct the right message. There are several general purposes that your message could possibly have, such as to request information or action or to convey specific or general information. Take a moment to think about why you want to communicate to your recipient. Determining the specific purpose lets you focus on your communications objective and develop a concise, clear, and accurate message.

Recipient

Think about who will be getting the message and visualize yourself delivering the message to them. A heightened awareness of the recipient will help you formulate a message that reflects their knowledge of the subject matter, your rapport and work experience with them, and why they need the message. If the recipient is someone you do not personally know, such as a customer or a top organizational official, envision what their concerns are and what they may be expecting in your message.

Content

Somewhere in your mind, you know exactly the details of the message you want to send. Your mind, which is a vast databank of thoughts, perceptions, and experiences, lets you process these and other numerous details quickly and subconsciously. When it is time to encode your communications message you must sort through this collection of information so you can accurately compose your message. In particular, remember to focus on the important and essential information and to eliminate the irrelevant and inessential, which can confuse the recipient or, even worse, cause your message to get lost.

Choose the Method of Delivery and Send Your Message

After you determine your message, the next step is to choose the best method of delivery and to send it. As in step one, it is helpful once again to consider the purpose of the message and its recipient. This will quickly allow you to narrow your selection by eliminating and tentatively selecting some of the available delivery methods. Although there are numerous ways to deliver your message, they fall into the two general classifications of spoken and written. Later in the chapter you will discover techniques for improving your delivery methods, but first you will examine these two methods. As is true with most skills they use, leaders vary their communications methods depending upon the leadership situation.

The spoken message is the most personalized method in which either you or someone you designate delivers your message to the recipient. If you personally deliver it, you can ensure that you quickly deliver it the way you intended without someone else mistakenly leaving out crucial information. You also get the opportunity firsthand to answer questions or clear up any confusion that the recipient may have. Designating a subordinate or someone else to deliver your message does not automatically mean that the above advantages turn into disadvantages. You just have to carefully prepare the messenger with as many details as you can so they can correctly deliver the message. The spoken delivery method can be used individually with one or a few people, in front of a group, or through devices such as a telephone or video camera.

The written delivery method is particularly useful when disseminating routine, permanent, nonsensitive, technical, or previously discussed information. It can be in numerous forms, such as a letter, computer file or electronic mail, news release, or organizational publication. The written delivery method lacks an important advantage of the spoken method in that it is more difficult to gauge the recipient's reaction to the message. This may not be important when informing your subordinates in writing about an upcoming meeting, but it could be critical when announcing upcoming customer service policies. As the leader, use your good judgment and select the proper method based upon your specific situation. Often, you will use both speaking and writing to communicate a message. A combination approach supplements each method and helps ensure that you effectively and clearly communicate the message to your subordinates.

Monitor the Receipt and Understanding of Your Message

Have you ever placed a telephone call that did not go through, the line was busy, or the answering party hung up because of a bad connection? Did you ever expect to receive a letter in the mail which never arrived, arrived late, arrived at someone else's address, or arrived torn up? Incidents similar to this happen every day when you communicate with people in your organization. Leaders can send the clearest message by the most secure method of delivery, but if no one receives it or understands it, the message is useless. You can imagine the calamity that would occur if your newly devised memo on emergency fire procedures was never distributed throughout the organization or if your customer service representatives did not know about the new product launch that occurred yesterday.

As discussed in Chapter 8, monitoring is one of many solutions to your leadership challenges. It also is a solution to proper communication. You must consistently check to see if your guidance, directives, and other forms of communication are received, understood, and retained. Regardless of whether you intended the message for a subordinate, superior, peer, or customer, it is possible despite your best efforts that someone may not receive or understand your communication. This occurs for various reasons, such as the receiver's willingness or ability to receive the message, the method of delivery, or some type of communications noise that interfered with the reception or understanding of the message.

It is extremely useful for a leader to pinpoint why the receiver did not receive or understand the message. Not only must you correct the specific incident that occurred, it could be a symptom of a deeper or personal organizational problem for you to remedy. An unwillingness to receive a message, for example, may suggest a recipient's low morale or disinterest. If you had asked a subordinate leader to get the word out about a policy change, they may have failed to do so because of an inability to know how to properly communicate; this would indicate a need for specific training from you. They also could have failed because of forgetting to clarify some assumption with you. If you determine that your delivery method was the reason for the problem, you can easily choose a better method or improve your writing and speaking skills, as you shall see later in the chapter.

Noise, which is any type of distortion, distraction, or interference with the communications process, is the broad category most often listed as the reason for ineffective receipt or understanding of communication. Examples of noise include:

▶ People not listening attentively to the message because they are busy thinking about other duties or problems,

> ► People making premature judgments and conclusions about the message before it is completely sent,

> ► Organizational issues and problems that preclude or cloud effective communications,

> ► Physical conditions that prevent the message from being understood, and

> ► Barriers to communication, such as psychological, social, semantic, or physical barriers.

Your objective is to constantly search for noise in your environment so that you can minimize or eliminate it and allow the communications process to continue.

Ten Methods for Improving Leadership Communication

You can dramatically increase your leadership effectiveness simply by improving your communications style. Here are ten methods especially applicable for leaders.

Improve Face-to-face Communications

One-on-one and small group situations are where most communication takes place. Try to increase the quality and quantity of your one-on-one and small group encounters because they are a most effective means of delivering your message. Here are other specific suggestions to consider.

Be Approachable

If your subordinates and others perceive you as openly warm and accessible, they will come to you when they need you and not avoid bringing up their concerns. Even though you and your subordinates may have remarkably different backgrounds, age differences, or communication styles, these are not reasons for you to be aloof and distant. Approachability also implies that you are not initially judgmental whenever someone talks with you but are open to others' ideas and suggestions.

One way to develop this approachability and rapport is to be aware of the person's style of speaking and adjust yours to more closely resemble theirs. This allows them to feel relaxed and more likely to engage in effective communication. For example, if someone's conversational grammar, speed, and tone are completely different from yours, speak more simply, slowly, and softly as they do. If they are reluctant to talk, ask leading questions that will give them the opportunity to express themselves, not simply answer with short, one-word responses. If they are using a particular nonverbal gesture, you likewise can periodically use it to gain their closeness and understanding.

Be Understanding and Sincere

When speaking with anyone, try to truly understand the motivations for their beliefs, express empathy towards them as you speak, and get a grasp of their true feelings. If you show a genuine concern for their needs and interests, they will reciprocate by better communicating and empathizing with your needs and interests. You will not diminish your position of leadership by developing a sincere and understanding communications session with others; you will enhance your position by effectively getting to what is truly important, good communication.

Avoid Mixed Signals

Sending mixed signals to others confuses them. For example, if you tell your subordinates to contact you anytime and anyplace, be receptive to them when they need to speak with you. If you have a particular style of communicating, be consistent in using it so your subordinates do not get confused. If you normally prefer to talk casually with someone before getting to the important information, avoid suddenly eliminating your chit-chat and becoming someone who wants to get to the point quickly.

Repeat Messages

Make it a habit to repeat your important messages from time to time to ensure that they were received and understood. This does not mean using the same exact words all the time but restating the messages in different ways to probe for comprehension. For example, you could inquire about a detail in a request you previously made to a subordinate; their response and your ensuing discussion will likely indicate whether they fully understood your request. If you have difficulty communicating with a specific subordinate, make sure that the instructions are simple and easy to understand. By repeating an instruction immediately after first giving it, you will help ensure that they comprehend it.

Listen To Others

Because communication is a two-way process between a sender and receiver, you as a leader should spend a significant amount of time actively listening to what people are telling you. The adage that a person should spend more time listening than talking is certainly a target at which a leader should aim because you can learn from everyone you are in contact with. Effective listening is much more than nodding your head while letting others talk. It is an active process in which your objective is to fully understand what the person is telling you by listening to their messages from their perspective, not yours; considering their feelings and interests, not just yours; and not interrupting them while they talk. It involves being patient, blocking out distractions, and pinpointing what the person is telling you.

Because it is impossible for a leader to know exactly what a subordinate is thinking — despite the natural human tendency to assume that you know — why not let them tell you? You have read of numerous situations throughout this book when leaders must get the assistance of others in defining causes of problems before deciding the solutions, such as in projects and training, for example. When you take the time to listen to others, they will become more motivated. They will enjoy working with an authentic leader who appreciates what they have to say and is not passively listening to them in order to manipulatively extract information and use it for themselves. They will see you as someone truly interested in their opinions, suggestions, and ideas, not because you have to listen but because you want to listen. This will pay you huge dividends through better communication that leads to better solutions, early identification and elimination of potential problems, and people who are more committed and loyal to you and your organization.

Speak Well

You will spend most of your communication time speaking to people in all types of roles and positions. It makes sense that if you speak clearly and precisely, your receivers will better understand you. If your message is garbled, grammatically incorrect, incoherent, or awkward, you will not only send a bad message but you will also send a negative impression of yourself that may counteract the positive leadership image you have been projecting. No matter how great your idea is, if you cannot communicate it effectively, it does you little good — and may even damage your success as a leader. Learn correct speaking techniques by allowing someone to coach you, by taking a self-study course, or by enrolling in a professionally-taught program.

Present Well

Delivering a presentation is a common method of sending your message to one or more individuals. You now know how critical it is to learn to speak well; this is a vital component of making presentations. However, you can go further and learn how to properly deliver a presentation so that it is most effective in conveying your message. Read a quick self-study booklet on the topic or attend a professional course of instruction, which is often offered in conjunction with a speech course. Augment this learning process by making practice presentations in front of someone who can knowledgeably evaluate you. This person can make frank comments on several areas, such as your organization, delivery, clarity, persuasive ability, and use of visual aids.

Here are some final points to consider when making your presentation, whether it is in front an audience of one or a hundred.

- ▶ Know your topic and audience extremely well.
- ▶ Practice several times by yourself and rehearse once or twice in front of someone who can critique you.
- ▶ Plan the use of visual aids carefully, use only what is necessary, and triple check all visual aids and equipment before the presentation.
- ▶ Be enthusiastic.
- ▶ Stay in control of the presentation.
- ▶ Speak naturally and be yourself.

Some leaders can speak more easily and deliver a better presentation than others. This comes through practice. Anytime you have an occasion to speak even a few words in front of people, take advantage of it. Regardless of whether you view presentations as anxiety filled chores or wonderful opportunities, commit to learning how to do them well since they are an inherent part of your duties.

Write Clearly

By improving your writing ability, you will be more able to clearly express and organize your information, eliminate ambiguity, anticipate the concerns of the reader, and decrease your readers' reading time. Your readers will better understand what you are attempting to communicate and will be better able to comply with your intent. Learning to write correctly is not difficult, but writing well takes more effort and commitment. You can approach writing improvement one step at a time, thanks to the dozens of self-help books and training materials that can easily lead you through the many nuances and rules of grammar that have been in existence for decades. Numerous confidence-building courses focus specifically on increasing your vocabulary or improving your spelling.

Until you start this training, here are a few specific tips to help you immediately improve your writing.

- ▶ Pinpoint the purpose and main points of your document before beginning to write it.
- ▶ Think about your readers' need for your information or persuasion, how knowledgeable they are about the subject, and what action you want them to take after reading your document.

> ▶ Use simple language, minimize jargon, and keep the document as brief as possible.
> ▶ Revise your document two or more times before sending it.
> ▶ Ask your assistant or a peer to review it for clarity, conciseness, and relevance as well as for grammar, punctuation, and spelling.

Use Leadership Words and Phrases

Avoid words or phrases that suggest incompetence, lack of common sense, or a reliance on excuses, such as:

> ▶ They never called me back.
> ▶ I don't know.
> ▶ That's impossible; we can't do that.
> ▶ That's not my job.
> ▶ I ran out of time.
> ▶ We're in trouble.
> ▶ I can't understand why this is happening.
> ▶ What we need is good luck.

If you use phrases such as these, or variations of them, you communicate the impression that you are willing to accept mediocrity instead of solutions. Remember you are the leader, not an obstacle to progress; therefore, your words must reflect your responsibility to move your subordinates and the organization forward toward progress and not to remain with the status quo.

Be Conscious of Nonverbal Communication

Nonverbal communication involves mannerisms or movements such as gestures, facial reactions, posture changes, or eye contact. These actions are easily observed by those around you. Whenever your nonverbal actions contradict that which you are verbally communicating, people notice. They rely strongly upon these symbolic messages and make correct and incorrect judgments about you, such as that you are lying, holding back information, uninterested, or nervous. Even when you are not speaking at all, observers often can surmise what you are thinking by observing your natural nonverbal actions, such as tapping a pen which indicates nervousness or blankly staring into space which suggests boredom. Subordinates look to their leaders for guidance, support, enthusiasm, and curiosity; nonverbal cues tell subordinates whether you have these or not.

The good news is that you can use nonverbal communication to your advantage in your leadership duties. By practicing using nonverbal communication correctly, you enhance your ability to communicate well. This will lead others to more accurately interpret these cues and help them better understand your meaning. Videotape one of your presentations to see yourself in action; you will notice positive and negative gestures and mannerisms that you did not know you used. Make intentional efforts to send positive nonverbal expressions as often as you can and minimize any negative behavior, unless, of course, you intentionally want to send a negative signal to someone. When speaking to someone, fully engage the person in the conversation by looking her or him in the eye and not looking all over the room, making ample use of appropriate facial expressions when reacting to what the person is saying, and asking questions to indicate that you are paying attention. To underscore your role as a leader, be alert, maintain great posture, and energetically stay involved with what is happening at the moment.

Increase Team Communication

You and your subordinates should regularly come together and communicate as a team. This could occur in team meetings, informal chats, or scheduled informational discussions. The purpose of these sessions is to give everyone the opportunity to raise concerns, ask questions, receive knowledge and guidance, and vent frustrations. You should routinely meet individually with people, but a group setting gives you the opportunity to show leadership by proudly standing in front of your team and taking charge of a session. As a source of information, you are the common link among your subordinates. Because some people are reluctant to raise issues as individuals, they welcome the occasion to see issues raised by more vocal people and to observe firsthand your responses to the concerns. Finally, instead of solely depending upon the use of one communications method such as a meeting, it is wise to develop multiple channels of communication to your team, such as newsletters, bulletin boards, or e-mail. This will help ensure that your team members clearly get your messages.

Improve Organizational Communication

By consistently using the communications process, you will greatly improve the effectiveness and efficiency of your personal communications. The details of designing an organizational communications program are beyond the scope of this chapter, but the subject is important nevertheless. It is critical for an organization to have a dependable internal communications program in effect. A specific individual usually coordinates this in large companies, while in some organizations it is a collective function of leaders at all levels.

Organizational communication is a challenging, complex process to control due to the volume of information and the multiple channels of communication that exist in an organization. It serves to promote a high degree of communication, morale, and understanding throughout the company. Good organizational communication ensures that the members are well informed in a balanced and straightforward way about all significant issues affecting the organization, such as business challenges, policy changes, and operational and strategic issues. Organizational communication also touches on other significant issues, such as organizational design, workplace improvements, customer service, and use of information technology. Organizations attempt to face these challenges through formal networks of communication, such as reporting channels, specific functional departments, and communication networks including voicemail and computer networks.

Despite the challenges at the organizational level, always search for opportunities to improve communications outside your immediate realm of responsibility. As a leader, you have an obligation to identify and correct any perceived communication problems that affect your department or subordinates. Do this by actively communicating with other departments to dig out any information that you need but is not given to you. While getting this information, you can make helpful suggestions for improvements to the responsible official. For example, you could recommend ways to streamline information dispersal such as an organization-wide newsletter, or you could make specific suggestions for topics in an already existing publication. If you feel that interdepartmental communication is stifled because of unfamiliarity with each other's employees, suggest a shared function like a potluck lunch or weekend social activity.

Understand Informal Communication Networks

In addition to formal networks of communication, the widely known grapevine does exist. When you know how it operates in your organization, you can use it when seeking or disseminating information. The grapevine is an informal communications network that both complements and detracts from the formal networks. Accept the fact that it is impossible to eliminate, hard to control, but easy to use. If you want to determine what is happening in your organization, such as how people feel about policies or what really concerns them, chat casually with your subordinates and others. Of course, you should be routinely chatting with them, but the point is that a vast amount of information in your organization is available if you simply talk informally with people. Try to see the grapevine as a tool that gives you an alternative means of communication, not as a threat that challenges your leadership authority. As a leader, correct and dispel any erroneous information that you discover in the grapevine. This response, coupled with an open and credible communications program, will ensure that you and your subordinates send and receive communication correctly.

The vital and frequently used skill of communication, the first of the relationship skills, is a simple skill to learn. As you have seen in this chapter, it also is one that requires your persistence, determination, and commitment to implement. Leaders must continually remind themselves that within the sphere of communication lie the solutions to many of your interpersonal and organizational challenges. Make proper leadership communication one of your highest daily priorities.

CHAPTER 11

DEVELOP YOUR TEAM

A team is a group of people who collaboratively accomplish specific goals. A team has numerous configurations, such as small groups working in close contact with each other, isolated groups working in different countries, a marketing department within a company, or the entire company itself. In some organizations, there are teams within teams. They have always existed in some form, and they go by names such as groups, crews, units, or squads.

Great teamwork, which suggests efficient, coordinated, collaborative, and successful operations, is a major goal of having a team because teamwork creates so many benefits for you, your subordinates, and your organization. Not only is teamwork the outcome of your efforts at closely organizing and coaching your team but it also is an enthusiastic attitude and set of skills that you use to lead your team to success. Your objective is to increase teamwork attitudes and skills throughout your organization.

The use of teams and teamwork skills has become increasingly relevant to a leader simply because it is an effective and smart way of getting things accomplished. A leader cannot resort to barking his orders to subordinates and telling everyone exactly what they should do. Not only is it an inefficient method of accomplishing your objectives but it is also not effective. If you are to thrive as a leader and take your organization to new levels of growth and achievement, you must seek innovative solutions to your increasingly complex challenges. It probably comes as no surprise to you that leaders do not individually have the right answers to all their challenges. They must pursue these solutions and implement them with the collective help of other people who have a variety of knowledge, skills, and interdisciplinary experience.

Teamwork means focusing less on what you can individually accomplish as a leader and more on how you can empower others to accomplish substantial achievements as a team. The idea of teamwork may scare some leaders who falsely believe they must surrender power to a group. In teamwork, you are sharing power with others to achieve greater levels of success. Leaders who have teamwork attitudes and skills recognize that they will be more successful by letting everyone contribute as much as they can.

Great teamwork allows the leaders to concentrate on the larger issues involved in leading the organization rather than on each individual issue. Even if you do not officially organize or recognize your group of subordinates as a team, you still can use the teamwork skills in this chapter and the teamwork attitude to guide them to success. Teamwork skills simply give you another perspective from which to approach your leadership duties.

Promote Teamwork

There are many reasons to promote teamwork in your organization. Teams help you do your job more easily because their members have less need for direct supervision since they become more autonomous. The camaraderie and group effort involved in team operations permit your subordinates to feel more satisfied with their work, resulting in fewer disciplinary problems, absences, and customer complaints. This sharing of ideas and talents can lead to better collective results. This is particularly true in fast-changing environments or situations involving technical issues.

Teamwork translates directly into bottom-line improvements in work processes, productivity, innovation, and safety. Even if you do not organize all your work into teams, the concepts are still applicable in a traditional work structure and can help you achieve your goals if you consistently use them. For example, teamwork can help you revise policies, solve a long-standing internal problem, or develop new products and services.

Despite the many excellent reasons in favor of teamwork and teams, remember that organizing solely by formal teams is not the only solution, nor is it always the best solution, to your leadership challenges. There may be several reasons for this.

First, if your group of people does not share a common goal that can be better achieved working collectively through a system of mutual interdependence, then formal teams are not the answer. Second, teams may not be necessary to improve your organizational performance. Some other action, such as improvements in communications or training, may better serve your needs. Third, if the organization's top leadership or your potential team members are not excited about or supportive of organizing by teams, they will need some convincing before you decide to implement the concept. Fourth, if the organization or department is undergoing or anticipating any major changes in key personnel turnover, strategic mission changes, or a relocation, for example, it may be best to delay implementation of formal teams until there is more organizational stability.

Be aware that some issues may surface that could cause resistance to your building a smoothly running team. Such issues could be fear of change, loss of control, or financial costs. During the creation of a team, there will be times when you and your team are not producing any tangible revenue, cost reduction, or results, even though each of you is still getting paid and undergoing team training. This temporary decrease in productivity, usually accompanied by an increase in training costs, is difficult to avoid but will be insignificant once you capture the benefits of teamwork.

Besides the economic costs, a leader at any level in an organization might perceive teamwork as a threat, because it involves sharing power not controlling it. This perception, fortunately, is not as pervasive as it once was due to the widespread recognition and publicity of the success of teamwork. Once the top leaders believe in and commit to the use of teamwork principles throughout the organization, the rest of the leaders will follow and allay their fears about the upcoming changes.

Finally, leaders or individual team members may have difficulty in accepting or understanding teamwork. They may have preconceived beliefs that they will not be able to work well in a group environment because they prefer to work alone, that they will receive too much responsibility in a team setting, or that they will have to learn too many additional skills. Some may doubt if the organization is really committed to teamwork, especially if leadership has shown in the past that it is not interested in rewarding fairly, eliminating organizational politics, or encouraging employees to assume greater responsibilities.

You can overcome these objections and others. Realize that a team structure is a major commitment by everyone because it involves changes in people's attitudes, work processes, and interpersonal relationships. For effective teamwork, the organization's operating systems and informal climate must be well developed and positive, particularly in the areas of employee morale, diversity, communications, training, and innovation. Then as you proceed to develop teams, play close attention to how you plan, organize, and optimize your team.

Plan Your Team

One of your leadership objectives is to organize the right teams and get them performing quickly and well. Before you organize your team, spend time deciding what you want to accomplish and what your vision is for the team. This involves considering your team's goals, its organization, and your role as leader.

Goals

Develop a clear idea of what you want to accomplish at the team level. At this point in the process, the goals are broad because later you and your team will more fully develop them both at team and individual levels. Make your team goals realistic, important and significant to the success of your organization, achievable, challenging to your team, time-specific, and measurable.

The primary reason to identify the team-level goals is to provide an unequivocal direction for your team. It will help your team members to know precisely what goals they must accomplish. Then they will attach importance and urgency to them, get excited about accomplishing them, focus more on activities that clearly support achievement of the goals, and develop personal goals that fully support the team's goals. Your team's goals will be the rallying point that you will invariably depend upon to refocus your team members when needed.

Organization

A well-organized team is critical for achieving team goals. The organization of a team is based on its general purpose. If the team changes its purpose, either temporarily or permanently, you can always reorganize it to better accommodate its new purpose. Three general ways to organize teams are around goals of problem solving, implementation, and innovation. You can use them independently of each other or together in a specially organized combination.

A problem-solving team is responsible for finding solutions to one-of-a-kind problems. It is best used when a functional department is unable for any reason to effectively solve a problem and is typically disbanded once you resolve the problem. A good example of a problem-solving team is a project team, which was discussed in Chapter 7. Others are known as task forces or by a unique name such as Team Alpha.

A problem-solving team is process oriented and is interested in logically arriving at a solution after, not before, debating and objectively examining the relevant facts and essential points. Due to the great amount of interaction among people of a problem-solving team, it functions best when the members can easily rely upon each other, when they have confidence in each other's abilities to contribute to an effective problem-solving work relationship, and when all are committed to the team's goals.

An implementation team is not concerned with finding solutions because it already has one — a plan that describes all the details of what everyone must do. An implementation team is committed to efficiently and accurately carrying out a clearly defined plan that has measurable standards and explicit operational procedures. This team functions best when it makes good use of its members' specialized skills, unambiguous job duties, and can-do attitudes to flawlessly implement its plan.

An innovation team is responsible for seeking new and creative ways of getting things done, such as improving processes, designing new products or services, or simply making suggestions. It has the freedom and the authority to seek out new possibilities and explore a variety of options. This team thrives when it is insulated from the systematic annoyances and constraints of the organization and when it is allowed to be informal and independent.

Leader's Role

Before you organize a team, it is helpful to understand the varying roles that you will soon have. Although your roles change throughout the life cycle of a team, you are still the leader who is responsible for achieving your team's goals. All the leadership skills you learn are needed in your team environment. Regardless of the role that you are in, always demonstrate by your words and actions that you are unrelentingly committed to the team and its goals.

By using the teamwork process, you can inspire and empower your team members to assume increasingly more responsibility, authority, and autonomy. Initially, you are the leader-in-charge, responsible for determining the direction for the team, closely supervising its formation, guiding the bonding of its members, and commencing the startup of the work. Then as your team organizes itself, you will use your relationship skills in the roles of conflict resolver, negotiator, and facilitator. You increasingly will rely upon participative leadership in which team members exercise their leadership abilities and take responsibility for certain aspects of the work.

Once your team is organized and begins performing, your role becomes that of a coach who encourages and oversees the team collectively and each of its members individually. At this point, your goal is to let the team members assume and maintain as much control over themselves as possible, while you monitor performance, maintain open lines of communication, and reward achievements.

Depending upon how successful the team is at directing its work, you may further distance yourself into the role of advisor, in which you are available primarily when the team requests your assistance.

Organize Your Team

As an effective leader you will want to follow a detailed outline when organizing your team. Given the fast-paced activities that occur during team formation and its initial operation, you and your team members must be organized, focused, and mission oriented.

The purpose of this nine-part outline is to guide you through the key actions needed to get your team up and running, quickly and correctly.

- ▶ Select team members.
- ▶ Determine your team goals.
- ▶ Teach the team attitude.
- ▶ Discuss team processes and details.
- ▶ Review the goals and develop a mission statement.
- ▶ Develop a plan.
- ▶ Determine and assign team roles and responsibilities.
- ▶ Obtain commitments.
- ▶ Build team trust, belonging, and spirit.

Select Team Members

There are selection principles to consider that are helpful in all types of team situations. The basic requirement is that all your team members be qualified. They must know how to do their job well and how to work with others in a team environment. What you want on your team are individuals who possess a variety of skills so that your team can thrive during challenging situations.

The current work location of your potential team members affects how you create your team. For example, if you are choosing solely from your own department of 10 people, you clearly have a limited selection. If however, you

ACTION

◆ 1 ◆

have a department of 200, or if you can choose from other departments within the organization, you have more selection.

There are two keys to guide you to the best qualified team. First, choose a mix of team-oriented people with the most important technical skills that you require. These are competent people who are extremely knowledgeable and experienced in crucial tasks and processes that will be used on your team. Second, look for people with the personal characteristics and values that you believe are necessary for membership on your team. Most team leaders obviously seek motivated, enthusiastic, ethical, hard working, intelligent, and goal-oriented individuals. On the basis of your particular requirements though, you may need someone who can assist you in leading the team during your absences or someone with particularly excellent communications skills.

If you are dealing with an innovation team, you may want a mix of more creative, independent thinkers and dreamers who can guide themselves if necessary, rather than the task-focused, by-the-book, and competitive people you will need on an implementation team. Similarly, a problem-solving team may need an extremely knowledgeable and people-oriented member or someone exceptionally skilled in a particular process. Identify your most important skill requirements for your team and start the selection process as described in Chapter 7.

ACTION	## Determine Your Team Goals
◆ 2 ◆	Let your team know what you consider to be their broad goals. Discuss the purpose of these goals and how they relate to organizational goals. Let the team know that within an hour or so, it will be their responsibility to collectively refine these broad goals into specific, prioritized, and realistic objectives. It is the collective belief in these objectives that will provide your team members the long-term determination that will turn them into a committed and cohesive team.

ACTION	## Teach the Team Attitude
◆ 3 ◆	Each of your team members must develop a team attitude. They must believe that a team can outperform individuals and that their team is going to win. Although most of them will naturally develop a positive team attitude over time, you can speed up the process by telling them what makes a great team attitude and by reinforcing it repeatedly over time. On the next page is a sample pep talk you can give your team members to teach the team attitude. Adapt it by using your own words to convey the same concepts.

The goals you have as an individual team member are linked to the goals of the team. Your performance, therefore, affects the performance of the team. On a team, you do not have to give up your ideas, opinions, individuality, personal ambition, or positive criticisms because we welcome them as contributions that can help the team accomplish our goals. However, you must give the team's goals highest priority on the job and always give your best effort for the team. Once our team reaches consensus, we expect you to support the decision and implement it. Achievement of the team's goals, your success as a team member, and the pursuit of excellence are the most important concerns for our team.

Do not let petty disagreements, self-serving behavior, personality conflicts, organizational politics, or any other irrelevant issues assume more importance than our goals, otherwise you will lose focus and concentration. This affects your fellow team members and, therefore, causes the team to lose focus. There is no problem or challenge that cannot be worked out if you are reasonable, open-minded, and respectful of others.

You are part of a team, and we want you to be a committed team member who supports the work of your fellow teammates, who recognizes your need for each other to accomplish our goals, and who unselfishly does your job well. Since we stress cooperation rather than competition, we believe in encouraging each other with positive regard and feedback. For the team to succeed, you must commit to being self-starting, motivated, hard-working, and responsible.

In return, as your leader I will see to it that you have opportunities to grow as a team and as individuals. You will participate in training and development activities that will help you grow professionally and personally as well.

Since the team needs your contributions and expertise, I will seek and use your contributions as best and as often as I can. I believe in participating and involving myself on our team, and I want you to participate and involve yourself.

I fully expect many of you will assume leadership roles in several aspects of our work. For those who want increasing leadership responsibilities, I will assist you. As a team member, you will have the autonomy and the authority to carry out your responsibilities. I will treat you fairly and appreciate you. Finally, as your team leader, I will do everything possible to help you achieve the team goals, as well as your professional and personal success.

ACTION

◈ 4 ◈

Discuss Team Processes and Details

Discuss all rules, policies, and procedures that will affect your team. Your team must establish procedures for dealing with communications, problem solving and decision making, conflict resolution, meetings, and training. Determine how much decision-making and implementation authority team members have at their individual or subteam level as well as what decisions are reserved for the team and team leader level. Let everyone know that all policies will be applied fairly and consistently.

ACTION

◈ 5 ◈

Review the Goals and Develop a Mission Statement

You and your team should freely discuss the team's goals that you described earlier. Your purpose is to give everyone the opportunity to raise questions, make comments, and offer suggestions on how best to achieve your goals. Analyze any relevant topic that affects your goals. In particular, examine why your organization needs the team to get these goals accomplished and why this team is the one to do this important work.

After determining the goals, set realistic but challenging standards that will inspire your determined team towards hard work and eventual success. These standards will be the gauge of how well your team achieves the team and individual goals. Consider what your clients or customers need from you and what level of quality they demand. Take into account any external issues such as regulation, resource availability, and the competition. As a team, compose and agree upon a mission statement that succinctly lists and prioritizes your major goals.

ACTION

◈ 6 ◈

Develop a Plan

Your team's goals may be extremely technical or could involve working with complicated measurements, processes, or quality standards. Alternatively, the goals may be comparatively simple, such as troubleshooting a customer service issue or simply providing quality human resources support to your organization. Regardless of the scope or complexity, you should spend sufficient quality time as a team discussing the details, using the problem-solving process, and developing a realistic plan of action to take you from where you are now to where you want to go, given all your resources and constraints.

If your team's goals involve areas that are unfamiliar to you, do some preparation for your planning meeting so you are aware of the particular issues involved. This will help you to guide your team in the right direction. Many professional societies, for example, have publications that give tips on how to structure a particular problem or list the steps involved in completing certain tasks. As you well know, there are hundreds of books on every aspect of organizational functions that can give you ideas and recommendations on any situation you may have. Use this expertise and the wisdom of your sub-ordinates to develop a plan.

Determine and Assign Team Roles and Responsibilities

ACTION
◈ 7 ◈

You and your team must clearly and fairly identify the responsibilities and roles of each team member if the team is to do its best. Superior team performance depends upon the superior performances of each of its members. If feasible, let the team members themselves determine individual roles and responsibilities. Spend adequate time to ensure they do this correctly and thoroughly, because the team members will own these responsibilities and the necessary authority after the assignment. Involving your team members with all the detailed planning at this stage will pay you huge dividends later as they develop into a cohesive, collaborative, and self-directing team.

You also want to ensure that all the team responsibilities are covered, that team members understand how their roles relate to each other, and that they know how their specific responsibilities contribute to the accomplishment of the team's goals. In addition, explain how subpar performance can adversely affect the team and that you will, therefore, monitor the performance of all individuals and hold them accountable for their responsibilities. Determine specifically how you will evaluate individual and team performance and how each person will know when they and the team are successfully performing. All the individual goals should be linked to high standards of performance. Set the tone now for the pursuit of excellence and your team members will pursue it until they achieve success.

Obtain Commitments

ACTION
◈ 8 ◈

Obtain explicit commitment from each team member to work hard to achieve team goals, pursue excellence, support their fellow team members, participate in team improvement, and maintain a great team attitude. Take the time to speak individually with everyone and together again as an assembled team. One of your primary goals as the team leader will be to maintain the commitment of everyone on your team. Keeping everyone inspired and enthused about being on their special team will be crucial in later ensuring your team's successful performance.

Build Team Trust, Belonging, and Spirit

ACTION
◈ 9 ◈

Your team will function most effectively if its members are secure enough in their relationships to openly speak to each other as equal members of a group with a purpose. It is particularly important during the first days of the team's existence that you take charge of the team and let them get to know you and the upcoming schedule of events. This starts the process that leads to a trusting team. Team members need each other, and if they are to fully concentrate on achieving the goals, each person must develop a high degree of trust for each other. This trust arrives quickly after team members share new experiences on the job and demonstrate that they can be counted upon to act with integrity.

Conversely, this requires that you be aware of factors that will diminish the trust levels in your organization, such as cliques, gossip, lack of follow-through on promises, hesitancies to delegate authority, and unfairness in any form. Loss of trust between team members is one of the most difficult problems to remedy. The loss can be minimized somewhat by removing the offending team member from the team. Although this approach is one of last resort, it may be necessary because if lack of trust becomes widespread, your team may not sufficiently recover.

As your team members identify with each other and the team grows, look for that spirited attitude that suggests that the focal point is the team, not any one person. Selfishness disappears and is replaced by a total commitment to and respect for the team. By spending hours with each other working on important activities, team members will grow emotionally attached to each other and will encourage one another to pursue excellence in everything they do. It is the collective result of these individual performances that drives a team towards success. If they perform well, they expect to perform even better next time. This relentless drive and inspiration to do everything first class is a pervasive attitude that will develop over time if you, the leader, set high standards for your team and hold them accountable to the commitments they make.

Optimize Your Team

Now that you have established your team, there are ways for you to capitalize on your many efforts thus far.

- ▶ Monitor the flow of information and resources.
- ▶ Promote communication and collaboration.
- ▶ Coach individual and team performance.
- ▶ Train your team.
- ▶ Reward your team.

Monitor the Flow of Information and Resources

Teamwork exists in an environment that is information- and resource-intensive. Your team members must have quick access to the quality organizational and external information that they need. Constantly check to see that your team members are getting reliable information so that they can make the best possible decisions. Maintain a log book to assist you in keeping an official record of the decisions and recommendations made by team members. This will serve as institutional knowledge and help you follow up on the ideas submitted by your team. In addition, you as the leader also must ensure that the team is logistically supported by the organizational staff and any other involved external agency. The team members count on you and other team leaders to help handle external relations so that they can focus on their daily work.

Promote Communication and Collaboration

As discussed in Chapter 10, communication is vital to any organization. It is particularly crucial for a well-functioning and collaborative team in which members spend so much time together and depend upon each other. Your team members must feel free to openly discuss issues and ask questions because this is how teams create and sustain a vibrant, collaborative, and trusting environment. Open lines of communication between you and the team members, and among the team members themselves, result in high team morale, pride, willingness to take reasonable chances, and adaptability to changes. The unequivocal sharing of information allows team members to better understand each other and know how they feel about issues. Doesn't it make sense that if all team members know that everyone is supporting each other, they will do their best for the good of the team? Can you imagine the possible successes for your team if every team member had this high level of confidence in each other?

Despite the inevitable conflict that will arise in a team environment, your team members should understand that they can positively resolve all disagreements. Regularly hold informal discussions and social activities so that team members can communicate and bond. Team training activities can increase the trust levels among members, especially if conducted soon after you organize the team.

Coach Individual and Team Performance

Use monitoring procedures to keep track of how your team members and team are performing. By frequently measuring progress against challenging but achievable standards then communicating this progress to your team members promptly and accurately, everyone will know exactly where they and the team stand in goal achievement and how their individual performance is helping the team. When giving feedback to your team members, remember to focus on details, facts, and team member performance. If you detect team performance problems, let your team members know and have them develop options that will improve the performance. The team then chooses the best course of action and implements it. Follow up to ensure that your team members are responding to your coaching; if not, repeat this coaching process.

Your team members appreciate your interest in what they do, and you will find that your relationship with each of them will grow stronger over time. In addition, by personally coaching your team members, you will diffuse any problems and concerns that they have.

If you find that a team member is not working collaboratively or has other performance problems, it is essential to change their behavior through coaching. Tell that person specifically how their attitude and performance are hindering the team, and find out why the person is not performing up to the agreed-upon standards. If their behavior does not change, you should remove them from the team because they will cause more damage than good — particularly when other team members become discouraged by the fact the disruptive person is not being penalized for counterproductive behavior, yet the team is bearing the penalty.

Train Your Team

Despite your having the opportunity to select a well-trained, motivated group of people for your team, once the team begins working you will notice additional needs for training. This does not mean that you made bad selections or that your leadership is ineffective. The reality is that team members need periodic training to maintain or improve the skills needed while participating on the team.

Specific training to include during team development is in the areas of individual jobs, problem solving, and team skills. Job training addresses those skills required of the individual to do their job or the jobs of the team members they support. Problem-solving training is important because this skill is inherent in most of the duties of a team, especially autonomous or self-directed work teams. It is crucial, therefore, to train team members to think logically so that they can participate equally in team decisions. This will help keep your team members enthusiastically involved in the team's activities and help avert the tendency toward ineffective consensus group thinking.

If you have team members who are inexperienced in working on a team, you should conduct specific training so that they can learn about teamwork concepts and practice team skills, such as communication and conflict resolution. Team training does more than just correct existing problems; it provides the means to empower your team so it eventually can carry out all its functions without the constant guidance of a leader. In addition, team training is specifically needed when you have an underperforming team or a group of people who have developed severe group hostility, low productivity, or low morale. Team training is an ongoing activity that will best help your team members if they have specific performance deficiencies. As discussed in Chapter 9, determine training needs by gathering preliminary data and surveying your team members. The key point is that in team training, all team members should be involved in assessing the training needs, developing training options, agreeing to the plan, and participating in the actual training. More experienced team members should help you lead these sessions.

Team training is a good opportunity for you and your team members to develop cohesion. The activities that you choose to help train your team can be of great benefit in accomplishing your training objectives if you plan the activities with your team in mind. As well as being relevant, the activities should be interesting and tailored to the character and personality of your team. The training should emphasize increasing expertise in specific skills that will allow the team to later develop practical solutions to support both team and organizational goals. Before the actual training, emphasize your role as a facilitator who wants to guide them through the training that they themselves selected and planned. Suggest that everyone be open-minded, relaxed, and enthusiastic about spending this time together.

Reward Your Team

Demonstrate that you appreciate your team members by rewarding them externally and internally. The reward system will be discussed more in the upcoming chapter on motivation, but there are some specific points that you can note now. Because you are truly interested in team performance, you should base your external rewards on the accomplishments of the team, not the individual. These external awards are many, such as the traditional bonuses, certificates, and public recognition. Find the rewards that most motivate your team and integrate them into your reward system.

More importantly, by being an involved, caring, and committed leader, you will enable your team members to create for themselves internal rewards, which some people value much more than most anything that can be awarded to them. Feelings of pride, belonging, self-esteem, and purpose will motivate people to great performance. It also will sustain them when their team is faced with difficult challenges.

Effective Meetings

You know that to effectively accomplish your leadership duties, you must rally subordinates around specific goals and then guide them to outstanding performance. Meetings are an excellent way to do this. Meetings can be quick or lengthy, scheduled or impromptu, and conducted with many or few people. To a leader, meetings are more than a method to promote communications, solve problems, or manage priorities. A meeting, in the broadest context, is a means for you to efficiently exercise your leadership responsibilities by working closely with others in a team setting. It is often the primary way that you as a leader collectively communicate with your team members, resolve conflicts, solicit opinions, and guide the group's efforts.

You most likely can recall times when you or others stated that meetings are ineffective ways of conducting work, a waste of time, and simply forums for opinionated attendees to dominate the discussion. You may even have wished that meetings be banned forever. It can be helpful to identify reasons why meetings are ineffective.

Nonproductive Meetings

Sometimes meetings may not be the right response to a problem. For example, do not use meetings solely for distributing or relaying information. Instead of asking ten people to give up two hours of their time, for a total cost of 20 work hours, write a memo or send information by mail. Second, meetings are often not the best means of checking progress on individual assignments if they waste the time of participants who must listen to routine updates that do not concern them. You may occasionally want attendees to hear what is occurring with each other, as it can promote communication and team building. Make an effort, however, to get individual updates from attendees at their job site, in your office, or on the telephone. Third, avoid having a meeting where everyone attends if a smaller group of attendees can meet and resolve the issues more effectively by itself. Finally, do not use a meeting for seeking opinions and comment on important new ideas if the participants have not had time to adequately form their opinions or to review relevant information. Instead, notify them in advance about the ideas and send them information to read before the meeting.

Too often meetings are convened with insignificant issues to discuss. Regularly scheduled meetings, such as the weekly staff meeting, can be useful if there are significant issues to discuss or resolve. They also permit the participants to make effective use of their schedule by being able to plan for attendance. It is best for you as a leader, however, to routinely assess the topics a day or two before each meeting. If you find that there is a need for the meeting, then keep it scheduled. If not, cancel it; the attendees will greatly appreciate your considerate and decisive action.

Leaders sometimes fail to establish or maintain control of meetings. If the participants sense that the meeting has no structure or control, or that the leader allows powerful participants to dominate the discussion, then they will lose interest, daydream, and not contribute during the meeting.

Despite the bad experiences that you or others may have had, effective meetings are essential to the success of the organization and to the individuals who need to get business accomplished with the assistance of other people. Although much work can be done by using the telephone, video conferences, and e-mail, the face-to-face communication involved in periodic meetings is crucial. Here are some suggestions for making your meetings useful and effective whether you are leading them or participating in them.

Use an Agenda

If after determining you really need the meeting, publish and distribute in advance a detailed agenda, then follow it during the meeting. Not only does an agenda help you remind the participants about the upcoming meeting but it also gives them some advance knowledge of the topics so that they can prepare for and make an effective contribution during the meeting. If you are planning an extended meeting of several hours, circulate a proposed agenda so that key participants can provide their comments or suggested topics. The agenda also gives you additional authority during the meeting to discuss the topics, and only those topics, and to remain on schedule.

Stay on Course

Encourage participation by seeking comments from every attendee, tactfully preventing individuals from dominating the discussion with their own concerns, and limiting digression. If you are leading the meeting, it is wise to minimize your direct participation in evaluating suggestions so as to encourage others to participate more freely. However, do speak up to get the meeting moving along, clarify issues, or make an outstanding suggestion. Evaluate your progress during the meeting to see if you are on course with your schedule and making progress towards achieving the meeting's objectives. Facilitate the meeting by asking leading and clarifying questions or by making statements that:

- ▶ Encourage participation — "How do you feel about that idea, Alyssa?"
- ▶ Rephrase comments — "So Max, you want brainstorming sessions, like Colette does?"
- ▶ Reward participants — "Good idea, Linda."
- ▶ Limit digression — "Let's see, since that important topic is not on our agenda and we have limited time, we should schedule it for the next time."

- ▸ Preserve civility — "Come on folks, let's keep the noise down while Alan is speaking."
- ▸ Maintain order — "Just a moment, Ross, let's finish hearing from Warren."
- ▸ Cause action — "Lindsey, can you and Kelley ask the vendor about that issue?"
- ▸ Summarize discussion — "Are we in agreement that finance issues are our priority?"

End the Meeting Positively and Assertively

Before adjourning, thank everyone for their valued participation and ask each person to make a brief summarizing comment of actions they will take or what they feel is important. Indicate on the agenda that you plan on seeking their comments so they will not be surprised. This will give the participants one last opportunity to offer any reluctant or strong opinions or what they feel is the most important result of the meeting. Close the meeting by mentioning any key point that was omitted from the individual summaries and ending with a positive statement about how you appreciate the high level of involvement by participants. Remember to retain your meeting notes so that you can later refer to them. If beneficial to you or the participants, prepare a summary of the meeting to distribute to participants.

Watch the Details

Pay attention to all the details, such as sending out timely notification, starting on time, inviting only those who are needed, scheduling breaks, and choosing the meeting room itself. Meetings are more effective when the temperature is pleasing, there are no noisy distractions nearby, and the room is clean. Every few meetings, ask someone to evaluate each of the details discussed in this section. Although as the leader you may believe the meetings are going well, it is helpful to have a participant confirm or refute your impressions of the meeting.

Actively Participate

If you are a non-leader participant in a meeting, be an active, involved, and informed contributor. If you have something relevant to say, say it with conviction. If you have a question, ask it, because someone else is probably thinking about the same question. The meeting's leader needs your positive suggestions and valued experience. However, it is not helpful to you or others if, during the meeting, you read unrelated material, distract the speakers by chatting loudly with others, offer negative or irrelevant comments, or doze.

Establish Goals

When you are solely the participant in a meeting and not its leader, identify before the meeting specific goals on how the meeting can serve your objectives, then actively participate to ensure that your needs are considered and your goals are accomplished. You may have little choice in whether to attend a meeting, but if it is scheduled, you can use it to accomplish goals related to your work, to resolve long-standing problems, to determine the views of other attendees, or to gain cooperation from others. Remember to think of solutions, not problems. Having such a positive focus in the meeting will give you the impetus to use the meeting to help you get your job done.

Remember that, by definition, a leader is one who gets the right things accomplished at the right time with the assistance of other people. These other people are your team members, whether they are people you supervise, peers or fellow volunteers, organizational staff members, clients, or family members. You are not necessarily the only team leader in each of these instances, but in every case you are working with others to achieve a common objective. Leadership through teamwork implies that you can harness the skills and talents of other people to create an environment where success becomes contagious.

MOTIVATE YOUR TEAM

Motivations are the reasons people act the way they do. Motivation is an intensely personal and emotional state wherein an individual feels compelled to act for any number of reasons or needs. It is because of these reasons and needs that people do superior work, fail to complete an assignment, offer to work overtime without pay, or quit an organization in disgust. So when you pinpoint why your subordinates do what they do, you are closer to establishing their motivation.

You cannot change others' existing motivations or create new ones by yourself; individuals have to do it internally themselves. Your primary goal is to understand what the general needs of your subordinates are as well as what their specific needs are when they work with their tasks and responsibilities at the job site. If you satisfy those needs, or even come close, then you are more likely to have motivated subordinates who will succeed.

After you take to heart and use what has been discussed so far in this book, you will probably have enthusiastic subordinates who are motivated to do their jobs well. This is because when leaders assume ownership of their responsibilities and lead in a caring and knowledgeable way, their subordinates will already have a basic level of motivation from which to do what is right.

It would be erroneous to think of motivation as a leadership skill that is isolated from your other leadership responsibilities. The motivation of a subordinate is affected by all the variables that exist every day: needs, emotions, job conditions and performance, interactions with people, as well as all the organizational issues such as morale and structure. Nevertheless, from a leader's perspective, people's motivations also are affected by your determined efforts to perform all your leadership skills well, to solve problems well, train well, communicate well, and maintain a team well, for example. This chapter will help you integrate these and the other skills you have learned into a practical, common sense approach to motivation. You will continue to build upon your motivation skills as you learn more during the remaining chapters of the book.

As a leader, don't settle for subordinates who are motivated to do their job adequately. You want to have the most motivated and energized team possible, because that is how you implement your strategy, negotiate the certainty of change, and achieve great successes. A committed and enthusiastic team will overcome obstacles of all types to accomplish its goals. Though it is a part of your job, you are not primarily responsible for motivating your subordinates to this successful job performance — it is ultimately their job to motivate themselves. You are responsible, however, for creating and maintaining a flourishing environment where subordinates have the opportunity to achieve a high degree of motivation, willingly strive to achieve their goals, and intensely want to do the best job they can. These are the purposes for increasing your motivation skills.

Principles Underlying Motivation

A leader depends upon influencing individual behavior so that organizational goals can be accomplished through the coordinated efforts of many people. Individual job performance is primarily a function of 1) the employee's abilities, 2) the support they get from their organization to carry out the job tasks, and 3) the employee's motivation to do that job. The first component, abilities, was addressed in Chapter 9 on the importance of training and developing a skilled group of subordinates. The second component, which is a premise throughout this book, is the effective use of leadership skills and how they can make enormous contributions to the success of your subordinates. The third component of job performance, motivation, consists of many personal factors.

Although motivation originates within the individual, you can significantly affect it if you understand six principles. You can use these principles to solidify your knowledge of motivation and help you determine the right actions to take. Later in the chapter are five steps to help you create and maintain an environment of high motivation.

These are the six principles underlying motivation that leaders must understand.

- ▸ People prefer positive rewards over punishment.
- ▸ Misused rewards cause people to act improperly.
- ▸ Meaningful contributions inspire people.
- ▸ People will pursue a worthy and achievable goal.
- ▸ People must believe and value your promises of reward.
- ▸ People want their leaders to act like leaders.

People Prefer Positive Rewards over Punishment

It is almost always better to reinforce your guidance and directives with the promise of a reward than with the threat of punishment. Both the lure of rewards and the certainty of punishment act as incentives, or things that cause a person to take action. Since this is true, do not be startled to learn that people act foremost for their own interests, not for yours or the organization's. This does not mean that your subordinates are second-rate because they are selfish — this is just a fact of human nature.

The rewards that you offer, which vary in importance for each individual, must be of primary benefit and value to your subordinate's current personal and professional priorities, not the organization's priorities. For instance, if you want someone to work hard on a project just because the organization will reap more profits, that will not necessarily increase your subordinate's motivation. To ensure a motivational opportunity, you must somehow relate the project to an individual reward that will act as a positive incentive to the person, such as a share of the company's profits, an increase in their stock price, personal recognition, or time off from work.

Be clear about punishment. You may need it as a negative incentive to ensure that some subordinates take the actions you want them to take. It is not, however, an effective means for maintaining high motivation. Do not punish subordinates because they are taking action and attempting to do the work but failing on the first try. Motivation by fear is not something you want to do. If you must punish, do so because they took action but are consistently yielding poor performance, a bad attitude, or some other undesirable behavior. Do not be afraid of punishment because you need it as part of your overall system of motivation. Like rewards, punishment has levels of intensity from which to choose, ranging from a mild conversation indicating your displeasure to progressively serious actions such as written reprimands and termination.

It is crucial that you do not overuse punishment by resorting to it for every undesirable occurrence in the workplace. To nitpick subordinates may only inspire more negative behavior or bitterness. Most of your subordinates do not require negative incentives to perform well, nevertheless, they must know what the consequences are for performance discrepancies and believe that you will firmly enforce the same fair standards for everyone. For example, if someone knows they will lose their job if they consistently are late for work, they will motivate themselves to show up on time. It is better in this example, though, for you to routinely de-emphasize the punishment aspects of showing up late and emphasize the rewards for showing up on time.

Misused Rewards Cause People to Act Improperly

Positive rewards will encourage people to do their best because it is in their self-interest to do so. When leaders misuse rewards, however, these incentives become disincentives that deter people from acting properly. For example, a company establishes employee bonuses as a reward system. However, if a leader threatens to revoke the bonus system if his subordinates do not perform better, it discourages them and negatively affects the trust that had been established. Other misuses include the overuse of praise and assigning credit for a job well done to the wrong person. Subordinates view their good relations with their leader as an incentive, and they expect the leader to consistently act maturely and responsibly. When leaders ignore their responsibilities or contradict good leadership practices, many subordinates will lose their hope, enthusiasm, and motivation to do well.

Meaningful Contributions Inspire People

When people believe what they are doing is important, they will feel good about their work and approach it with enthusiasm and determination. They will believe that the organization, their boss, and their coworkers are depending on them to do the job to the best of their ability because it is a crucial part of everyone's success. Since their work is important, they will motivate themselves to do it well because they feel important. If they do not believe their work involves significant responsibility, they will more likely take shortcuts in quality or not be much of a team player.

When meaningful and challenging work is combined with the opportunity to participate in workplace decision making, your subordinates have powerful incentives to maintain a high level of motivation.

People Will Pursue a Worthy and Achievable Goal

When subordinates believe strongly that they can achieve a goal that is worthwhile, they are more likely to pursue the goal with gusto and achieve it. This shows you how pivotal you are as a leader when you guide your subordinates to expect to achieve fair and challenging goals. The more convincing and inspiring you are, the more they will believe in the worthiness of the goal and link their effort with its achievement. This, in turn, promotes a valuable commitment to you and your organization. As discussed throughout this book, you must ensure that the subordinate understands what he must do and why he must do it. One effective way to do this is to clearly communicate with the subordinate during goal setting and coaching sessions.

People Must Believe and Value Your Promises of Reward

A firm bond of trust between you and your subordinates is key to keeping them motivated. If they know that you will do what you promise, then they will not doubt you. This trust will cause your subordinates to form positive conclusions about what to expect under your leadership. In addition to believing your promise of reward, subordinates must value and desire the reward you offer. If they don't, the lure of the reward will not stimulate them to expend the effort to attain it.

People Want Their Leaders to Act Like Leaders

Most people do not like uncertainty, indecision, disorganization, or lack of direction in a leader. They feel unmotivated to achieve great acts when they believe that no one is in charge, that the leader does not care about their needs or appreciate them, or that the leader does not desire their comments to help achieve organizational goals. Your subordinates count on you not only to provide clear direction and purpose but also to not retreat when you are confronted with tough decisions or difficulties.

It is imperative, therefore, that you understand the important connection between your subordinates' motivation and the exercise of your leadership responsibilities. All your leadership skills are vital components of a highly motivating and well-functioning work environment. No subordinate expects you to do everything correctly, but they expect you to do your best since you are the leader. It is reassuring and comforting to them that you understand your mission. They want you to determine the right things to do and lead the way, then they will follow you.

Motivational Goals for Leaders

Now that you understand the basic principles of motivation, you can use these five steps to create and maintain an environment of high motivation.

- ▶ Know what motivates your subordinates.
- ▶ Be a sensitive leader.

▸ Reward properly, immediately, and equitably.

▸ Reward desired behavior and punish undesirable behavior.

▸ Eliminate demotivators.

Know What Motivates Your Subordinates

Since people are motivated by different things, find out what motivates each of your subordinates and use this information to sustain a high state of motivation. If you communicate well with your employees, you naturally will find out their hopes and dreams, their needs and core values. You may uncover talents and abilities that were suppressed but can now be used for the benefit of both your subordinates and the organization. Motivations are shaped not only by personal and professional experiences, age, and tenure in the work force but also by expectations of what will happen as they perform their job under your leadership. Once you determine what motivates your subordinates, modify your formal and informal reward systems so you can effectively reward your subordinates based on what they value.

Not all people are motivated by usual formal rewards, such as automatic pay increases, fringe benefits, and expense accounts. Some are motivated more by the informal rewards that exist or that you as a leader can initiate. For example, some subordinates enjoy a sense of control over their jobs that they have not had before. For others it may be nurturing, peer support that helps them achieve their goals. These informal rewards and benefits can be extrinsic, which are given by others, such as recognition or fair treatment. At other times the rewards are intrinsic, meaning they are primarily internal feelings, such as feelings of self-esteem and of satisfaction in a job well done.

Staying in touch with your subordinates' motivations will allow you to react quickly when you notice that their needs have changed or become satisfied, thus prompting you to find new motivators. What motivates individuals this month may not motivate them next month. By keeping up with what motivates your subordinates, you will always be able to align their needs with the organization's needs. You do this by helping subordinates see exactly how they can achieve their needs by being a productive part of your organization, a win-win situation for them and you.

When you know more about your subordinates, you will understand them better. Know details about each subordinate's family such as the names of the spouse and children, challenges that the family faces, and what the family does for recreation. These are indeed personal details, but great leaders know these things about their subordinates, and your subordinates probably want you to know them; if they do not, they will tell you so. Remember these details by jotting them down in a notebook, and refer to them periodically so that you can use them in conversations with your subordinates.

STEP

◈ 2 ◈

Be a Sensitive Leader

Your subordinates are, above all, individuals, and then they are your employees. They each have different degrees of sensitivity and will require, therefore, varying amounts of attention. For example, people react differently to criticism or lack of praise. Some demand periodic comment from you on how well they are doing their job or otherwise they will believe you are ignoring them. Some subordinates are insulted if you start discussing work without saying good morning or if you forget to say please when asking for assistance. Many high achievers feel slighted if you spend more of your coaching time with the underachievers than with them.

Being pleasant to your subordinates will help them maintain a high state of motivation if the pleasantries are used in conjunction with good motivational skills; it will not accomplish much by itself. If you are perceptive, empathetic, and sympathetic of others' sensitivities, your subordinates will see you as less of a threat and more of an ally. If you value, respect, and not take for granted your relationship with each subordinate, you will help them attain high levels of motivation.

STEP

◈ 3 ◈

Reward Properly, Immediately, and Equitably

There are many ways to structure a reward and recognition program. For a leader's purposes, such a program includes any formal or informal means of recognizing an employee who has performed well on the job. Several books are available on this topic, some even list hundreds of rewards you can give subordinates. The key points to remember are to reward properly, immediately, and equitably.

Proper rewards include a mix of external and internal awards large enough to motivate all your subordinates to great achievements. Besides using monetary rewards such as bonuses, incentive pay, or cash awards, it is important to include other kinds of rewards. These might include public recognition, time off from work, or gifts. Vary the rewards by using some that relate to the job, such as professional seminars or training, and some that do not, such as a weekend trip or lunch. Probably the most appreciated reward that you could give someone is simple praise or thanks that comes from the heart.

The types of rewards you give are based on what you want to achieve, what works best for your organization's culture, what is financially and operationally feasible, and what suggestions you solicit from your subordinates. As discussed in the previous chapter, if your subordinates are organized as a team, the rewards should be based on the team's accomplishments. If your organization depends heavily on individual contributions, reward individuals. To keep everyone oriented to your strategic objectives, long-term rewards can be linked to long-term performance such as growth, not on short-term earnings or sales.

Reward as soon as possible after the achievement so as to encourage a repetition of the behavior. For example, if you recognize someone as employee of the year, this obviously is done annually as soon as the competition ends. With more frequent activities, such as monthly sales contests or periodic projects, tie in the reward to the culmination of each activity. To keep the winner motivated, other subordinates geared for the next award, and everyone's performance level high, give the reward as soon as possible after the achievement becomes known. Informal rewards can be more spontaneous, such as when you praise a subordinate for outstanding work or a great idea.

One excellent motivator is to set a goal for yourself to praise in some way all your subordinates several times a day. If you think about it, most people do good things throughout the day. Wouldn't it be great for you to let your subordinates know that you appreciate them? Your subordinates want to know when they are doing a great job, and one way of ensuring that they know is to tell them. You do not need to offer gushing praise every time. Simple statements such as, "You've done a great job," "I am proud of you," or "I appreciate what you've done" will be impressive enough to your subordinates.

The rewards system should be equitably devised and operated. This is because subordinates will compare their experiences with the rewards system to the experiences that other people have with it. Naturally, they will become unhappy if they perceive inequities or if rewards are not uniformly available to everyone. Areas of concern include reward systems that are too complicated; that are not appropriate for your particular industry; that do not reflect differences in geographical areas; or that do not reward the desired performance over and above low performance.

Although you may not have primary responsibility for the organization's formal reward system, you can provide your influential comments to the people who do. As you detect inequities or inconsistencies in the reward system that affect the motivation of your subordinates, take solutions to the responsible officials. You need to resolve these issues because if you do not reward your subordinates properly, you will see an increase in undesirable performance behavior.

Reward Desired Behavior and Punish Undesirable Behavior

It seems obvious but remember to follow through on your promises of reward and threats of punishment. Your subordinates will get your message a lot quicker when your actions support your words. When subordinates perform satisfactorily, reinforce this behavior by rewarding them in some way.

STEP

❧ 4 ❧

To strengthen their motivation and encourage them to achieve super performances, it is crucial to have some sort of merit system in which they will receive more reward when they perform better than the standard. The key is to reward the desired individual or team behavior that you want. If you want close and collaborative team behavior, do not reward individual performance within the team. If you need creativity, then provide incentives for your subordinates to make creative suggestions.

It is important to punish in some way an undesirable behavior and deter its repetition by clearly letting subordinates know when their behavior is wrong. If you do not punish them, you are by default rewarding their negative behavior and giving them the message that their undesirable behavior is allowed. It is more likely, therefore, that they will repeat this behavior.

STEP

◆ 5 ◆

Eliminate Demotivators

Most anything in the work environment can potentially affect the level of a subordinate's motivation. One part of your job is to continually identify and eliminate demotivators that cause dissatisfaction. Demotivators could include stifling, controlling, or nonsensical policies and procedures; a too formal benefits-and-rewards systems; the career management system; or even the work environment itself. If you see a problem, do not ignore it but seek instead to find its solution.

Simply removing demotivators will not necessarily create motivation, but it can lead to a more positive work environment that will help eliminate negativity among your subordinates. This can eventually lead to higher levels of satisfaction in your organization.

When your subordinates evolve to the point where they are more excited about being a contributing, responsible member of a winning organization than about the amount of the next bonus, you indeed have a motivated team. Your leadership efforts will have created an abundance of internal rewards as important as any external reward.

CHAPTER 13

DEVELOP A DIVERSE TEAM

Diversity means having differences. You may no doubt have strong diversity beliefs, such as the best age or gender for a certain type of profession or that you prefer to work with someone from a similar background and heritage. It would be naive to expect you to disregard years of socialization about the variety of issues related to diversity. This chapter is not a minicourse on diversity awareness, but is intended to show you how you can be a better leader simply by considering the impact of diversity upon your responsibilities, then taking steps to capitalize upon the diversity you have in the workplace. As with all your leadership skills, you can use these diversity ideas and skills in any organization where you have a leadership role, such as at work, in your community, or in your family.

Your diversity goals as a leader are two-fold.

- ▶ Personally exhibit, and lead your subordinates to exhibit, understanding, acceptance, respect, and tolerance in your behavior and attitude toward diverse groups.
- ▶ Use diversity as a valuable catalyst to increase the performance and motivation of all your subordinates so that they can achieve their full potential.

Diversity as it pertains to your leadership role refers to the human differences that exist in your organization in eight major areas:

- ▸ Gender
- ▸ Age
- ▸ Race
- ▸ Ethnic group
- ▸ Physical appearance
- ▸ Physical abilities
- ▸ Background
- ▸ Lifestyle

The last four categories are vast, and conceivably could contain within them scores of further classifications, such as the educated and less educated, factory workers and office workers, sports participants and sports viewers, as just a beginning. Because most people could claim membership in several diverse groups, it is realistic to think of diversity as a characteristic that permeates your work force, not as a separate challenge that you must handle differently, less intensely, or more delicately than your other leadership duties.

There is some debate as to whether some diversity classifications are more important than others. Some scholars attach more importance to gender and race than lifestyle choices and background because the first set constitutes a more permanent and significant part of daily living. This line of reasoning concludes that lifestyle choices, background, and abilities are less important because they are supposedly more fluid and easily changed.

There are several reasons why it is foolhardy for leaders to try to assign importance to diversity categories. First, leaders cannot accurately make those types of subjective decisions when it is the individual, not other people, who determines the value of such differences and must decide, for example, whether to think of oneself more as an Asian-American or as a young single parent. Of course, the legal system forces you to make these distinctions in certain categories such as race and gender, but that still does not mean that people value their racial differences more than their educational differences. Second, because there are so many conceivable classifications of diversity, it would be highly impractical and ineffective for leaders to assign a relative importance for each category. Third, if subordinates perceive their leaders as favoring one classification of diversity over another, they could have resentment that may fester and create new workplace problems.

Leaders should not think of diversity in terms of a hierarchy of importance but rather should value all diversity equally. An effective leader will use these differences to create a better work environment for subordinates and more success for the organization.

The Relevance of Diversity

You or your fellow leaders may wonder why there is a need to learn diversity skills or even consider the topic, especially since handling diversity has not been seen historically as a vital leadership skill. There are several significant reasons why a leader must go beyond simple indifference to diversity.

Realize Dramatic Demographic Changes Are Occurring

The demographics of the work force — your most important resource — will continue to change dramatically into the next century. Your subordinates, peers, customers, and supervisors will increasingly consist of diverse people who no longer fit conveniently into what was once considered the traditional majority: married Caucasian males with three children. Although you may already notice this demographic shift, expect it to be more pronounced in the next century.

This change will dramatically affect you as you attract and retain the best employees for your organization. If you consult organizations that predicts U.S. workforce demographic trends from the year 2000 onward, most foresee even greater diversity in the workforce. These diversity forecasts are similar to the expected general population trends, which undoubtedly affect your responses to customer service, marketing, and community interaction.

Because competition for the smaller pool of younger, diverse employees will increase, entry level workers will most likely examine very closely how a potential employer handles diversity issues. Those organizations that effectively utilize their diversity will be viewed as progressive and attuned to the needs of the labor force, while those organizations that do not will be seen as inferior places to work. This inevitably will create challenges for the recruitment and retention efforts of organizations lagging behind the times.

Do Not Ignore Change

Diversity, just as with any other challenge you face as a leader, is a part of your environment that is here to stay. Although you may be able to change customer opinions about your product, increase the quality in a manufacturing facility, or successfully ignore naysayers when launching a new service, you cannot significantly change the diversity that exists in your environment. Ignoring it will only cause you to miss opportunities for you and your subordinates and increase the level of dissatisfaction in your work force. As a leader, you must respond.

Consider the Benefits of Diversity

The concept of a diverse workforce parallels the discussion in Chapter 11 of the advantages of having team members who possess a wide range of knowledge, skills, and experience. By actively seeking and using the varied ideas, opinions, and talents available, you will leverage your workforce. Diversity then becomes an advantage, a competitive edge. As a result, you will better understand the needs of your domestic and international customers, the potential applications of your existing or new products and services, and the right approaches to targeting diverse customers in the entire marketplace.

Remember that one aspect of your responsibilities as a leader is to bring all your subordinates together as a team to get the right things done. As you hone the leadership skills presented in this book, you will make tremendous progress toward building and maintaining a high-performing team of subordinates. If you incorporate the issues of diversity into your leadership activities, you will make more progress because these issues represent a vital dimension to your success.

When your subordinates and others know that you are not just tolerant but completely accepting of their diversity, your job will be much easier because they will respect you as an empathetic, concerned leader. Your subordinates are all individuals with unique personalities, needs, heritages, and backgrounds. Your subordinates will respond better to your leadership if they know that you value them personally, not just for what they can do for you and the organization. This does not mean that you tolerate unacceptable performance from subordinates because you fear they may label you as a racist, sexist, or intolerant leader. Nor does it mean that you have to relearn all your leadership skills so that you can treat or lead diverse groups differently than others. It does mean that you consider your leadership responsibilities in the context of the diversity that exists in your organization. It also requires that you exercise your duties fairly, comply with legal requirements, and treat everyone with dignity and respect.

Acknowledge, Understand, and Respond to Diversity

Many leaders assume that it is safest to treat all subordinates the same and avoid the issues of diversity. Although this approach may have been successful in the past for some leaders, it does not work well as a general leadership tactic, and it certainly will not work well in a diverse environment. As is true in any leadership challenge, avoidance is usually not the best solution because it will eventually cause further disruption. Ignoring diversity and doing nothing, therefore, will lead to critical performance problems, such as increased interpersonal conflicts, overt discrimination, tension, low morale, and high turnover, and thus to increased financial costs for the organization.

You can avoid or minimize this by proactively addressing the issues of diversity. It is important for you and your subordinates to recognize and acknowledge the differences that are inherent in your diverse organization. An environment where diversity communication is open, not closeted, will be an impetus for widespread respect for diversity among your subordinates. This will lead to a team of subordinates who will commit to your diversity efforts and desire for organizational success.

Diversity Issues for Leaders

It is beyond the scope of this chapter to fully explain differences among diverse groups or unique discrimination histories or particular cultural nuances. You can research this information later in as much detail as you want. Yet it is important for you as a leader to understand some basic diversity issues so you can immediately begin developing a solid plan of action to address diversity within your organization. There are five important points regarding diversity with which leaders concern themselves.

POINT

◆ 1 ◆

Diversity Shapes People's Perceptions

Even though your subordinates may work together on the same tasks, this does not mean that they perceive their work in the same way. Their background and differing characteristics shape their views on everything, such as how to do work, how much they enjoy the work, and whether they are willing to improve work processes. These things also affect a subordinate's ability to concentrate on the job and relate with others. This leads to stereotypes that often interfere with your subordinate's ability to form objective opinions about diverse coworkers and customers. As you lead your subordinates, remember that each person is a complex individual with specific needs and perceptions.

POINT

◆ 2 ◆

Quotas, Affirmative Action, and Diversity Programs Differ

Because there is widespread confusion as to the meanings of certain terms, understand their differences so you can eliminate the confusion among your subordinates and fellow leaders whenever possible.

Quotas are an inflexible and fixed allocation of opportunities, for example in job positions or training opportunities, based upon a diversity classification such as race or gender.

Affirmative action is a program that attempts to correct diversity imbalances that exist in workplace positions. It may or may not include quotas, but it still has as its objective the search for qualified — not unqualified — people from diverse backgrounds.

A diversity program approaches these issues from an entirely different perspective. It emphasizes naturally proactive, long-term, and fundamental organizational changes so that there is eventually no need for quotas or affirmative action. In a well-designed diversity program, everyone is seen as an individual with unique contributions to offer, and people are judged on the quality of those contributions, not on subjective or irrelevant conclusions based on a diversity classification.

Assimilation Is Outdated

For years leaders have assumed that it is better to encourage assimilation, which makes individuals in the organization adapt to each other's behaviors, express less individuality, and become similar or homogenous. Leaders typically have done this by treating everyone the same and ignoring differences. In return, people were expected to conform and follow the example of successful role models and leaders within the organization.

The main idea behind assimilation is that it is better to treat all employees equally in the same manner than to treat one group differently. In recent years, assimilation has been legally supported by affirmative action programs. Assimilation also serves to maintain the organization's original norms and culture. The mainstream employees, members of the traditional nondiverse groups, usually welcome assimilation because it is not a threat to them. Assimilation often continues indefinitely within an organization because existing policies and systems perpetuate it.

An overemphasis on assimilation encourages diverse people to blend into the dominating group and to suppress their individuality. This eventually deprives the organization of the creativity and contributions of people with a lot to offer. It results in underutilization of people and unnecessary anxiety, division, and resentment in the workplace.

Some conformity is necessary for the survival of the organization, such as in following safety rules, learning to use certain types of equipment, or obeying organizational directives. The key is for leaders to recognize where assimilation has gone too far and then make a committed effort to correct it.

Behavior that encourages homogeneity, occurring for years in many organizations, affects the long-term success of the organization. For example, if dominant groups in your organization establish policies and procedures in a vacuum without the assistance of others, the resulting solutions probably are not the best and may not meet the needs of your diverse workforce nor your customers. Since organizational culture often frowns upon people challenging decisions, change is seldom ever made even though it may be needed.

POINT

◆ 3 ◆

One response has been the development of support networks for diverse groups, which are a natural reaction to the stifling effects of assimilation. These networks encourage communication, networking, and camaraderie among the members and provide a means for members to seek the emotional support and mentoring that are often unavailable in an organization that encourages conformity. However, these groups are not in support of the organizational culture, and they are perceived by nonmembers as suspicious activities or hotspots of conflict. The irony is that if the culture encouraged everyone to participate and contribute despite their differences, there would be much less need for these networks.

If you as an organizational leader choose to, you can slow down assimilation considerably with a widespread committed effort. As an alternative, emphasize the existing strengths of all your subordinates and encourage them to be more successful. By recognizing the benefits of diversity, you can redirect your efforts to capitalize on the varied talents and expertise of your subordinates, instead of forcing them to conform. You will see an upsurge in cultural awareness because of more interaction and less isolation among the diverse groups. This, in turn, will promote cooperation, trust, and understanding. Eventually you will have more fulfilled individuals who will build a harmonious and successful organization.

POINT

◆ 4 ◆

Prejudice and Stereotyping Are Destructive

Almost everyone has prejudices and uses stereotypes occasionally. Prejudices are prejudgments or conclusions that people make before they know or accept the facts. In the organizational setting, prejudice refers to the overstated and sometimes intense personal beliefs and bias that irrationally perpetuate the dominance of certain groups over others. Examples are the beliefs that older workers are less vigorous than the younger ones or that men are better workers than women. Stereotypes are highly oversimplified generalizations made about certain groups of people. An example of a stereotype would be that younger workers have no loyalty to the organization or that they like to stay up all night dancing and drinking.

There is much danger to the organization and your subordinates if prejudices and stereotypes are allowed. These destructive forces undermine certain individuals in the workplace, thus hampering your efforts to promote diversity on a large scale. In addition, they will disrupt your leadership activities that involve relationship building, such as teamwork, innovation, and effective communication.

Since these beliefs and generalizations seem to be formed from early socialization and reinforced continually in life, you cannot force everyone to eliminate their prejudices and stereotypes from their minds. You can, however, slowly make progress in limiting them by taking several actions. First, coach your subordinates so they avoid making generalizations and focus instead on the facts before they make conclusions. This will help them develop solid alternatives to the off-the-cuff remarks that may be stereotypical. Also, whenever you hear someone make these comments, let them know immediately that what they just said is prejudicial or stereotypical. These people will learn over time to suppress remarks that interfere with working relationships.

Make sure that you as a leader never resort to voicing prejudices or stereotypes, as certainly there will be subordinates who will mimic your behavior, or worse yet, lose respect for you. Read up on typically listed stereotypes so that you can immediately spot them in your company policies and procedures. You then can teach your subordinates how to better recognize prejudices and stereotyping among themselves, realize its negative impact, and change their behavior.

Finally, the close interaction and teamwork you develop among your subordinates will help you eliminate these detrimental ideas and statements. It may take you a while, but you can reduce the problems of prejudices and stereotypes over time.

Communication As a Vital Component of Diversity

POINT
❖ 5 ❖

The way people communicate adds to or detracts from an environment of diversity. The most important point to remember about the impact of communication on diversity is that anything you or your subordinates communicate, either verbally or nonverbally, is subject to offending someone — whether you intended to or not. By taking just a few actions, however, you can dramatically increase the quality of your communications so there is a more positive effect upon your diversity efforts.

There are many well-known examples of obvious racist or sexist language, ethnic slurs, or lifestyle comments. Although their use has decreased tremendously in recent years because of better awareness and new legal constraints, they still appear more covertly, particularly among close-knit members of similar groups. Your job as leader, is to promote an environment where these actions are not tolerated.

Just as harmful, though, are subtly inappropriate comments and expressions due to ignorance about diverse styles of communication. Many people may not notice this at first, but they negatively affect the work environment. Following are some suggestions for avoiding unsuitable uses of the language. These suggestions can be helpful to you as well as to anyone whose behavior you can influence.

► Eliminate any silly or joking comment to anyone — friends and superiors included — when it relates to diversity classifications, despite how humorous you think it may be.

► Refer to people in your organization by their name, and avoid describing them in terms of their diversity, such as our Chinese payroll supervisor, that black man, or our wheelchair-bound employee. Never characterize others in a mean-spirited or degrading way, such as sissy man, manly woman, or our shell-shocked military veterans.

► Stay current on lists of words that are considered offensive or unsuitable to others, such as the terms minorities, blue-collar workers, Negroes, gals, or handicapped. Use instead more positive references, such as Asian-Americans, first-line supervisors, people of color or African-Americans, women, and physically challenged.

► When speaking to an individual or to groups, use varying examples and comparisons that reflect all types of diversity, such as international and minority leaders, successful women, and ethnic role models. Avoid relying on overly used analogies from less diverse sources, such as sports or the military.

People of all diversities have different communication styles. It is important to realize this as you send or receive messages so that you do not misinterpret information, offend others, or have unrealistic expectations. Styles differ in numerous ways, but five significant, easily observable factors include: use of formality, rationality, and logic in conversations; tendency to dominate or submit during conversations; degree of assertiveness in conflict resolution; characteristics of speech; and personal openness, physical contact, and space boundaries during conversations.

Since anyone can exhibit various combinations of these factors, it is important to understand that no one will be exactly like you and that differences in styles of communication are all right. The key is to recognize that there are differences and adjust to them whenever you encounter them. You then will be less likely to draw inaccurate conclusions about people based on their style of conversation. With better awareness of communication styles, you will learn to base your opinions of people on facts and performance results, not upon faulty assumptions or stereotypes.

When you encounter someone who has a different communication style, you do not have to drastically change your style. It would be helpful, though, to occasionally mirror the other person's style to make both of you more comfortable. In addition, by being more aware of your own style of communication, you can better recognize how others might misunderstand your communications. You then can better attune yourself to the perceptions of others during conversation to make sure your messages are properly sent and understood.

Diversity As a Long-term Process

The term most often used for handling the issues of diversity is managing diversity. Managing diversity implies that there is a certain process involved. Most proponents insist diversity management is more a process than a program. This is generally true if the organization's top leadership commits to promoting diversity. All too often, though, people fear diversity because it symbolizes change, uncertainty, or too much of a commitment. Leaders may prefer short-term programs, such as affirmative action or valuing differences, because they produce more immediate results and pacify some people. Consequently, diversity management never reaches its potential as a solution to the needs of the organization or the individual.

A better term might be maximizing diversity. It connotes achieving the most from what diversity offers both the organization and the individual, rather than simply managing a process. Maximizing diversity still involves management processes and selected programs, but the design and implementation is approached from the bold, equitable, and win-win perspective of a leader — not from the narrow perspective of traditional programs. This process of maximizing diversity can be so complementary to your leadership efforts that it gradually replaces short-term diversity programs.

Leadership Actions to Maximize Diversity

There are specific steps you can take to introduce diversity concepts and practices into your organization. You do not have to accomplish them all at once, but they can be part of a comprehensive program to maximize diversity. When the process involves several functional departments or when someone else is leading an official diversity effort in your organization, consult with other leaders so you can devise a program correctly and collaboratively.

Here are eight leadership actions you can take to maximize diversity.

- ► Approach diversity as a resource, not as a problem.
- ► Use your leadership skills.
- ► Get the facts on diversity.
- ► Assess conditions in your organization.
- ► Determine specific and measurable goals.

- ▶ Involve diverse groups in developing your program.
- ▶ Communicate and get commitment.
- ▶ Align your organization with diversity.

ACTION

◆ 1 ◆

Approach Diversity As a Resource, Not As a Problem

Diversity is not a sacred or taboo subject. It is a fact of life that should concern you as much as competition, inflation, or customer service. Convince yourself until you truly believe it that your organization's diversity is a resource as valuable as a brand name, geographical location, or any other competitive advantage that you can imagine.

You now must do everything in your power to exploit this advantage in all your responsibilities. Whenever you solve problems, brainstorm, or deal with your subordinates, remember to consider diversity as a strategic resource that is part of the solution. Teach the benefits of this diversity philosophy to your leaders and subordinates so that everyone will understand and accept this attitudinal approach.

ACTION

◆ 2 ◆

Use Your Leadership Skills

You can make great strides in maximizing your organization's diversity simply by focusing daily on doing the best job that you can as a leader and encouraging other leaders in your organization to do so as well. One primary reason that organizations do not maximize diversity is that leaders do not clearly see or act upon the opportunities that diversity provides. You and your subordinate leaders will not overlook these opportunities if you:

- ▶ Communicate well with your subordinates and fully understand their concerns.
- ▶ Create and maintain an environment where teamwork, fairness, mutual respect, personal and organizational excellence, and goal achievement are the standards.
- ▶ Stay closely involved in empowering, coaching, and developing your subordinates.
- ▶ Monitor and share information about what goes on in your organization and where it is headed strategically.
- ▶ Fully communicate your vision and gain commitment from your subordinates to support it.

Remember that proven leadership skills — not trendy gimmicks — will help you achieve any of your leadership challenges, including those pertaining to diversity. It is your responsibility to use your skills to pursue what diversity has to offer you and your organization.

Get the Facts on Diversity

It would be a superb investment of your time if you perused diversity material that is available commercially or in your library. This knowledge, which is crucial to the development of your leadership diversity skills, will give you specific ideas to help maximize diversity. In addition, you will get valuable insight into the diverse groups within your organization. If you knew just a little more about a religion that has followers in your organization, or a specific country that has contributed skilled workers to your department, you will probably be more empathetic of their customs and beliefs. Most importantly, this knowledge and concern could lead to better communication between you and them, increase their performance on the job, and generate innovation along the way.

ACTION

◈ 3 ◈

Assess Conditions in Your Organization

Before you prematurely create a diversity program, assess the status of diversity within your organization or help the responsible department to assess it. This will give you an accurate basis for planning and gauging your progress in maximizing diversity.

The initial step is to determine what specific information you need. Address the areas of policies and procedures, skill levels, attitudes, perceptions, diverse group interaction, and obstacles to diversity. Such information will orient you to the right diversity solutions as well as give you a true appraisal of the current environment, which can tip you off to other challenges to address. Seek different perspectives from as many people and job levels as possible. In addition to your survey of workers, remember to analyze existing data that may be of use. This includes personnel data and employment statistics on recruitment, terminations, the rewards system, race, gender, or age.

Several diversity questionnaires are available commercially that you can use as a guide in designing your own questionnaire. During the assessment, be on the watch for people who are truly interested in diversity and who may later be resources for your program.

ACTION

◈ 4 ◈

Determine Specific and Measurable Goals

Diversity awareness training as a sole solution to the challenges of diversity has received mixed reviews in the workplace. It does not accomplish as much as a more comprehensive approach to diversity. Most awareness training lacks specific follow-up requirements, therefore, the training is ineffective. After listening to a seminar, viewing a film, or participating in a discussion, people often go their separate ways with no requirement to implement what they have learned. Your subordinates do need to have knowledge of diversity

ACTION

◈ 5 ◈

issues, and education is a required part of implementing organizational change. It is necessary, however, to have your subordinates apply that knowledge in specific ways. It is unrealistic to hope that information alone will result in changes in attitudes.

Examples of specific goals may be to increase the gender or ethnic diversity in a particular department, to develop diverse leadership for your future staffing needs, or to better serve diverse international markets. All training, however, must be linked to specific goals that support your overall diversity program and specific business objectives.

ACTION

◆ 6 ◆

Involve Diverse Groups in Developing Your Program

While developing and implementing your diversity program, remember to include representatives from all groups at all organizational levels. Explain that you need their advice and cultural knowledge to make the best decisions. They will give you valuable insight into what they perceive to be relevant diversity issues, such as barriers to achievement that exist in the organization, current relations among diverse groups, culture clashes, and policies and procedures that promote assimilation.

ACTION

◆ 7 ◆

Communicate and Get Commitment

As you do with any of your plans and programs, communicate your diversity objectives to everyone in your organization. Diversity is one of those topics that scares some people. People will feel anxious if they perceive themselves as targeted for criticism or blamed for injustices. Consequently, it makes sense to explain to your subordinates the actions that you are taking. At the same time, seek their commitment to diversity. While not everyone will completely agree with your reasoning, ask for and expect their support in making changes.

ACTION

◆ 8 ◆

Align Your Organization with Diversity

A commitment to diversity as an organization-wide value must permeate all levels if the organization is to truly reach its potential. This is an evolutionary effort that must be piloted by the top leaders in the organization. To truly take advantage of the enormous benefits of diversity, your organizational objectives must be aligned with your company's diverse culture, not in conflict with it. Maximizing diversity in an organization is a long-term goal of three years or more that will evolve from the many short-term changes described in this chapter.

By now, it should be of no surprise to you that traditional workplace policies, procedures, and systems will not effectively support the needs of a diverse workforce. You will need to redesign and continually monitor all your systems so that you can elicit the best performance and behavior from all your subordinates. The following are just three examples of actions that you can take after you gain input from your subordinates about their diversity concerns.

Revise the Benefits Program

Ensure that your subordinates value the benefits that you offer. You could alter the program to reflect the diversity of your workforce and include innovative benefits such as flexible work hours, self-selected holidays, child care, or elder care.

Diversify Organizational Social Events

Instead of exclusively entertaining clients at sports events, which are viewed by some people as male-oriented events, also use restaurants, museums, exhibits, or the theater.

Monitor Human Resource Programs for Trends

By continually evaluating the selection, training and development, promotion, and rewards programs, you will better maximize and recognize your talented pool of diversity. The diversity statistics from these areas will tell you much about the success of your inclusion efforts. In addition, you will more quickly identify and correct diversity barriers that are impeding your efforts at organizational change.

Leaders at all levels have a responsibility to respond correctly to the diversity that exists in their organization. This does not mean you can decree that everyone in your organization will coexist in a harmonious state in which all diverse needs are satisfied, every policy reflects the unique concerns of everyone, and no one is ever offended again. Such goals are unrealistic, and it is not necessary to aim for such perfection. It does mean you should focus on those things that you can change to help your subordinates and your organization grow. By looking for ways to use diversity to everyone's benefit, you are acting responsibly as a leader.

CHAPTER 14

PROVIDE CONFLICT RESOLUTION

You see every day how conflict exists all around you and in all types of leadership situations. It is practically impossible for leaders to avoid conflict — and undesirable as well, since conflict often leads to the changes that you and your organization need. Thus it makes sense to learn all that you can about handling it, particularly given the effect that conflict has on your own success or failure.

As you learned in the previous chapter, human differences are certain and many. Differences in culture, perspective, skill and knowledge levels, goals, and in communication styles, for example, affect the varying levels of agreement and disagreement among people. Conflict is synonymous with disagreement, whether it is at a slight or an intense level. In the workplace, people can conceivably disagree over anything, such as policies, decisions, ideas, strategy, the brand of coffee to use, or how well they like coworkers. Disagreements are not necessarily bad because they can lead to better decisions, innovation, and bonding among people.

Despite the inevitability of conflict, the way people respond to these differences is their choice. People can choose one of three responses during conflict situations. They can:

- ▶ Compromise amicably to turn disagreements into agreements,
- ▶ Continue to privately disagree but fully support the final agreed-upon decision, or
- ▶ Continue to disruptively disagree.

Your objective as a leader is to resolve conflicts in one of the first two ways. This chapter will guide you by suggesting simple techniques applicable to any leadership situation at work, in the home, or in the community. This chapter will first provide the foundation for conflict resolution by showing you four specific steps to a satisfying resolution. It then will strengthen this foundation by introducing the skill of negotiating, which you can use to help resolve many other types of conflict that you encounter as a leader.

Follow these four steps for successful conflict resolution.

- ▶ Separate misunderstandings from conflicts.
- ▶ Create a positive environment for conflict resolution.
- ▶ Focus on people's interests, not their positions.
- ▶ Communicate clearly.

Separate Misunderstandings from Conflicts

STEP ❧ 1 ❧

Many of the perceived disagreements that occur are not really disagreements but misunderstandings. Misunderstandings can be easily remedied. Before you assume that you have a conflict, find out what the other person believes about the situation. You may find they are misinformed or do not have all the facts about the situation and may be willing to change their position. Conversely, you may find that it is you who misunderstands the situation. In any event, if both of you can come to a quick agreement based upon a clarification of the facts and assumptions, you have resolved the misunderstanding. If you cannot agree and there remains a conflict, go to the next step.

Create a Positive Environment for Conflict Resolution

STEP ❧ 2 ❧

You can create a positive environment in two ways. First separate the problem from the person. Stay problem-oriented by retaining a clear and vigorous focus on the problem and not conveying an adversarial notion that the person is the problem. If you communicate to the other person in the conflict that both of you are part of a team that must collectively solve a problem, then you will more effectively frame your attitudes and respond to the upcoming challenge. You still are concerned about the person's needs, feelings, or emotional condition, but by objectively concentrating on the problem and not personally attacking the other person, you can find solutions that will solve the problem without antagonism. This will, in turn, reduce the tension built up between the two of you.

For example, if you want to convey to a subordinate that he or she is not performing well, avoid hostile opening phrases such as, "You are not doing a great job." Instead, focus on the problem by saying, "Your job position requires that all customers be treated with respect." You then can discuss the criteria for effective job performance from a less confrontational approach and be more successful at defusing the conflict and improving behavior. When examining the problem, remember to spend time looking at it from your subordinates' perspective. Understanding their point of view and accepting their feelings are not going to make you a weak leader or negotiator, instead it helps you resolve the conflict more quickly, efficiently, and permanently.

Second, portray an attitude of win-win. Win-win means that a solution is found in which you win and the other person wins and no one feels they are the loser. Win-win means that everyone walks away from a conflict feeling good, not frustrated or angry, about having successfully satisfied their needs in an environment of cooperation. If you help people achieve what they want to achieve, you also will benefit by better performance and increased loyalty to you and the organization. You convey a win-win attitude when you let people know that you are looking for a mutually beneficial solution, one that is unifying and highly acceptable to both of you.

A win-win attitude is so crucial in a leader that everything discussed throughout the remainder of this chapter centers upon finding and applying win-win solutions.

STEP

◆ 3 ◆

Focus on People's Interests, Not Their Positions

In a conflict situation, you want to resolve it not just with any agreement at hand but with a durable and fair arrangement in which everyone is reasonably content. To do so, it is best to focus not on people's positions, which are their stated demands, but on their interests, which are their real needs.

A position is what people state they want, such as more salary, more vacation days, or fewer hours at work. Individuals view their position as the best possible solution to their needs. This may or may not be the case because their position may be embellished to strengthen an argument or they may not be clearly defining their needs or examining their alternatives.

Interests, on the other hand, are the true, underlying reasons behind why a person wants something. If you both focus only on your own stated positions, you become emotionally and sometimes irreversibly attached to them and will find it difficult to compromise. But if you focus on your interests in a nonadversarial way, you will develop many more creative solutions that are fair and rewarding to you both.

For example, your subordinate may want a higher salary and more vacation time. In probing further, you discover that their true interest is a desire to spend more time with family — hence the increased vacation time request — and a desire to place his or her child in a more expensive day care center that is closer to work and home — hence the higher salary request. Once you know your subordinate's true interests, you can compare them to your interests and see how far apart you are on the issue. Your interests in this situation may be that you want the subordinate to do the job well without disruption to anyone else's work. Once you and your subordinate confer, you both can discuss the problem in detail and collaborate on solutions that will allow you both to achieve your interests. Possible solutions could be for the subordinate to arrive earlier and leave earlier on certain days, to telecommute one day a week, or to study the feasibility of an on-site day care center for the organization.

Deeply held and valued interests are ultimately what concern most people, not arbitrary, quickly formed positions that result in temporary solutions that may or may not help them obtain their interests. If satisfaction of everyone's underlying interests is your objective, everyone will be much happier when practical, innovative, and realistic solutions are mutually agreed upon. In many cases, you have to question people thoroughly to determine their interests because they intentionally and unintentionally mask them from you and from themselves. Once you find out why they want something, you will best be able to mutually decide how they can obtain it. Then they will believe that you can help them meet their needs and the conflict will soon be resolved.

Communicate Clearly

STEP
❖ 4 ❖

In addition to the communication principles discussed in Chapter 10, there are some additional suggestions that are particularly well-suited for conflict resolution. The main point to remember is that good communication builds trust which then helps to resolve conflicts, while ineffective communication will hinder agreements and complicate problems.

Keep a Positive, Agreeable, and Relaxed Attitude

Although you as the leader are in a higher position of authority than your subordinate, it is not helpful to misuse this relationship when resolving a conflict.

This principle also applies to any other conflict situation you may have, such as with a client, in a contract negotiation, or with a peer. Since emotions will probably be intense in a conflict situation, it is always best not to be swept up into an atmosphere of anger, fear, or resentment. Avoid this by recognizing that both of you will be somewhat emotional but that emotions can be kept in check by understanding them and acknowledging them openly.

As you begin your discussion, always open with a positive statement, such as referring to the interests you both have in common. Maintain this positive approach throughout the discussion. By keeping a respectful, empathetic, and caring attitude towards the other person, you will be seen as someone who is interested in resolving the problem. Avoid using *you* statements; instead use less accusatory *I* statements. This transfers the focus away from the other person and towards yourself, allowing you to express your needs and interests while subtly encouraging the other person to express theirs.

Never resort to negative accusations, disagreeableness, or losing your temper. Although you may temporarily feel better, it will not help you to resolve the conflict. If you convey to your subordinate that you are committed to resolving the problem while trying to understand their feelings and needs, they will be more open to win-win thinking.

Stay on Course

So you both can stay focused on specific issues, determine and agree upon what the problem is at the beginning of the discussion. If either one of you begins to stray from the topic, refer back to the stated problem to get you back on course.

Once you identify the issues involved in the conflict, avoid lamenting about the what has happened in the past; focus instead on solutions for the future, which is something you have control over.

Be an Active Listener

Your subordinates want their views heard, so remember to demonstrate visibly that you are actively listening, as described in Chapter 10. Remember to allow others to speak without interruption, acknowledging what they say, questioning them when needed, and repeating exactly the key points to prevent misunderstanding. Whenever anything is unclear or omitted, ask for clarification. There is nothing wrong with occasionally nodding agreement with what is said. This is assuring because it conveys respect and acknowledges them as a person, even though you may disagree with some of what they say. Eye contact is particularly important during discussions because it conveys honesty and trust to the other person.

Listening will give you the means to examine the other person's perceptions about the conflict. These perceptions are important to you because they will help you better understand the person so you can help develop viable solutions for their needs and interests. By allowing the person to talk freely, you gain information you may not have obtained had you talked instead. You also will gain insight by analyzing what is not said and the areas which are avoided.

Negotiation and Conflict Resolution

Most of the ordinary and routine conflict that you face can be resolved using the four steps previously discussed. Other situations will require a more structured approach using negotiation because they involve issues that are not easily resolved through a four-step method. It is extremely useful to understand how negotiating interacts with conflict resolution because the two are not at all separate. Conflict resolution — not negotiating — is one of your leadership goals. Negotiating is simply a highly effective process and skill that you can use to resolve certain types of conflict.

Knowledge of how to apply negotiating skills to your everyday leadership responsibilities is invaluable in resolving routine conflicts such as interpersonal friction or performance problems. Sometimes these negotiations will be quick five-minute encounters with subordinates; at other times they may be a three-week session with international clients. Negotiating skills, therefore, will assist you as you increasingly confront greater responsibilities, such as resolving contract disputes, organizational change issues, or strategic alliance questions. As you think of negotiating, try not to limit it to its more glamorous or well-known areas such as corporate mergers or large contracts. Instead, relate it broadly to all the routine situations that you encounter everyday at work, home, and in the community, with your subordinates, peers, supervisors, customers, and family members.

Much of the discussion so far in this chapter concerning conflict resolution has implicitly contained some elements of negotiation. The topics of attitude, interests, positions, and win-win solutions, for example, are fundamental negotiation concepts that are invariably mentioned whenever negotiation is taught. The remainder of the chapter will build upon what you have learned so far and show you how to use the essential skill of negotiating to resolve conflicts the best way that you can.

A Leader's Approach to Win-win Negotiations

As you practice the skills necessary to be an effective leader, you are simultaneously practicing the skills necessary to master a win-win style of negotiating.

You believe in not only getting the job done correctly but doing it by focusing on objectives that you and your subordinates have in common and by maximizing the outcomes for both of you. This involves using your many technical, analytical, and relationship skills to accomplish with others what might not have been possible individually. As a result, everyone benefits and no one loses. Since you believe that the feelings, opinions, and knowledge of other people must be considered during negotiations, you are willing to completely involve them in the process, to listen objectively, and to compromise when necessary. You are interested in solving the problems that are identified during the negotiation by developing alternatives that can satisfy all of the parties involved.

It will be quite simple for you to develop your negotiation skills because there are so many resources available to increase your knowledge. There are scores of excellent, informative books, tapes, and seminars with detailed techniques that can be tailored to your particular needs. You can learn numerous tactics involving everything from room layout to the prevention of stonewalling. You also can explore all that is discussed in this chapter in much more detail. Any specific challenge you may have is probably addressed in one or more of these resources. Until you choose to invest your time in additional study, you can adapt the basics in this chapter for use in any of your negotiation situations.

A leader's approach to win-win negotiations consists of seven steps.

- ► Explore your objectives.
- ► Prioritize your interests.
- ► Improve your negotiating position.
- ► Finalize your negotiating strategy.
- ► Recognize the distributive negotiator.
- ► Respond to the distributive negotiator.
- ► Create a win-win solution.

STEP

◆ 1 ◆

Explore Your Objectives

Clearly identify the primary objectives that you want to achieve from the negotiation. Objectives are similar in concept to the positions that were earlier described. Clear, precise, realistic, tangible, and intangible objectives are crucial to later developing the planning aspects of your negotiation, such as your shorter-term negotiating tactics. The objectives also will guide and focus your efforts when you are in the middle of a quickly moving or complex negotiation. As with any other challenge that you have as a leader, if you spend a little time at the beginning of the process thinking about your objectives, you will later more easily achieve them.

Develop a range of primary and secondary objectives so you will have flexibility in negotiating. Primary objectives are those that are of the greatest importance to you; they usually include such areas as price, salary, job description, deadlines, and terms of purchase. Secondary objectives could include anything else that is related to the negotiation, such as options for additional purchases, discounts for bulk purchases, salary incentives, or public relation issues.

Once you have identified your objectives, establish how you would most and least like to achieve them, that is, by determining alternatives which represent best and worst case scenarios of what could actually happen. Doing this will give you the courage and confidence to approach the negotiations with the right attitude. If you do not reach an agreement in which you achieve an ideal objective, you will know that all is not lost because you have identified a range of acceptable alternatives. These alternatives also will increase your negotiating power and the likelihood of a successful agreement because you will not be forced into accepting an unfavorable deal.

These alternatives are placed in what is called a range of acceptable agreement. It is in this range that you find your most-preferred alternative and your least-preferred alternative for each of your objectives. For example, if you are about to negotiate with a subordinate concerning a pay raise, you would identify in advance several objectives and their respective most- and least-preferred alternatives. These could be a pay raise ranging from $2,000–$5,000, a bonus potential ranging from one to three percent, a workload increase ranging from a major increase in responsibilities to a minor increase, or an expense account increase ranging from $500 to $3,000 per year. Naturally, you would prefer an agreement that is closer to each objective's most-preferred alternative than to its least-preferred, but this is not realistic nor is it mutually advantageous to you both, as you will soon see. Adding mystery to this process is not knowing the most- and least-preferred alternatives of the other person.

Here is an example of a simple negotiation involving only one objective. You are negotiating a deadline extension that a team member has requested. You may ideally want to approve a one-week extension but would settle for up to a two-week extension. The request may be for a four-week extension, but the person would settle for a two-week extension. The negotiating process allows you to close this gap and reach an agreement within the range that benefits both parties. Most likely, the agreement will be close to or exactly at the two-week extension. However, if the person's least-preferred alternative is three weeks instead of two weeks, there is an additional gap of one week that you must address. By having only one objective to negotiate, the extension, you both must change your expectations to resolve the gap or there could be ill will between you or, even worse, the deadline extension might not be approved even though it is probably needed.

This reliance on a single alternative, which is synonymous with a bottom line, protects negotiators somewhat from yielding to intense pressure during the heat of a negotiation. At the same time, however, it also constrains you into falsely thinking there is only one way of reaching your agreement: by achieving or doing better than your bottom line. Having additional objectives, each with their own set of alternatives, or at least having a single objective along with a broad mix of alternatives you are willing to accept, increases the opportunity for agreement. You can then negotiate combinations of solutions, some variation of which may be acceptable. For these reasons, always attempt to negotiate with more than one objective.

In more involved negotiations, the stakes may be higher for you or your organization, and you may not be as willing to change your expectations as with a simple deadline extension. That is the reason to know your least-preferred alternatives because if you absolutely cannot achieve them, individually or in combination with other alternatives, you might be just as well off not reaching an agreement and continuing to operate as usual or pursuing further options. Otherwise, you could end up worse off than your current situation.

It is always good to know, therefore, what your alternatives are if you choose not to negotiate an agreement. By explicitly identifying no-agreement alternatives to choose from if you fail to reach an agreement, you will be able to analyze the final offers in terms of how they compare to the certainty of these no-agreement alternatives, not just how the final offers compare to your least-preferred alternatives. In addition, establishing your no-agreement alternatives before negotiation begins will reassure you that you do not have to accept an agreement if it is not in your best interests.

When you have viable and realistic no-agreement alternatives to choose from in the event of not reaching a negotiated agreement, you will add to your negotiating power. For example, despite your best attempts at negotiating and reaching a win-win solution, a key supplier of resources may give you a final offer — which actually may not be his or her true final offer — of a 20 percent price increase. Your least preferred alternative is 15 percent. Examine a 20 percent increase in relation to your no-agreement alternatives. If you find that there are no other companies to supply you, a 20 percent price increase is more acceptable than lost sales or bankruptcy. On the other hand, if you have many suppliers from which to choose or if you have an enormous inventory of these supplies that will last several months, it may be more advantageous for you to reject the final offer or to attempt again forcefully and confidently to negotiate a better settlement.

Prioritize Your Interests

Interests are those individual matters that are of underlying concern to you and to the other party. Using the assistance of someone on your negotiating team or someone else you trust, analyze in detail why you want to achieve the objectives you have identified. It is important to note that interests are a matter of perception, as are people's needs, values, or preferences for rewards. What may matter most to you could matter least to others while something they value could be of no practical concern to you. This is why you always want to identify your interests and continually seek to determine the interests of the other party. It is the two-way, progressive, and mutually beneficial discussion of all these differently valued interests that will be the heart and substance of your negotiation.

Once you have identified your interests, prioritize them according to their value to you and their relative value to each other. For example, your objective may be to lease a particular office suite for under $1,000 a month. After analyzing why you want this objective, you find that you have a limited budget, you value the suite's proximity to your house, there is an abundance of nearby restaurants for client lunches, you will need an office within six months, and the office building is well maintained. These are your interests. After prioritizing these interests, you find that their order of importance is rental price, location, condition, and availability. In addition, price may be only a little more important than location, but it may be much more important than the condition, and it may be extremely more important than availability. You can develop any type of ranking system as long as it makes sense to you.

During the negotiation for the lease, take specific action to identify the interests of the other party, the leasing company. Now that you know your interests, you can negotiate based upon your four interests and their interests. This is far preferable to negotiating on your overall position, which in this example has only one objective. You may discover that the leasing company is willing to reduce your monthly rent to under $1,000, which is your primary interest but not their big concern, if you can move in quickly and generate immediate revenues, which is their primary interest but not a big concern for you.

As you can see, a thorough knowledge of your interests is extremely valuable in evaluating the cost of giving up one interest compared to the value of gaining agreement on another interest. It is also helpful in predicting how interests interrelate with each other and how each interest is affected when the other interests are negotiated. Before the negotiations begin, approach your negotiating team members or other responsible officials and discuss what you have determined about your interests to this point. They will give you valuable input or verify how you prioritized your interests.

During the negotiations, you will either negotiate each interest separately or in combination with your other interests and theirs. More often than not, the combination approach will be your best alternative simply because it gives you more flexibility and will more likely lead to a win-win situation. To make this approach work well for you, develop values for different combinations of interests so that you can forecast the results if you agree to a particular combination. Knowing the values will later assist you to quickly make objective decisions based on the other party's offers and counteroffers.

For example, your perception of the value of Combination A, which specifies $1,100 rent, no availability for eight months, and free janitorial services for one year, may differ from how you value Combination B, which specifies $1,000 rent, immediate availability, and six months of janitorial services.

STEP

◆ 3 ◆

Improve Your Negotiating Position

The best way to improve your negotiating position is to thoroughly analyze those elements that most affect your situation. Three such elements are information, time, and power.

The old saying that knowledge is power is especially pertinent during a negotiation. This means knowing everything you can about what you are negotiating well in advance of the negotiations so you can develop your objectives, interests, and strategy. A well-informed negotiator will know all the minor and major details about such things as values, costs, and previous negotiations on the subject. You certainly will want to spend more effort researching those negotiations that are more important or risky to you. It is always wise, though, to prepare just as thoroughly for routine negotiations because the more knowledge you have, the better you will perform during the negotiation. Because information is exchanged during a negotiation session, the quality, quantity, and indisputability of your information will give you enormous negotiating power in promoting your interests, countering arguments, and making as few concessions as possible.

Information gathering is an ongoing habit that occurs daily through conversing with everyone you meet, including subordinates, clients, supervisors, and peers. The best time to gather information about upcoming negotiations is before the negotiations are scheduled or even conceptualized because people are much less defensive then and will more likely give you the information you need. People are used to leaders inquiring about all sorts of topics, so you probably will be able to methodically and inconspicuously approach anyone that could possibly give you information. Remember that astute people will not continually give you information unless you give them some information in return; therefore, be prepared to reciprocate by sharing some knowledge with them.

Of particular interest to you are the people with whom you are negotiating. If these are people you already know, such as a colleague, subordinate, family member, or client, you are at an advantage because you understand how they think and behave. If you have little knowledge of them, find out what others think about them, their reputation, negotiating tactics, needs or problems, and authority to make decisions. Information about their organization's financial condition, strategic intentions, or competitive pressures is beneficial. Any information is good because it gives you valuable insights that you may use during the negotiations. At this stage of the negotiating process, brainstorm and then analyze the other party's potential objectives, interests, and arguments using the same process as you used earlier for yourself. This will help you in case you need to adjust your objectives, the value of your interests, and your negotiating arguments.

Time is a resource that affects your negotiation in two significant ways. First, it tells you how many days or hours you have until the negotiation begins. If more time is available, you can better prepare for the negotiation. Conversely, less available time means that you have to work quickly and prioritize your negotiation plan. Second, it is vital to know the approximate duration of the negotiation because the process of negotiation occurs in stages. Adjust your expectations and strategy to account for these stages.

For example, as the negotiations begin, very few concessions will occur because both of you are staking out your positions and attempting to uncover each other's interests. Most significant concessions occur at the very end of the process near or after the deadline. If both parties have the same deadline, negotiations will move forward with the goal of closure at a defined moment, and concessions likely will be mutually made in tandem. If, however, one of the parties has a more flexible deadline or does not reveal it, then they can proceed at a relatively relaxed pace and delay making concessions. This will increase the pressure on the other party, who will more likely make final concessions earlier.

Power, in the context of leadership, is the ability to influence or exercise control over some aspect of your duties. You have seen throughout this book the power you have as a leader in making things happen and in convincing others that you can help or harm them. Confidence in your power is not something you should abuse but is something you can generally use as a leader and specifically as a negotiator. Knowing how the other person perceives your position of power will help you craft effective negotiation strategies and respond better during the negotiations. If you understand how you are perceived, you can likewise use this information to reassure or dispel those beliefs. The sources of your negotiating power are numerous, including the power to help or harm; to convince or compel; to garner more resources, such as time, information, or money; to exercise leadership or supervisory authority; or to inspire complete respect and trust in you.

You can emphasize any of these sources of power depending upon the situation in which you are involved. Every party in a negotiation has some type of power, but the key here is to identify the relative positions of power before the negotiations and to develop your strategy with these conclusions in your mind. You may want to emphasize one source of power over another because you believe it will be more effective in changing the negotiating behavior of the other person and be less likely to damage your relationship.

For example, if you are negotiating with a subordinate for a one-week deadline extension, you have several sources of power that you could draw upon, either overtly or covertly, during the discussions: reward power, punishment power, positional power, and coercive power. It is unlikely that you would want to use all the sources during the discussions, and you may not have to. Subordinates vividly know the power that you, the leader, have over them, and they are unlikely to challenge it because they recognize their obligation to comply with your directives. From a negotiating perspective, this is good for you and bad for them. However, subordinates can draw upon their sources of power to assist themselves in the negotiations. This person may be the only one in your department who can expertly complete the assignment, or the project may not be needed for several more weeks. The negotiation for the deadline extension will involve these power considerations but will not ultimately depend upon them. What are more important are your interests and your subordinate's interests and how you can best satisfy as many as possible. Since your only interests are that the project be finished reasonably soon and without error, you may have no objection to the subordinate's request as long as they can satisfy your concerns.

STEP

◆ 4 ◆

Finalize Your Negotiating Strategy

Before the negotiations begin, look over all your information and finalize your strategy. If someone is on your negotiating team, it is helpful to conduct one or more sessions and discuss the details of your strategy. Go over everything you have determined so far about your interests and objectives, the facts, the other party, and your negotiating situation. Talk over the tactics that you will use during the negotiations including opening statements, your opening offer, who will speak for the team, and any other procedural rules. Once you map out your strategy, spend some time rehearsing it alone, with your team, or with someone whom you can trust.

The opening hours of the negotiation can be fruitful because this is the time when you discover the tactics and interests of the other party. You can follow a few guidelines to make certain that you take full advantage of this period. Verify before you begin the negotiations that the other party has the authority to make the decisions that will lead to a negotiated agreement. If not, you will waste your time because you will end up making most of the concessions and offers, and you will probably end up having to negotiate again with someone else.

It is usually best if you let the other party make the initial offer because it is preferable to first know what they are thinking before you reveal what you are thinking. A key tactic during a negotiation is to make ample use of questions whenever you see the opportunity since they often bring you the answers you need. In addition, the other person may be less threatened by probing and thoughtful inquiries than they would have been had you simply made counteroffers or forceful declarations. Any time that you can get information, rather than give it, is usually good.

It is a common occurrence in negotiations for opposing sides to begin negotiations with distant stances and then make gradual concessions to arrive at a more realistic and mutually acceptable agreement. Win-win negotiating does not preclude these wide differences in offers. For this reason, your initial offers on the issues should be high, relative to their offers, to give you both plenty of room to negotiate towards each other's offers. This approach will also allow you both to feel that you are indeed accomplishing something. This will help minimize deadlocked negotiations, which often occur when one or both sides are unwilling or unable to make more concessions. A high offer, as long as you can justify it, is an acceptable tactic during a negotiation and is somewhat expected; otherwise your low offer could be perceived as a sign of weakness or of your having inadequate negotiating information.

Recognize the Distributive Negotiator

As previously suggested, it is best for a leader to use a win-win approach to resolving conflicts. Not only will a win-win attitude and an interests-oriented approach consistently yield you better overall solutions but you will also gain esteem in the eyes of the other party. This will lead to later successes both in negotiating and in your other duties. Despite the increasing acceptance and use of win-win negotiating over the years, there are many who will use distributive negotiating, which is the accepted name for a highly competitive win-lose style.

A win-lose style of negotiating, whether done informally with a subordinate or formally in high-stakes discussions, is not the optimal way of solving a conflict. It often is used in traditional positional bargaining situations, such as purchasing a home or buying items at a flea market. More

STEP

◆ 5 ◆

importantly to you as a leader, it is used in the workplace, in the family, and in other organizations with whom you affiliate. It may appear to be the best style to use when there are limited resources or the positions of the negotiating parties are in direct and obvious conflict with each other. Because most people in these situations naturally believe they should get as much of those limited resources as possible, they will negotiate in a manner that they believe helps them achieve that objective, a distributive approach.

Distributive negotiating frequently breeds mistrust, injures relationships, and can easily, although not always, revert to misleading statements or outright lying. This type of negotiating is more successful when there is a limited relationship between parties and when they have little regard for ethics or fair play. It is, therefore, not a style typically used by leaders who have high regard for their subordinates and others. However, your purpose is to immediately recognize when someone else uses this style so that you can develop actions and strategies to effectively conduct your negotiations to everyone's benefit.

Distributive negotiators are not all alike in the intensity of their style and certainly do not all conform to a stereotypical description. Most, however, are usually fixated with winning at all costs under their own terms. They are not concerned with how you feel, whether your needs are satisfied, or whether you are treated fairly. Their objective is to defeat you. Although you may not initially notice that you are dealing with this type, certain tactics will eventually tip you off.

For example, note whether the person:

- ► Has unreasonable and extreme initial positions;
- ► Uses intimidating emotional and psychological actions such as guilt projection, outbursts, threats, insulting laughter, or periods of silence;
- ► Does not believe in making reciprocal concessions;
- ► Claims not to have the authority to negotiate an agreement; or
- ► Refuses to establish rules or later disregards rules that organize the negotiations, such as those pertaining to etiquette, deadlines, and good-faith bargaining.

An important conclusion to make about distributive negotiators is that their tactics work, sometimes well and sometimes not so well. Since all participants in a negotiation are human and have their own feelings and comfort levels when confronted with such tactics, each person responds differently. So this type of negotiator is sometimes successful when confronting the meek and uninformed, but not as successful with others. The fact remains, though, that they are content using these tactics because they like them and, for the most part, they are successful at using them. Despite the obvious disadvantages of dealing with a distributive negotiator, remember you have the choice not to play their game.

Respond to the Distributive Negotiator

STEP

◆ 6 ◆

The best way to respond to a distributive negotiator is to persistently continue to negotiate based upon the principles of win-win negotiating. Even in the face of attacks, positional bargaining, and other distributive techniques, you can still make progress by attempting to turn positional statements into expressions of interests and needs, which are the basis for win-win negotiating. When faced with unreasonable, illogical demands, do not fight or dismiss them as impossible but acknowledge the point and continue to use calm, rational persuasion and other win-win techniques.

When you treat people as though they are interested in problem solving, even though their actions clearly suggest otherwise, they may begin to negotiate in a constructive manner. Probe by questioning about their positions; in doing so, you can uncover a wealth of information about their interests. Let them think you are considering the unreasonable demand as a possible option as you question and try to understand their reasoning for proposing it. There is nothing wrong with ignoring and side-stepping callous or ridiculous remarks then continuing with your negotiating strategy.

The reactions and other information you uncover through effective, nonthreatening questioning will help you explore ways to use the proposed alternatives as a starting point for more mutually acceptable alternatives. Ask the person for advice on anything related to the alternatives, such as what they think about certain solutions or how business has been previously done. Ask exploratory, open-ended questions, such as how would this alternative work, why not use another particular method, or why this has not worked in the past. Use this information to present improved alternatives. You may have your alternatives criticized, but do not take the attacks personally; instead use them to continually improve upon the alternatives. Even when faced with the most determined and hard-bargaining negotiators, eventually you will progress towards an agreement.

If you find you are making absolutely no progress, resort to other methods. Although you can certainly attempt to negotiate distributively, avoid this because it is inefficient and does not produce optimal agreements. One good alternative is to expose the tactics by directly or indirectly letting the person know that you will not respond to them. Simply questioning the tactics may cause them to cease. If ultimatums are issued, ignore them as if they did not occur. You may even patiently and selectively employ some of the same tactics — not the mean-spirited ones, though — such as laughing at the person's comments, allowing several moments of silence, saying you do not have the authority to approve such requests, or taking your time in negotiating.

You can always deflect frequent attempts at confusing you by saying these newly raised concerns are separate issues from what you are discussing. Once the people realize you are wise to their tactics and are willing to call their bluff, they may start to negotiate more sensibly. If they do not, halt the negotiations, make an issue of the tactics, and firmly negotiate over what processes and procedures will be used during the negotiations. After you both have agreed on how best to conduct the negotiations, you then can return to substantive and problem-solving negotiating.

If they are unwilling to make any concessions or their hard-headedness is blocking all progress, you can try to break the impasse through one effective method: the use of objective standards and procedures that are fair, reasonable, readily obtained, and acceptable to all parties in the negotiation. This technique provides the parties with a shared goal, that of determining the standards or procedures, and lays the groundwork for increased trust, persuasion by facts, face-saving if necessary, and unselfish, long-lasting solutions.

Most people successfully use objective standards and procedures in many aspects of their daily lives. Tax assessors, for example, do not individually bargain with car owners over the tax they owe for a tag; they simply compute the tax based upon predetermined and preannounced factors such as the location of the vehicle, its age, and its model type. Some retail stores promise that if you can produce evidence that one of its items can be purchased elsewhere less expensively, then they will sell it to you for that price; otherwise, they will not negotiate the price with you.

You can use the same technique in your negotiations. Here are some examples.

> ► Resolve disagreements over annual price increases by basing them on the government's inflation calculations.
> ► Create procedures to follow if one party later breaks an agreement by agreeing in advance on mediation by a neutral party.
> ► Set merit pay increases based on a standard of productivity measurement that applies to everyone.
> ► Arrive at the cost of several items of used equipment by calculating purchase price minus depreciation.

Make sure you frame your offer around an objective standard with which you are willing to agree. Your task then is get the other party to also agree to it. Be open minded yet firm in your conviction not to yield to threats, intimidation, or any other pressure that the distributive negotiator may send your way. You are offering a fair and objective way to help both of you reach a mutually satisfying agreement — which is a great alternative to endless arguing.

Create a Win-win Solution

The conflict resolution process discussed throughout this chapter is the foundation for the win-win approach to negotiating. More than anything else, it is a mind-set in which everyone can achieve more of what they want if they establish an environment conducive to conflict resolution, if they focus on interests and not positions, and if they truly want a mutually satisfying agreement. Some final suggestions will help you reach your negotiating objective of a win-win solution.

Rely upon your interpersonal skills. Negotiating involves interpersonal skills that are identical to those that you use as a leader. Just because your subordinate, client, or supervisor is now in an opposing position does not mean that you should become uncivil, insensitive, or inconsiderate. Assertiveness, clarity, and resolve are the behaviors for you to portray in a negotiation. If you are perceived as being timid, apologetic, or lost in thought, the other person may view you as weak and attempt to steal your power.

A negotiation is an excellent opportunity to show your self-confidence as a negotiator by treating the other party with respect, trust, and courtesy throughout the negotiation. One of your objectives is to get the other person to identify with you so that he or she will easily understand your negotiating arguments, empathize with your concerns, respect you as a person, and maintain a positive long-term relationship with you.

Keep your ego in check. Avoid pretending that you are more knowledgeable about the negotiation facts or anything else. When negotiating, do not assume your version of facts is the correct version, but rather ask for concurrence when it is believed the facts are true. Attempt to genuinely understand the other person on a personal level, but do not bother with obviously insincere or contrived conversations that will simply offend. Disregard anything you may have been told about negotiation tactics that emphasize rudeness, foul language, unreasonable demands, shouting, or threats because these actions do not portray you as a leader; they damage your reputation and are ineffective as well.

Create solutions that will satisfy everyone's interests, not just yours. The solutions that you both generate, besides being innovative, numerous, and effective, must be mutually beneficial. Be open to any solutions that will satisfy both of your interests. Develop possible solutions before the negotiations begin by brainstorming with your team. As the negotiations progress and you learn more about the other party's interests, you will be able to generate more ideas.

You also can brainstorm with the other party, even though the thought of doing so may upset you. Remember that both of you are sitting down together to agree to solutions that will benefit you both. Since both of you have invested significant time in negotiating, there is a good chance there will be a willingness to generate new alternatives. Brainstorming can help you collaborate on solutions as long as you are careful not to reveal any of your confidential information. As discussed earlier in this book, do not evaluate the worthiness of the suggestions until after brainstorming is finished; otherwise, you may prematurely eliminate some alternatives. The more solutions you develop, the more chance you will have of finding mutually acceptable solutions.

Look closely at the commonalties and differences you share. They could actually generate ideas for solutions. For example, if you and a subordinate share an interest in getting a project quickly finished, talk about it and attempt to develop mutually acceptable solutions that will accomplish just that. If you and a key supplier are in disagreement over price, talk about your shared interest in preserving your long-term relationship. You each might fervently differ over how you expect future events to unfold or how risky one course of action is.

The key is to structure a solution based upon these differences, in which a low-cost concession by you could be a highly advantageous solution for them, and vice-versa. If the disagreement is over price and future events, for instance, you could develop price schedules based upon different economic or political scenarios, thus minimizing the risk for both of you.

Stay alert and reassess your negotiating situation. As the negotiation continues, evaluate everything that occurs, the words that are spoken and not spoken, the nonverbal communication attitude, interests, and needs. You may not have much time to do an extensive evaluation so be prepared to think clearly and rapidly.

Remind yourself during the negotiations that you have something that they do not have and that they want, otherwise they would not be sitting there in the room negotiating with you. Of utmost interest, therefore, are their needs and interests; never lose track of these. It is important to note the reasons they need an agreement with you. These are leverage points that indicate how badly they want an agreement, how much of a concession they may make, or how highly they value the items that are being negotiated. In particular, determine what alternatives you both have if you do not reach an agreement. You both will rely upon these alternatives as leverage in the negotiation. By using your leverage points to your advantage, you will better hold on to your convictions and retain the courage to negotiate with strength and confidence.

Remember that the negotiating picture is constantly changing because both sides are yielding points, making concessions, gaining concessions, and divulging new information. Every tactic you use is probably being used by them. You must, therefore, constantly reassess your negotiating situation or you may become too overconfident. Take your time and do not rush through the negotiations. A step-by-step, deliberate approach will allow both sides to follow the negotiations and achieve incremental successes. These, in turn, will give both of you the confidence that a final agreement can be reached through a win-win attitude. Once you determine that you have achieved a mutually satisfying agreement, conclude the negotiations and commit yourself to honoring it.

CHAPTER 15

COACH YOUR TEAM

Coaching is the process of guiding and encouraging your subordinates to achieve superior performance results. It is an active and participatory skill that allows you to become involved with the goals and work activities of your subordinates and to encourage them to succeed at what is best for them and the organization. In practical terms, coaching gives you a method to change behaviors so that subordinates start or continue doing what they are supposed to do, cease doing what they are not supposed to do, and progressively perform better over time.

Coaching is not a skill that stands alone, but it integrates all the leadership skills you have learned so far in this book. It is the pinnacle of the six relationship skills. Having just studied a total of eleven leadership skills, you now can consolidate these skills into an inclusive process that you can use every day to inspire great performances from each of your subordinates.

You might wonder why you need a coaching process, particularly if coaching represents skills you have just studied and learned. There are two primary reasons. First, your job is to lead. Of all your leadership skills, coaching is the one that comes closest to defining what leadership is all about: getting the rights things accomplished at the right time with the assistance of other people. Coaching provides a workable and easy-to-use process of immediate value that will enable you to use all your leadership skills to focus on getting the right results. Individual leadership skills by themselves will not ensure great leadership. It is the coordinated and correct application of all these skills that results in great leadership. Coaching, when it is performed consistently and enthusiastically by you the leader, will result in immediate and tangible results for you, your subordinates, and your organization.

Second, your subordinates need someone to routinely encourage them to take advantage of opportunities to achieve the most they can; to set high and achievable expectations; to steer them in the right directions and give them the power and authority to move forward; to listen to them and support them as they encounter difficulties and challenges along the way to achieving their goals; and to advise them based upon knowledge, skills, and experience. Leaders are in an excellent position to coach subordinates because leaders interact so closely with them and are ultimately responsible for their performance successes and failures. What better person is there to be the coach than the most responsible individual?

A Coach's Attitude

A coach is a leader. A coach's attitude is a leader's attitude, and a coach's skills are a leader's skills. If you acquire the knowledge and practice the leadership skills throughout this book, you will lay the foundation to become a great coach and a great leader. The purpose of this section is to emphasize three key characteristics of a great coaching attitude.

A great coach commits to and gains commitment from subordinates. As a coach you understand and accept the pivotal responsibility for preparing, teaching, and guiding subordinates to success through the coaching process. Belief in the positive benefits of coaching is so great that you are committed to investing whatever amount of time and patience it takes to personally coach each subordinate. You expect the best from subordinates but are not upset, discouraged, or punishing when they try and fail. In return for these strong convictions, you gain the commitment of subordinates to cooperate with the coaching process, to take responsibility for their work, to increase skills and improve performance, and to focus on the best ways to achieve goals.

A great coach is willing to co-develop performance plans and check progress. The coaching process heavily relies upon your comparing a person's performance with the job standards and goals. It is incumbent upon you as the coach to meticulously develop and monitor performance plans with each subordinate. These plans become the official yardstick against which you analyze performance problems, discuss concerns with the subordinate, suggest areas to improve upon, and decide together with the subordinate on what positive actions to take.

A great coach feels comfortable communicating face-to-face. Since coaching is foremost a communications process, it is vital for you to understand and be comfortable with all aspects of face-to-face communication. You must be able to question, listen, and give performance feedback without creating resentment. For the coaching process to work best, you and the subordinate must be capable of communicating with each other easily with openness and honesty.

The Coaching Process

The coaching process in this section is based on an important assumption: that you and your subordinate have previously developed and agreed upon job standards and goals. It is after this point in the performance management process that you use coaching to achieve these goals. Since coaching should become one of your most natural and frequently used leadership activities, it is helpful to have the acronym COACH for the process so you can easily remember each step.

The coaching process (COACH) can be separated into five steps.

▶ Compare performance with standards and goals.
▶ Offer feedback.
▶ Ask for comments and analyze the performance.
▶ Collaborate on a solution.
▶ Honor your subordinate.

STEP

◈ 1 ◈

Compare Performance with Standards and Goals

Two reliable tests of whether your subordinate has a performance problem are to see if they are deviating from a standard of performance or not making progress toward their goals. If there is no problem in these areas, you still should use the coaching process to review the performance with the subordinate because people need to hear the positive news as well as the negative news. In addition, this will lead to opportunities for you to coach your subordinate to higher levels of performance by increasing his or her expertise and job knowledge. Coaching helps you prevent potential problems by identifying those areas before they become worse. If the subordinate is not on track for achieving standards or goals, for example, you can use the coaching process to discuss performance behavior, develop solutions, and agree on a corrective plan of action. Due to your limited time and the importance of correctly coaching for improved performance, do not spend time on your subordinate's insignificant or irrelevant behavior issues; focus instead on critical performance-related issues.

You learned in Chapter 5's problem-solving section that it is a straightforward process to observe and then determine that your subordinate has a performance problem. What is less easy is determining the cause of the performance problem. At this stage of the coaching process, you can only speculate on possible causes. Despite your gut feelings or leadership wisdom, avoid concluding what the causes are until you investigate further; otherwise you could make seriously erroneous assumptions. During your face-to-face coaching session with your subordinate is the time to delve into these potential causes.

After exploring possible causes, if you determine that the subordinate is not primarily the cause of the performance problem, seek to eliminate the true cause of the problem and not take the coaching process any further. Why should you coach a subordinate on improving their behavior when the behavior is not the cause? For example, you may find out from another subordinate that none of the team members has been officially trained in the skill that is related to the performance problem. Your solution, therefore, is to schedule the training so that performance levels can improve. In another example, you might determine that organizational barriers, such as a shortage of resources, prevent the subordinate from accomplishing the tasks. Again, the leadership solution is to spend your time finding the necessary resources, not coaching the subordinate.

Offer Feedback

STEP
◈ 2 ◈

The next step is to immediately begin the face-to-face portion of the coaching process by offering feedback. Schedule some uninterrupted time alone to speak candidly with the individual about his or her performance. The best places are in your office, since you can block out potential interruptions such as the telephone or visitors, or at the employee's location if it is completely private. To prevent misunderstandings, focus quickly on the problem and describe specifically what you think the problem is. Use good communication techniques to minimize apprehensiveness and defensiveness, and explain specifically your observations, such as, "You missed your sales goal by $500," not "Your sales are off this month." If someone is not following an office rule, for example, say, "The policy is for everyone to have four ten-minute breaks per day, and I noticed that you have been away from your desk for over twenty minutes each time." Support your comments with objective facts, such as reports, performance observations, and measurable job standards.

Ask for Comments and Analyze the Performance

The objectives of this step are for you and your subordinate to recognize and acknowledge that there is a problem with performance, to jointly identify the problem, and to determine its cause. The easiest way to see if your subordinate is aware of a performance problem is to ask about it. You could do this separately after you finish offering your feedback in step two or in conjunction with step two. For example, you could ask, "Did you know that you have been taking twenty-minute breaks this week when the allotted time is ten minutes?" It may be that the person is aware of the behavior but assumes that the ten-minute rule is only a guideline.

More often than not, if you just state that this behavior is undesirable and explain how it affects the team's operations, it will be corrected. Explain how subpar performance has consequences on others, such as when team members must cover the work or when delays keep meetings from starting on time. It is important to get your subordinate to verbally acknowledge a performance problem. This is a crucial part of the coaching process that must be done before you continue any further.

When the subordinate acknowledges a performance behavior problem, determine why he or she is not performing to standard. As with any problem, there could be numerous causes, so avoid prejudging or losing your composure until you have completely identified the true cause. Question the person to find out whether they understand the details of what must be done and how it must be done. You will soon determine the cause of the behavior problem, such as a miscommunication of the scope of the task, a misunderstanding of what you needed, personal challenges that affect performance of the duties, or motivational issues.

Collaborate on a Solution

Your objective in this step is for both of you to find a solution that eliminates the unsatisfactory performance. This means linking the behavior that must be changed to specific actions that will result in your subordinate doing things correctly. As in all problem-solving sessions where you are open to various suggestions, jointly identify as many possible alternative actions as you can. Discuss each in detail and agree on the best course of action that will solve the performance problem by a specific date.

After the coaching session, both of you should clearly know how you define satisfactory and unsatisfactory performance. Not only will this help you later as you monitor your subordinate's performance but it will also be one last reminder of what kind of behavior you expect. Make your final statement one that expresses your complete confidence in the person's ability to implement the solution.

Honor Your Subordinate

Throughout the coaching process, approach your subordinate with an attitude of respect, a desire to resolve the problem, and much optimism about
the future. By honoring the person as a human being and as a contributing
team member, you will reinforce their efforts to succeed. Part of this honoring process is your continued commitment to guide the person in achieving
his or her goals.

Respect is an aspect of honor. The coaching process may initially
intimidate your subordinates. Reassure them that coaching is a productive
process that furthers the concerns of both the individual and the organization.
Assure them that coaching focuses on improving performance, not on
demeaning people or changing people's personalities.

Following up is also an aspect of honor. As you learned in Chapter 8,
monitoring ensures that your leadership efforts are effective. This is particularly crucial in coaching, because if you do not check to see if your subordinate does as agreed, acceptable performance may not be maintained over the
long run. Within hours or days after the coaching session, let your subordinate know how you perceive their progress. If the person's behavior is
acceptable, say so — positive recognition has been earned. As discussed in
Chapter 12, the sooner you recognize positive behavior, the better are the
chances at sustaining it, which is your objective.

Even if the person is only making progress and has not yet passed the
threshold to acceptable performance, encourage the behavior by acknowledging you are pleased with his or her progress. Occasionally examine whether
the performance continues to be acceptable because some people will resort
to prior behaviors if they are not periodically checked. Remember, subordinates learn from their mistakes, as does everyone, so there is no need for constant reminders of past mistakes. Honor subordinates for their commitment to
improve their behavior.

During follow-up, if you discover your subordinate has not responded
well to the coaching process, repeat the process and explore the reasons why
the person has not changed as agreed. You are not again trying to solve the
original problem, but now you are trying to solve the new problem of the
subordinate not taking the agreed-upon action.

If subordinates do not comply with agreed-upon solutions in the first
couple of sessions of coaching, they probably have ignored the consequences
their actions have had on team members or on themselves. It may take repeated
coaching sessions for your subordinate to completely understand the effects of
under-performance. You may need to eventually resort to punishment, such as
docking pay, reprimanding, transferring, or replacing the person.

You have a responsibility as a leader to ensure that you do everything possible to improve your subordinate's unsatisfactory performance. This means that you do not give up when the first session of coaching does not result in perfect behavior. Each person will respond differently to coaching, but because coaching works, almost everyone will eventually respond favorably to your coaching efforts.

Honor your subordinates by consistently coaching all of them. Coaching is not something to start doing and soon forget — it is too important and effective as a leadership skill. Your leadership obligation to your subordinates demands that you honestly, courageously, and consistently offer the best leadership you can.

The Coaching Results

Coaching is at the heart of leadership, because when two people can come together to discuss performance behavior and develop positive solutions, they can improve their organization. All your subordinates routinely need your involved attention, whether they are doing a mediocre, average, or outstanding job.

Although the discussion in this chapter has focused primarily on coaching a subordinate who is performing poorly, it is important that you coach all employees at all levels of performance. A subordinate who performs adequately can be coached to perform outstandingly, and a superb performer can be coached to perform better in some areas or to assume responsibilities in new and challenging areas. Few things motivate a person more than praise from their leader when they deserve it. As a leader, you can always show them how they can help themselves and their organization do better.

PART IV

STRATEGIC
SKILLS

Upper-level Leadership Skills

CHAPTER 16

FINE TUNE YOUR VISION

Vision is the ability to perceive the many possibilities that are available to your organization and to create an ideal picture of where your organization will be at a future point. Vision is much more than setting a goal, writing a statement of purpose, or planning for the long term. Vision is setting a clear, focused, desirable direction that will take your organization to some specific destination.

This direction is the culmination of your efforts at observing, analyzing, and consulting with others. It entails a clear understanding of your existing situation and where your organization is currently headed, a continual assessment of the possibilities that could move you forward in the same or different direction, and the courage to act upon the best of these possibilities to produce change.

The exciting direction that you envision places an emphasis on what can go right, not on what may go wrong. As a visionary leader, you often think about the future and attempt to influence in advance your organization's place in it, not simply to react as the future unfolds. The vision you create is bold, energizing, and exactly where everyone wants to be one day; therefore, your followers will do their best to help get there.

As a leader, you need vision because it is imperative for your organization to frequently reassess the present and the future, particularly since change is constant. You must periodically adjust the direction in which you lead your subordinates. Be open-minded, curious, committed to the organization, and capable of articulating the vision to people whose support you need. You can be a visionary leader at any organizational level — not just at the top levels. Your vision does not have to be original or brilliant; however, it must be a well-developed, sound, and realistic conception that rallies and focuses organizational members everyday towards specific objectives.

The Visioning Process

You can become highly skilled at the visioning process by developing some simple habits and by practicing proven techniques, many of which have been discussed in this book. Following a five-step process will help you create and achieve the right vision for your organization.

- ► Acquire a visionary attitude.
- ► Understand your organization.
- ► Develop your vision.
- ► Communicate your vision and obtain commitments.
- ► Support your vision.

Acquire a Visionary Attitude

STEP
✦ 1 ✦

To acquire a visionary attitude, you must begin to think like a visionary and then practice that attitude as often as possible. Here are some examples of visionary thinking.

Visionary leaders think about the possibilities in almost everything they do. They know the power of an idea and how the right ideas can lead to enormous success for them and their organization. Even though they focus on the future, they are not unhappy with the daily responsibilities of implementing ideas or other more routine functions; however, they believe in giving their subordinates the autonomy to assume more and more of the important daily responsibilities. This frees their time for imagining and shaping the direction of their organization.

Visionary leaders know that the future is not preordained but is influenced daily by people like themselves. Since they believe in the power of innovation, they regularly improve their creative thinking skills and encourage others to unleash their creativity. They realize the right vision will develop more quickly if they are completely involved with the ideas, concerns, and needs of everyone with whom they operate — subordinates, customers, peers, and competitors. They openly encourage subordinates to come forward with their ideas, thus inspiring their confidence. They constantly inform everyone as to where they and the organization are going.

Understand Your Organization

You must thoroughly understand the nature and challenges of your organization at your own level and at other levels. This understanding includes a knowledge of culture, values, financial condition, competitive situation, customers, and strategy. As a visionary leader, develop a habit of routinely questioning all significant organizational areas by considering general questions for which the answers will lead you to profound conclusions.

Examples of inward-oriented questions might include:

▸ What does our organization do best?

▸ What systems, strengths, and factors cause us to perform so well in these areas?

▸ What are our organizational values and how can we sustain them over the next decade?

▸ What would be an ideal type of organization?

▸ If I had the power to influence the future, what would it look like and what type of organization could we become?

More outward-oriented questions, which are also important in understanding your organization and its environment, include:

▸ What is our competition doing in response to market changes?

▸ How is our industry changing?

▸ What markets should the organization be in?

▸ What are our customers telling us about their needs?

These are just some of the questions that you can develop and pose to yourself and your subordinates. The questions will give everyone the opportunity to think creatively and freely, and they will stimulate hopes and aspirations that will start you on the path towards shaping a vision. You cannot determine the answers overnight because many of them have to be experienced and developed over time. But once you are in touch with the answers, you will reap much benefit from them.

Take the time to routinely and thoroughly examine everything that affects your organization because it is these discoveries that will lead you to visionary conclusions. If you ignore doing so, you will make erroneous assumptions about the status of your organization, and this will cause you to miss opportunities or take the wrong path. Armed with this knowledge and a complete understanding of your personal values, you can proactively think about the best ways to help your organization and to lead your subordinates to do the same. If you know where your organization is going, you will more easily spot opportunities each day. Only by truly understanding your organization, will you create a vision that is aligned with your organization's core values, culture, and potential.

Develop Your Vision

With an understanding of your organization's environment and your personal commitment to maintaining a visionary's attitude, begin the process of developing your vision for the organization. Imagine the ideal futuristic state for your organization including what it will look like, what environment will you operate within, and how you can take advantage of the countless opportunities that exist. Develop a specific, clear, and simple-to-understand vision for your areas of responsibility. The vision should evolve from what you believe is possible, right, and needed for your organization; what will support your higher organization's strategic direction; and what will inspire your subordinates to succeed despite the inevitable obstacles that they will encounter.

As is always true when solving problems, managing projects, or making decisions, you will greatly benefit from consulting with members of your organization as you develop your vision and its details. No leader has the responsibility or capability of designing a vision alone. Also, you alone will not achieve your vision without the committed efforts of your subordinates. People must believe in the vision if they are to achieve it, and they must participate in its development if they are to believe in it. Using the assistance of others also will reveal any erroneous assumptions and help you develop the specific details of the vision. For the vision to be realized, your subordinates must voluntarily assume responsibility to own it and to achieve it — you cannot forcibly cause this to happen. Part of your visioning skill is the ability to elicit from others their visions for the organization.

If you desire a high level of subordinate involvement in the process, you could even formally ask them to jointly develop and approve the vision. This will give everyone the opportunity to incorporate their personal visions and dreams for the organization, describe the work environment necessary to achieve the vision, and increase their long-term commitment to it. They will realize that they indeed have control over their own future and that the vision can help them meet their own needs. After your subordinates develop a common vision and realize how they can reach it through cooperation and collaboration, they will become a stronger, more unified team.

Vision statements are a means of communicating your vision. They are useful if you truly intend to do what is necessary to realize your vision;

STEP

◆ 3 ◆

otherwise, they are useless and could cause more harm than good if people perceive them as another catchy gimmick of the month. Vision statements can be of any length, ranging from one paragraph to several pages, and can address solely the overall vision or explain in detail the subareas that relate to it. Statements that are precise and succinct, however, are usually best.

Here are examples of simple but powerful vision statements for two organizations.

> ► We resolve to be the service leader in the computer industry and always do what is right for our customers, employees, and shareholders.

> ► Our organization will pursue excellence and will be recognized as the best chain of grocery stores in the United States.

Since vision involves a yet-to-occur reality, not all details can be set forth. With a clear statement of the direction that you want to set for the organization, however, you and your subordinates later can concern yourselves with the details and inevitable uncertainties involved in implementing the vision.

STEP

◆ 4 ◆

Communicate Your Vision and Obtain Commitments

If your subordinates are to achieve your vision, they must clearly understand it, believe it is an important and worthwhile cause, see exactly how it will benefit them and the organization, and fully commit to achieving it. As you might expect, aligning your subordinates in such a manner is more complex than simply telling them about the vision or writing them a memo.

You have to treat vision in a nonroutine way because vision causes more fundamental change to your organization and its employees than do routine events. Properly communicating your vision must result in people lining up to support it and to achieve it. That is why it is almost always better to get your subordinates involved early in developing the vision. When you and your subordinates understand the vision in its entirety, you will minimize any uncertainty and resistance.

As your subordinates come to believe that they have the responsibility and authority to step outside of traditional boundaries to move the organization towards its vision, then they will continually take those actions and risks that you need to achieve your vision. Explicitly ask for and obtain commitment from all your subordinates to work toward achieving the vision. Determine which other members within the organization are crucial to realization of the vision, including other staff members and your supervisor. Since these people are integral to creating and sustaining the alliances you need, they also must commit to your vision.

Support Your Vision

After you properly communicate your vision, your actions now become the proof that you are intent upon following it through. Your subordinates will watch you closely for evidence that you are personally committed to the vision and will not arbitrarily change your views or back away from it. They want you to set the example by leading them through the unknown and by showing them that you are willing to share the hazards and the rewards of charting these new paths. If they know that you are courageously in front of them, they will loyally and enthusiastically support you.

You will need to continually repeat your vision during casual conversations, meetings, speeches, and all organizational communication. Whenever you interview new subordinates, remember to speak about your vision and the opportunities that lie ahead. Because your actions will prove to your subordinates that you are intent on achieving your vision, remember to view everything you do as being either supportive or detrimental to achieving that goal. In particular, watch closely your comments, reactions to everyday occurrences, and your attitude.

Update Your Vision

The visioning process is an evolutionary one that never ends because of the constant change that you face; therefore, do not hesitate to review and adapt your vision. Look for opportunities to broaden its scope throughout your organization so the vision becomes not just a concept but an achievable, credible, and accepted reality that permeates all your operations and all facets of the daily lives of your subordinates.

If your organization is to survive and thrive, it needs you to be the catalyst to initiate vision, seek others' input, and align your subordinates behind it. You then can move on to develop an innovative framework, or strategy, which is the means for implementing that vision.

CHAPTER 17

DEVELOP YOUR STRATEGY

S trategy is an integrated, extensive, and long-term way of thinking, decision making, and acting that produces viable plans for achieving the vision set for your organization. By establishing a vision, you are thinking strategically. To lead your organization strategically, you must take this thinking process further and apply it to all aspects of your organization. When using your strategy skills, you are considering the broad issues and factors that affect your organization's future in all areas, including long-term competition and growth, marketing, manufacturing, finance, operations, customer service, and responsibilities to your subordinates and shareholders.

Planning and Strategy

Planning is a necessary and important part of any leader's daily responsibilities, whether done informally throughout the day or formally with a staff or other assistance. It permeates all your leadership skills because it is an essential activity that provides the structure needed to accomplish daily organizational activities. Planning, however, is associated primarily with the managerial aspects of a leader's responsibilities because its objective is to keep the organization functioning well without major disruptions or problems. If an organization is to achieve what it sets out to do, it must plan.

Leaders agree with this philosophy but also approach planning from a different angle, believing it is strategies, not plans, that provide the framework and guidance that result in successful organizations. While recognizing that most activities require planning, leaders do not overly rely on planning at the expense of developing strategies. Leaders realize that, in a fast-paced and constantly changing world, plans are not the definitive answer to the challenges of an organization because plans are time-consuming to prepare, quickly become obsolete, and cannot possibly prevent all challenges or problems from occurring. Leaders do invest an appropriate, not excessive, amount of time in planning, yet they also take calculated risks that could result in achievement of the vision, keep an anticipatory eye on the changing big picture, and respond to events as they unfold.

In other words, leaders develop a series of nimble strategies — not detailed and rigid long-term plans — that allow them to achieve their vision. Planning will naturally follow the development of strategies, but the best plans will be short- to medium-term in nature, well-guided by clear and focused strategies, developed with the assistance of knowledgeable subordinates, and inherently adaptable to changing conditions.

The Strategy Process

When selecting ways to create and implement strategies, you have many methods from which to choose. Several excellent commercial books and programs exist that can guide you through the strategy formulation process for either specific functional or broad organizational areas. If your budget can handle it, it is helpful to employ strategy consultants to help guide you and other top leaders to the right decisions for your organization. Besides outside sources, your organization may have its own systems that use some of the proven techniques of strategic planning or strategic management. Even with all these resources available to you, there is no consensus as to which techniques or planning systems are best. You decide what is best based upon what works well for your particular organization.

As you get more experience in this area or if you later use strategy experts, you will become increasingly effective as a strategist. Regardless of what strategic systems that you may have available, the best initial approach is to concentrate thoroughly on the strategic thinking before you begin the strategic planning and implementation.

Thinking strategically involves seeing the connections in apparently unrelated happenings and understanding how myriad trends and occurrences interrelate to affect your organization. You should think strategically every day and encourage leaders and subordinates throughout your organization to do the same. As you learn and use the strategy process that follows, strategic thinking will be the underlying skill that you develop.

> ► Know your environment and its relationship to your vision.
> ► Involve subordinates and others in strategy building.
> ► Develop strategies.
> ► Align your day-to-day mission with your vision and strategy.

STEP

❖ 1 ❖

Know Your Environment and Its Relationship to Your Vision

In the visioning process, understanding your organization was a key step to realizing its potential. Now that you have pinpointed some exciting possibilities for your organization, you must understand as much as you can about those internal and external factors that will help you achieve your vision, as well as any factors that might get in your way.

You have a duty to recognize and promote your organization's strengths and other advantages because these assets will increase opportunities for developing and implementing winning strategies. Likewise, it is essential to anticipate and react to factors that could threaten your organization and prevent it from achieving its vision. Knowing your environment involves understanding the four key areas of assumptions, resources, market, and external environment.

Identifying assumptions that you and others make about your organization will help you corroborate facts and avoid wasted time and effort. Few things are more discouraging to people than to discover, after investing large amounts of time, that their ideas and recommendations are useless because they were founded on unrealistic or false assumptions. Imagine the wrong directions strategy development could take if people were not aware that the organization was eliminating a major product line, was planning to reorganize sales districts, or was about to become a public corporation. This is why it is always wise to discuss assumptions before developing strategy.

Assess the resources that you currently have available or could acquire for use during the strategic timeframe. Compare this with the resources that you require to achieve your vision. In addition to examining typical resources, such as equipment, employees, and skills capabilities, look at others such as the time you need during the strategic period and the quality of relationships you have with suppliers and customers.

Staying in touch with your market will help you identify threats to your organization's survival in addition to opportunities to pursue. A thorough understanding of your market means knowing:

> ► Your customers, such as what they think about your organization, who they are by category, and what services and products they want now and in the future.

► Your competition, including what they offer or do not offer in the market, their competitive strategy, how might they react to your competitive actions, and their strengths and weaknesses compared to your organization.

► Your competitive position within the market, such as how your organization presents or differentiates itself, what value it offers, and what features distinguish you from the competition.

Anything external to your organization has the potential to affect it positively or negatively. Avoid tunnel vision by staying aware of political, economic, sociological, cultural, technological, and industrial events and trends. This up-to-date knowledge will permit you to evaluate the impact of an external issue upon your organization and then to develop the right responses.

Involve Subordinates and Others in Strategy Building

STEP
◈ 2 ◈

As was true in developing your vision, it is wise to involve your subordinates and others in developing the strategy to achieve that vision. Your strategy will be more viable and innovative if you use a variety of available expertise, and if you truly listen to what everyone tells you. There was a time when organizational strategy building was often centrally controlled and developed, and it still is in many instances. But if you develop strategy only at the highest levels of your organization or if you fail to adequately consult with those people who have the knowledge and experience to help, you will probably end up with an inadequate or failed strategy. That assuredly will later jeopardize your organization's survival. Avoid this by involving a variety of people in strategy formulation, such as customers, resource providers, outside experts, and people from multiple organizational levels.

Develop Strategies

STEP
◈ 3 ◈

To achieve your vision, you must translate it into specific strategies. These consist of understandable, achievable objectives and plans that are long-, medium-, and short-range. The strategies will apply to multiple organizational levels and functional areas, each with its own details of implementation, and will be developed with the assistance of your subordinates and other members of your organization. A strategy addresses the issues of breadth, depth, objectives, and implementation.

Breadth signifies the organization's top-level intentions across a wide operational range that will enable it to succeed in a variety of areas or businesses. These broad aims usually are referred to as a corporate or organizational strategy. It seeks to address what specific products and services will be offered, where the organization will function or compete, what the growth plans are, and what resources will be allocated to subordinate organizations.

The typical organization does not rely upon one overall corporate strategy to achieve its vision but it implements several strategies in depth so that multiple objectives can be met. These strategies belong to specific organizational levels, business units, or autonomous units. The strategies at major business levels are usually referred to as business strategies. Strategies at this level are in alignment with their corporate strategies but also address more specific actions that the major business unit must take to achieve its mission. As is similar with the operations of a team and its members, it is the collective efforts of many business strategies that help the overall organization succeed at its strategy. If you and other top leaders effectively integrate the diverse business units within the organization and take advantage of complementary resources and synergistic capabilities, your organization will function much more effectively at each strategic level.

Functional strategies support specific business strategies through such functional areas as human resources, marketing, finance, innovation, production, or operations. Each of these functional strategies has its own set of tactics, or implementation plans and procedures, that detail the daily work that must be done to achieve the functional strategy.

You can develop winning business and functional strategies by using your experience, research, and consultation with experts. Since every organization faces unique competitive challenges, explore wisely all available resources so that you and your organization can examine a range of alternatives before making final strategic decisions. Fortunately, there are numerous resources including books and strategy consultants to help you think through this process and guide you to the best decision.

One of your major strategy challenges as a leader is to ensure that all your organizational strategies are consistent with each other in breadth and in depth. It is not enough to develop a hierarchy of strategies; they must all support attainment of the overall corporate strategy. No matter what level of organization you lead, you must be unrelenting in keeping your organization on track. When you notice inconsistent strategies, bad judgment, or a need to revise a previously approved strategy, speak up.

For example, if part of the overall organizational strategy is to increase revenues 10 percent a year, then the business and functional strategies should support and reinforce, not contradict, this growth objective. In this example, individual business strategies should focus on competitive markets that can produce sales growth, or they could focus on regular introduction of new products and services. In turn, the functional strategy of marketing would similarly reinforce strategies. The sales strategy should encourage and reward high performance; the advertising and promotion strategy should bolster high potential markets; and the quality and customer service strategies should focus on product excellence and customer loyalty and retention.

As with any leadership undertaking, you must clearly establish prioritized objectives that will unequivocally show you and your subordinates what everyone has to accomplish to achieve the vision. This is particularly important at the strategic level because, if the objectives are missing or unclear, all related activities will be similarly flawed. Your organizational objectives address the many areas of strategic concern to your organization: profitability, growth, competitive performance, innovation, quality, and concern for customers, employees, shareholders, or society. Regardless of the objectives that you choose, they should each have specific targets that can be periodically evaluated by measures of performance, such as return on investment, sales increase, market share, cost savings, product defect rate, or customer satisfaction.

Develop enough objectives within realistic time frames for each of your strategic intentions. Start first with your long-term organizational objectives of two to ten years, then develop them into medium-range objectives of one to two years and short-term objectives of one month to one year. Each unit within a division, a product line, functional department, or international operation will in turn develop its own long-, medium-, and short-term objectives that are compatible and consistent with its higher level in the organization.

It would be naive to think that implementation of a strategy can be effectively summed up in a few paragraphs. The process leading up to strategy formulation involves meticulous thinking, planning, rethinking, and decision making. This also is true as you implement the strategy because internal and external organizational changes occur, causing you to periodically adjust your plans. All this exists in an environment of economic uncertainty, competitive pressures, and change. Fortunately, your leadership efforts at a strategic level succeed with the same skills that you use daily at team levels. The main differences with strategic issues tend to be their broadened scope, lengthier time frames, increased complexity, and higher levels of uncertainty. You are still dealing, however, with human beings who want to be properly lead, who must be given the support they need to achieve your vision, and who want to make meaningful contributions.

The keys to implementing your well-developed strategy are based on the main points you have learned throughout this book.

- ▶ Develop viable but flexible plans using the assistance and wisdom of your subordinates.
- ▶ Communicate your strategy to your subordinates, gain their commitment to the strategy, and give them the responsibility and authority to achieve it.

▶ Provide your subordinates and organizational units the resources they need to achieve strategic objectives.

▶ Ensure that organizational processes, policies, and reward systems encourage your subordinates to assume the long-term focus necessary for successful strategy implementation.

▶ Monitor both your organizational environment and the market, then reassess and adjust elements of your strategy as needed.

Continual monitoring is particularly crucial to strategy implementation because it is your swift reaction to the short-term and incremental changes that will help you successfully adjust your strategy. During the implementation phase, many things can cause your strategy to falter or deviate from your initial expectations. These could be changes in assumptions, lack of progress in the tactical plans, increase in barriers, change in environmental factors, or a need for organizational redesign. If you assess organizational performance, environmental conditions, or progress on strategy implementation only twice a year, for example, you will not be able to react quickly enough to successfully adjust a failing strategy, react to impending problems, or make any needed tactical changes.

STEP

⊰ 4 ⊱

Align Your Day-to-day Mission with Your Vision and Strategy

A mission statement expresses why your organization exists, specifying its purpose, what it does best, and what it does daily to serve its customers, employees, and shareholders. Unlike the future orientation of the vision statement described in Chapter 16, a mission statement is a detailed guide of one paragraph to several pages that focuses on the present. You develop it after realistically examining the strengths and competencies of your organization and deciding what you have to do each day to continue to survive and progress.

Your organizational mission probably has had months or years to be tested and refined to a logical, accurate reflection of what your organization chooses to do and what it does best. You even may have a viable mission statement for your organization that seems to be working well. Having just recently identified the right vision for your organization, however, you should now review your mission statement to ensure that it is in alignment with your vision.

Although your mission statement is oriented towards daily challenges, it is a pivotal link to your efforts at implementing your strategy and achieving your vision. It is not sufficient for you to loudly and periodically proclaim what your organization intends to accomplish; you must wisely ensure that everyone is marching in the same direction every day. It is your responsibility, therefore, to align the daily focus of your subordinates with your vision. This is where the detailed and unambiguous guidance of a mission statement is particularly helpful. Because most of your subordinates naturally tend to concentrate on the daily aspects of their jobs, a focus on the mission will not be difficult for you to instill. Current daily operations are quite important to you, so your mission statement must accurately reflect the level of excellence that you expect from your subordinates and your organization as a whole. Not only will an emphasis on the mission help everyone accomplish the right things every day, but the resulting incremental successes from a committed workforce will collectively lead to the long-term achievement of your vision.

Winning Strategies

Your purpose for developing strategy skills is ultimately to produce winning strategies for your organization. As a leader, you implicitly recognize your full accountability to the core constituencies of employees, shareholders, and customers. That is why you take seriously your responsibility to know what is happening strategically with your organization. Otherwise, the organization will not thrive in the long run. It is up to you as a leader, therefore, to develop and practice your strategy skills so that you can have a positive and long-lasting impact upon your organization.

CHAPTER 18

GUIDE DURING CHANGE

Remember the definition of a leader as one who uses all their skills to get the right things accomplished at the right time with the assistance of other people. This implies that leaders guide their subordinates from where they are to where the leaders want them to be. This process of leadership, therefore, is fundamentally one of change. Your objectives for change are to perceive the need to leave today's status quo, to recognize the opportunities involved with change, and to muster the confidence to calmly lead your subordinates and others along the uncharted path of change. You accomplish these objectives by integrating your leadership skills with the specific change skills discussed in this chapter, which are to prepare for, initiate, and implement change.

Prepare for Change

If you know that something is certain to change at a future point, doesn't it make sense to proactively use your time now to prepare your subordinates and your organization for the change? While the change process involves all of the skills you have learned in this book, there are four key skills involved in preparing for change that you should grasp.

▶ Understand the different perspectives of change.

▶ Maintain a positive attitude toward change.

▶ Promote continuous learning.

▶ Be aware of your environment.

Understand the Different Perspectives of Change

Change can be seen from the differing perspectives of the environment, the organization, its members, and its leaders.

Anything in the environment external to the organization can be a catalyst for change, so prepare yourself to anticipate and respond to these known and unknown events. Notable examples of external changes include changing customer needs, technological innovation, domestic and global competition, market maturation, and regulatory requirements. Many of these external changes are out of your control and may challenge your organization's very survival; however, most can be handled well through thoughtful anticipation and the right responses by you and your organization, such as a willingness to improve your performance and increase innovation.

Organizational change is a pervasive and long-term process that results in significant widespread changes in the behaviors of its members and the organization as a whole. Examples of these changes include environmental changes, strategy implementation, and the integration of technology into the workplace. Ideally, any needed changes should support attainment of the organizational vision within the context and constraints of the environment. It is usually a challenge to change ingrained attitudes, beliefs, and culture within an organization, but you can most assuredly change them over time.

As for the members of an organization, it is natural for most people to prefer little or no change because change typically upsets order and stability, threatens people's self-interests, increases stress, and involves risk. Whenever personal or organizational change occurs, whether it is a reorganization, a bold new strategy, a change in leaders, a revised benefits policy, or a tragedy, people tend to exhibit a certain response. This response to change follows a four-part pattern that:

▶ Begins with fear and denial,

▶ Continues with feelings of loss and grief about the old ways,

▶ Improves with acceptance of the change and release of the old ways, and

▶ Ends with implementation of the change.

By recognizing that this change process is perfectly normal and healthy, people should strive to limit, not eliminate, the time they spend in the first stages and instead focus on the last two stages. By using the leadership skills that you have developed and by creating the organizational structures and systems to support change, you can lead your subordinates deliberately through this process. Your subordinates are depending on you and your decisive leadership to reduce the personal and organizational upheaval that is expected to occur.

Frequently, it is not the final changes that scare people but rather the confusion and upsetting consequences that the changes produce along the way. Since each stage of the response pattern cycle is important but varies in significance to each person, you must encourage free-flowing information related to the changes, promote specific change assistance programs, and allocate sufficient resources. For example, to help ease and hasten the release of the old ways, your subordinates might appreciate nonstructured informational meetings, question-and-answer sessions with experts, access to counselors, or specific customs such as kickoff or farewell ceremonies. To help your subordinates cope with the uncertainty that exists throughout the change cycle, intensify your leadership presence by being unambiguous, reassuring, and positive about what they must do to implement the changes.

Leaders are aware of the reactions that change causes in others, but, as you would expect, effective leaders choose not to let change provoke a similar response in themselves. See change as an opportunity to help everyone achieve greater success in new, exciting ways. Since change is a fundamental part of your leadership responsibilities, whether you are envisioning and initiating the changes, implementing the changes, or reacting to unexpected changes, make sure that the change process works well.

Maintain a Positive Attitude Toward Change

You learned in Chapter 3 how important the right attitude is for a leader. Since change is such a frightening process for many people, it is essential for you to maintain a great attitude and then promote this positive attitude with your subordinates so that they can better understand change and see it as an opportunity.

Change is inevitable. Like the challenges you face in your personal and professional life, change will occur whether you want it to or not. Although you may have felt more comfortable and safe when changes were infrequent or more manageable, you cannot live and work by yesterday's reality. It is more realistic and less stressful to adapt to today's realities. Even though change requires that you lose something, such as the old way of doing things or a perceived security, it replaces what it takes with new ways of doing things or a different type of security. Instead of blaming someone or something for causing a change or instead of completely ignoring or avoiding the changes, accept your professional responsibility to embrace change and respond to it by maintaining an optimistic, solution-oriented attitude and behavior.

Change is good. Change is often feared because of the effect it has on some people, the naturally upsetting and stressful feelings of uncertainty, failure, loss of control, or conflict. The healthy attitude to have about change is that it is good because, if it is properly handled, it helps promote personal and professional growth, new opportunities, and increased fun and satisfaction on the road to achieving your organization's vision.

Change is conquerable. Despite the inevitability of change and the destabilization that it brings, you can control how you react to it and thus, in essence, control the change. The right reactions are curiosity, enthusiasm, flexibility, confidence, and a willingness to take action and possibly make mistakes. Such responses allow you to overcome the challenges of change and use them to your advantage. Wrong reactions, such as ambivalence, skepticism, negativism, second-guessing, blaming, retreating, risk aversion, and a desire to maintain the status quo, almost always guarantee failure. Part of the solution is keeping a positive attitude, believing there is no change that you or your subordinates cannot overcome. This is the belief component of the solution. The other part is seeing the superb results that change brings, which is the proof component of the solution. As a leader, it is essential for you to keep the belief and proof levels high among your subordinates.

Promote Continuous Learning

Continuous learning — itself an exercise in change — will help your subordinates better anticipate and react to changes. As discussed in Chapter 9, if your subordinates constantly seek new and better ways to carry out their responsibilities, they will continually expose themselves to new ideas and methods. This intellectual stimulation will lay the foundation for them to acquire the skills and knowledge to successfully anticipate change, recommend solutions, and implement changes. Everyone must realize that they alone are responsible to prepare themselves for the certainty of change. You as the leader, on the other hand, have an ongoing responsibility to identify and support any special training needs that develop as conditions change.

Be Aware of Your Environment

You have learned throughout this book the importance of knowing your internal and external organizational environment. If you commit to regularly updating this knowledge and applying what you learn, you will better anticipate changes. You also will lessen your own and others' anxiety about the future by constantly gathering more information about trends and upcoming changes. For example, if you regularly quiz your customers or study their purchasing habits, you will know their preferences, opinions, complaints, and suggestions. You then will have more time to respond correctly to their changing needs. Likewise, if your organization relies heavily upon catalog orders, you should notice and react when you hear that postal rates will increase next year or that your competition's sales over the Internet are increasing dramatically.

This principle of knowing what is going on around you applies to everything in your internal and external environments — customers, members of your organization, the competition, technology, the economy, and politics. You are not expected to be clairvoyant, but it is helpful to have dependable sources of information, such as technology experts, trusted and frank advisors, and news publications on business, industry, and the world in general. There is no point, however, in being a news hound who indiscriminately collects information. The key is to stay alert to and in touch with those areas that influence your organization and to use relevant information to help you make better and timelier leadership decisions.

Initiate and Implement Change

When a leader believes that change is needed for any reason, it is better to initiate the change instead of waiting for someone else to discover the need and start the process. Because leaders accept the inevitability of change, they do not delay in initiating needed changes nor do they wait until the last moment to react to impending changes. They confidently take action to incorporate the changes and benefit their constituencies of subordinates, shareholders, customers, and others. They also create opportunities for change when no one else can or will.

Change is not something you can separate from your other responsibilities but is a pervasive aspect of everything you do. It may be so pervasive you may overlook the fact that you have some power over the process of change. Approach change proactively by following these four guidelines.

- ► Realize many roads lead to your destination.
- ► Eliminate barriers to change.
- ► Monitor your change efforts.
- ► Pre-empt change with innovation.

Realize Many Roads Lead to Your Destination

Since you have already developed your vision, strategy, and implementation plans, your responsibility now is to move forward. If you keep a steady focus on your vision, you will realize that there are many ways to achieve it, some that you anticipated and some that you did not. Be adaptable to adjustments in your implementation plans based upon changing environmental conditions, unexpected resource surpluses or constraints, and new developments that you had not anticipated. As with your other duties, know exactly what changes you want to accomplish and how you will measure your success in achieving them, while leaving open for modification the various paths inbetween.

Long before any changes begin, seek the input of your subordinates and others so that you can develop consensus on the need for change, demonstrate the rewards of change, collaborate on the best overall change decisions, and obtain the commitments to support and not resist the changes. One of the common reasons that change implementation fails is from a lack of a commitment for change throughout the organization. Everyone — subordinates, top leadership, and staff — must unequivocally accept and support the changes. While not everyone will completely agree on the details nor be equally enthusiastic, it is imperative that you and your subordinates collectively support the change efforts.

Eliminate Barriers to Change

Expect to encounter resistance and obstacles to change because it is natural for this to occur. But as a leader, you must persistently work to remove any barriers that will prevent you and your organization from handling change and achieving your vision. Anything can be a potential barrier, such as a subordinate's attitude, a top leader's lack of commitment, political infighting, resource constraints, or economic conditions. Continually reevaluate conditions so that you are always alert to any potential barriers.

To turn a change barrier into a change booster, use your array of leadership skills to:

- ▶ Communicate the consequences of failing to change,
- ▶ Overcome people's doubts,
- ▶ Gather input from all those effected,
- ▶ Gain everyone's commitment to support the changes,
- ▶ Form energized, winning teams of change stakeholders,
- ▶ Hold people accountable to their change responsibilities and results,
- ▶ Solve unexpected problems and conflicts quickly, and
- ▶ Collaborate to create win-win solutions.

Communicate the need for change throughout your organization by clearly explaining why change is necessary and achievable and by expressing your confidence that everyone is capable enough to tackle the upcoming changes. You will rarely be able to convince everyone all the time about your change ideas, so avoid setting yourself up for disappointment. A more realistic objective would be to ensure that, by using all your leadership skills, your subordinates and others will understand 1) where they are now, 2) why change is needed, and 3) how change will occur. It might take several attempts for everyone to understand these three things, but persistence will pay off.

During periods of change, particularly those intense changes with a high degree of long-term uncertainty such as a reorganization, it is helpful to keep your subordinates focused and busy working on those things that you are certain of, including your short-term objectives, excellence in performing their day-to-day duties, and priority customer service.

Monitor Your Change Efforts

Monitoring is particularly crucial during the change process primarily because of the many forces that will challenge, resist, or disrupt your efforts, despite the change momentum that you create. Additionally, as your organization undergoes change, there is still the need to effectively maintain day-to-day functions, which adds to the complexity of change implementation. However, the long-term implications of not monitoring your change efforts are enormous for you and your organization. If, for example, your subordinates perceive that you or other top leaders are more interested in starting new programs than in the necessary follow-through that monitoring requires, they will be less willing to commit their efforts. They will lose confidence in your ability to lead them and will be tempted to ignore your future change ideas.

While monitoring your changes, remember to:

▶ Give your subordinates the authority to implement changes,

▶ Continually inform subordinates on the progress of changes,

▶ Listen to their needs and concerns, and

▶ Reward them as they support the change efforts and achieve milestones.

You must stay attuned to everything that is happening in your organization so that you can quickly make adjustments when needed. There is no magic formula to help you monitor change in your organization. However, it may help you to review the discussion in Chapter 8 of monitoring skills, with an eye toward how they can help lead you through change. The key is to stay closely involved with what is happening with your subordinates by communicating well, demonstrating your concern for their welfare and goal achievement, and committing to do whatever is necessary to make the change successfully. If you do these things while continuing to practice great leadership skills, you will attune yourself to how well the changes are progressing and will react quickly with any adjustments as needed.

Pre-empt Change with Innovation

You can use innovation to get the jump on change. An organization-wide focus on innovation means that there is widespread acceptance of creating and applying new ideas that relate to your vision and strategy. Your organization must constantly update itself by searching for new ways of operating, such as with new products and services, customer service improvements, and new technologies. The competitive importance of change requires your organization be as proactive and anticipatory as possible in developing the right responses to upcoming or yet-to-be-determined changes, or else other organizations will jump in ahead of you to do the job. Innovation is not a simple and quickly implemented event, but it is a deliberate, well conceptualized strategy that lays the foundation for changes to occur naturally.

As a leader in your organization, you are responsible for creating and fostering a climate of innovation. Innovation results not only in organizational success but also in benefits to your subordinates that allow them to think creatively, make meaningful contributions, and feel fulfilled at the end of the day. As you enthusiastically lead your subordinates through the challenges of change by using your leadership skills to model innovative thinking, you will increasingly become a great resource for your organization.

Although people feel most comfortable when changes are slight or infrequent, no one can live and work by yesterday's reality. For an organization's top leaders to successfully design and implement change, they must, with the assistance of other organizational members, identify the right changes to make, credibly communicate these changes throughout the organization, provide resources to support the changes, and allow enough time and flexibility for the changes to take place. With the widespread commitment of people throughout the organization, change efforts will succeed. Change, therefore, does not substantially alter the way a leader leads; change only reinforces that leaders must always use their skills to lead well every day.

Benefit From Change Leadership

By applying the knowledge you gain from this book, you will without doubt become a better leader. As a result, your subordinates will have higher levels of trust and respect for you and your ability to successfully lead them through any unknown or changing situation. This, in turn, leads to exactly that which you seek to obtain every day from your subordinates: a strong commitment to you, your organization's vision, and all aspects of their jobs.

With this high level of commitment comes a responsibility for you to regularly deliver proof of your leadership promises. As you do, you will find yourself consistently, fairly, and caringly practicing great leadership skills, showing an unrelenting desire to achieve your vision, and demonstrating commitment to the welfare of all your subordinates. As an added benefit, you will see your own abilities unfold while tremendously improving the lives of your subordinates.

INDEX

ESTABLISH A FRAMEWORK
for excellence
WITH THE SUCCESSFUL BUSINESS LIBRARY

OASIS PRESS SOFTWARE
BOOKS&
Celebrating 25 Years

The Oasis Press®
PSI Research

P.O. Box 3727
Central Point, Oregon
97502-0032

Call Direct
1-800-228-2275

Fax Line
1-541-476-1479

Email Address
info@psi-research.com

Fastbreaking changes in technology and the global marketplace continue to create unprecedented opportunities for businesses through the '90s and into the new millennium. However with these opportunities will also come many new challenges. Today, more than ever, businesses, especially small businesses, need to excel in all areas of operation to complete and succeed in an ever-changing world.

The Successful Business Library takes you through the '90s and beyond, helping you solve the day-to-day problems you face now, and prepares you for the unexpected problems you may be facing down the road. With any of our products, you will receive up-to-date and practical business solutions, which are easy to use and easy to understand. No jargon or theories, just solid, nuts-and-bolts information.

Whether you are an entrepreneur going into business for the first time or an experienced consultant trying to keep up with the latest rules and regulations, The Successful Business Library provides you with the step-by-step guidance, and action-oriented plans you need to succeed in today's world. As an added benefit, PSI Research/The Oasis Press® unconditionally guarantees your satisfaction with the purchase of any book or software application in our catalog.

THE OASIS PRESS® ONLINE

More than a marketplace for our products, we actually provide something that many business Web sites tend to overlook... *...useful information.*

It's no mystery that the World Wide Web is a great way for businesses to promote their products, however most commercial sites stop there. We have always viewed our site's goals a little differently. For starters, we have applied our 25 years of experience providing hands-on information to small businesses directly to our Web site. We offer current information to help you start your own business, guidelines to keep it up and running, useful federal and state-specific information (including addresses and phone numbers to contact these resources), and a forum for business owners to communicate and network with others on the Internet. We would like to invite you to check out our Web site and discover the information that can assist you and your small business venture.

ALL MAJOR CREDIT CARDS ACCEPTED

CALL TO PLACE AN ORDER
— or —
TO RECEIVE A FREE CATALOG **1-800-228-2275**

International Orders (541) 479-9464   *Fax Orders* (541) 476-1479
Web site http://www.psi-research.com   *Email* sales@psi-research.com

PSI Research   P.O. Box 3727   Central Point, Oregon   97502   U.S.A.

The Oasis Press Online
http://www.psi-research.com

Where Business Talks To Business

From The Leading Publisher of Small Business Information
Books that save you time and money.

If you can't remember the last time you found yourself smiling at work, it's time to read *Joysticks, Blinking Lights, and Thrills*. A refreshing approach to running your business or department within a business. Shows where, how, and why most small business problems could occur and what can be done to resolve them. Sherlock brings humorous examples from his own business experiences to identify over 45 specific problem areas in business and their easy-to-implement solutions.

Joysticks, Blinking Lights, & Thrills   **Pages: 275**
Paperback: $18.95   **ISBN: 1-55571-401-3**

This innovative book provides managers with an entirely new way of looking at information that can save time, money, headaches, and maybe even their jobs or companies. It provides cutting-edge principles and concepts that will help people work far more effectively and easily with all sorts of data.

Information Breakthrough   **Pages: 250**
Paperback: $22.95   **ISBN: 1-55571-413-7**

Focuses on developing the art of working with people to maximize the productivity and satisfaction of both manager and employees. Discussions, exercises, and self-tests boost skill in communicating, delegating, motivating, developing teams, goal-setting, adapting to change, and coping with stress.

Managing People   **Pages: 260**
Paperback: $21.95   **ISBN: 1-55571-380-7**

Author Luigi Salvaneschi clearly shows how studying eight specific liberal arts principles can help nurture your own leadership skills within — and make you an asset for the business world of the 21st century. Each chapter leads you through his new concept in management thinking and tells how it applies to both the business world and your own personal life. Includes exercises to explore at home, work, and while traveling.

Renaissance 2000   **Pages: 345**
Paperback: $22.95   **ISBN: 1-55571-412-9**

From The Leading Publisher of Small Business Information
Books that save you time and money.

Managers and business owners will learn exactly where to draw the line on sexual harassment. How to draw the line firmly, so that employees understand and respect it. Clearly spells out the procedures that are most effective if a lawsuit is lodged and gives tips on enlisting a good attorney.

Draw The Line **Pages: 172**
Paperback: $17.95 **ISBN: 1-55571-370-X**

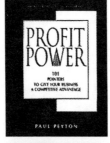

This useful guide discusses techniques for developing a solid foundation on which to build a successful business. Includes many real-world pointers that any business can implement into its day-to-day operations. Contains 30 checklists, evaluations, figures, and charts that will give you the power to drive your business' profits in the right direction.

Profit Power **Pages: 272**
Paperback: $19.95 **ISBN: 1-55571-374-2**

Saves costly consultant or staff hours in creating company personnel policies. Provides over 70 model policies on topics such as employee safety, leave of absence, flex time, smoking, substance abuse, sexual harassment, performance improvement, and grievance procedures. For each subject, practical and legal ramifications are explained and a choice of alternate policies is presented.

Company Policy & Personnel Workbook **Pages: 350**
Paperback: $29.95 **ISBN: 1-55571-365-3**
Binder: $49.95 **ISBN: 1-55571-364-5**

Surviving Success presents a program for those who wish to lead their companies from promising startup to industry dominance. Meet the challenges of business growth and transition with new insights. Learn from success stories. Be prepared to take proactive steps into your company's next growth transition.

Surviving Success **Pages: 230**
Paperback: $19.95 **ISBN: 1-55571-446-3**

ORDER DIRECT FROM THE PUBLISHER

The Oasis Press®

The Leading Publisher of Small Business Information

— 1-800-228-2275 —

[U.S. AND CANADA ONLY]

HOW TO ORDER

Mail:	Send this completed order form and a check, money order or credit card information to: **PSI Research/The Oasis Press®, P.O. Box 3727, Central Point, Oregon 97502-0032**
Fax:	Available 24 hours a day, 7 days a week at **1-541-476-1479**
Email:	**info@psi-research.com** (Please include a phone number, should we need to contact you.)
Web:	Purchase any of our products online at our Website at **http://www.psi-research.com/oasis.htm**

Inquiries and International Orders: Please call **1-541-479-9464**

Indicate the quantity and price of the titles you would like:

4/99

TITLE	ISBN	BINDER	PAPERBACK	QTY.	TOTAL
Advertising Without An Agency	1-55571-429-3		☐ 19.95		
Before You Go Into Business Read This	1-55571-481-1		☐ 17.95		
Bottom Line Basics	1-55571-329-7 (B) ■ 1-55571-330-0 (P)	☐ 39.95	☐ 19.95		
BusinessBasics	1-55571-430-7		☐ 16.95		
The Business Environmental Handbook	1-55571-304-1 (B) ■ 1-55571-163-4 (P)	☐ 39.95	☐ 19.95		
Business Owner's Guide to Accounting and Bookkeeping	1-55571-381-5		☐ 19.95		
businessplan.com	1-55571-455-2		☐ 19.95		
Buyer's Guide to Business Insurance	1-55571-310-6 (B) ■ 1-55571-162-6 (P)	☐ 39.95	☐ 19.95		
California Corporation Formation Package	1-55571-368-8 (B) ■ 1-55571-464-1 (P)	☐ 39.95	☐ 29.95		
Collection Techniques for a Small Business	1-55571-312-2 (B) ■ 1-55571-171-5 (P)	☐ 39.95	☐ 19.95		
College Entrepreneur Handbook	1-55571-503-6		☐ 16.95		
A Company Policy & Personnel Workbook	1-55571-364-5 (B) ■ 1-55571-486-2 (P)	☐ 49.95	☐ 29.95		
Company Relocation Handbook	1-55571-091-3 (B) ■ 1-55571-092-1 (P)	☐ 39.95	☐ 19.95		
CompControl	1-55571-356-4 (B) ■ 1-55571-355-6 (P)	☐ 39.95	☐ 19.95		
Complete Book of Business Forms	1-55571-107-3		☐ 19.95		
Connecting Online	1-55571-403-X		☐ 21.95		
Customer Engineering	1-55571-360-2 (B) ■ 1-55571-359-9 (P)	☐ 39.95	☐ 19.95		
Develop and Market Your Creative Ideas	1-55571-383-1		☐ 15.95		
Developing International Markets	1-55571-433-1		☐ 19.95		
Doing Business in Russia	1-55571-375-0		☐ 19.95		
Draw the Line	1-55571-370-X		☐ 17.95		
The Essential Corporation Handbook	1-55571-342-4		☐ 21.95		
Essential Limited Liability Company Handbook	1-55571-362-9 (B) ■ 1-55571-361-0 (P)	☐ 39.95	☐ 21.95		
Export Now	1-55571-192-8 (B) ■ 1-55571-167-7 (P)	☐ 39.95	☐ 24.95		
Financial Decisionmaking	1-55571-435-8		☐ 19.95		
Financial Management Techniques	1-55571-116-2 (B) ■ 1-55571-124-3 (P)	☐ 39.95	☐ 19.95		
Financing Your Small Business	1-55571-160-X		☐ 19.95		
Franchise Bible	1-55571-366-1 (B) ■ 1-55571-367-X (P)	☐ 39.95	☐ 24.95		
The Franchise Redbook	1-55571-484-6		☐ 34.95		
Friendship Marketing	1-55571-399-8		☐ 18.95		
Funding High-Tech Ventures	1-55571-405-6		☐ 21.95		
Home Business Made Easy	1-55571-428-5		☐ 19.95		
Improving Staff Productivity	1-55571-456-0		☐ 16.95		
Information Breakthrough	1-55571-413-7		☐ 22.95		
Insider's Guide to Small Business Loans	1-55571-488-9		☐ 19.95		
InstaCorp™ Book & Software	1-55571-382-3		☐ 29.95		
Joysticks, Blinking Lights, and Thrills	1-55571-401-3		☐ 18.95		
Keeping Score: An Inside Look at Sports Marketing	1-55571-377-7		☐ 18.95		
Know Your Market	1-55571-341-6 (B) ■ 1-55571-333-5 (P)	☐ 39.95	☐ 19.95		
Leader's Guide: 15 Essential Skills	1-55571-434-X		☐ 19.95		
Legal Expense Defense	1-55571-349-1 (B) ■ 1-55571-348-3 (P)	☐ 39.95	☐ 19.95		
Legal Road Map for Consultants	1-55571-460-9		☐ 18.95		
Location, Location, Location	1-55571-376-9		☐ 19.95		
Mail Order Legal Guide	1-55571-193-6 (B) ■ 1-55571-190-1 (P)	☐ 45.00	☐ 29.95		
Managing People: A Practical Guide	1-55571-380-7		☐ 21.95		
Marketing for the New Millennium	1-55571-432-3		☐ 19.95		
Marketing Mastery	1-55571-358-0 (B) ■ 1-55571-357-2 (P)	☐ 39.95	☐ 19.95		
Money Connection	1-55571-352-1 (B) ■ 1-55571-351-3 (P)	☐ 39.95	☐ 24.95		
Moonlighting: Earning a Second Income at Home	1-55571-406-4		☐ 15.95		
Navigating the Marketplace: Growth Strategies for Small Business	1-55571-458-7		☐ 21.95		
No Money Down Financing for Franchising	1-55571-462-5		☐ 19.95		
Not Another Meeting!	1-55571-480-3		☐ 17.95		
People-Centered Profit Strategies	1-55571-517-6		☐ 18.95		

Sub-total for this side:

TITLE	ISBN		BINDER	PAPERBACK	QTY.	TOTAL
People Investment	1-55571-187-1 (B) ■ 1-55571-161-8 (P)		☐ 39.95	☐ 19.95		
Power Marketing for Small Business	1-55571-303-3 (B) ■ 1-55571-166-9 (P)		☐ 39.95	☐ 19.95		
Proposal Development	1-55571-067-0 (B) ■ 1-55571-431-5 (P)		☐ 39.95	☐ 21.95		
Prospecting for Gold	1-55571-483-8			☐ 14.95		
Public Relations Marketing	1-55571-459-5			☐ 19.95		
Raising Capital	1-55571-306-8 (B) ■ 1-55571-305-X (P)		☐ 39.95	☐ 19.95		
Renaissance 2000	1-55571-412-9			☐ 22.95		
Retail in Detail	1-55571-371-8			☐ 15.95		
The Rule Book of Business Plans for Startups	1-55571-519-2			☐ 18.95		
Secrets of High Ticket Selling	1-55571-436-6			☐ 19.95		
Secrets to Buying and Selling a Business	1-55571-489-7			☐ 24.95		
Secure Your Future	1-55571-335-1			☐ 19.95		
Selling Services	1-55571-461-7			☐ 18.95		
SmartStart Your (State) Business	varies per state			☐ 19.95		
Indicate which state you prefer:						
Small Business Insider's Guide to Bankers	1-55571-400-5			☐ 18.95		
Smile Training Isn't Enough	1-55571-422-6			☐ 19.95		
Start Your Business	1-55571-485-4			☐ 10.95		
Strategic Management for Small and Growing Firms	1-55571-465-X			☐ 24.95		
Successful Network Marketing	1-55571-350-5			☐ 15.95		
Surviving Success	1-55571-446-3			☐ 19.95		
TargetSmart!	1-55571-384-X			☐ 19.95		
Top Tax Saving Ideas for Today's Small Business	1-55571-463-3			☐ 16.95		
Truth About Teams	1-55571-482-X			☐ 18.95		
Twenty-One Sales in a Sale	1-55571-448-X			☐ 19.95		
WebWise	1-55571-501-X (B) ■ 1-55571-479-X (P)		☐ 29.95	☐ 19.95		
What's It Worth?	1-55571-504-4			☐ 22.95		
Which Business?	1-55571-390-4			☐ 18.95		
Write Your Own Business Contracts	1-55571-196-0 (B) ■ 1-55571-170-7 (P)		☐ 39.95	☐ 24.95		

Success Series	ISBN		PAPERBACK	QTY.	TOTAL
50 Ways to Get Promoted	1-55571-506-0		☐ 10.95		
You Can't Go Wrong By Doing It Right	1-55571-490-0		☐ 14.95		

Oasis Software	FORMAT	BINDER	PAPERBACK	QTY.	TOTAL
Company Policy Text Files	CD-ROM ☐		☐ 49.95		
Company Policy Text Files Book & Disk Package	CD-ROM ☐	☐ 89.95 (B)	☐ 69.95 (P)		
Financial Management Techniques Standalone	Floppy Disks ☐		☐ 99.95		
Financial Management Techniques Book & Disk Package	Floppy Disks ☐	☐ 129.95(B)	☐ 119.95 (P)		
Insurance Assistant	Floppy Disks ☐		☐ 29.95		
Insurance Assistant & Buyer's Guide to Business Insurance	Floppy Disks ☐	☐ 59.95 (B)	☐ 39.95 (P)		
Winning Business Plans in Color CD-ROM	CD-ROM ☐		☐ 59.95		

Ordered by: *Please give street address*

NAME _____ TITLE _____

COMPANY _____

STREET ADDRESS _____

CITY _____ STATE _____ ZIP _____

DAYTIME PHONE _____ EMAIL _____

Ship to: *If different than above*

NAME _____ TITLE _____

COMPANY _____

STREET ADDRESS _____

CITY _____ STATE _____ ZIP _____

DAYTIME PHONE _____

Shipping:

YOUR ORDER IS:	ADD:
0-25	5.00
25.01-50	6.00
50.01-100	7.00
100.01-175	9.00
175.01-250	13.00
250.01-500	18.00
500.01+	4% of total

Subtotal from other side	
Subtotal from this side	
Shipping	
TOTAL	

PLEASE CALL FOR RUSH SERVICE OPTIONS.
INTERNATIONAL ORDERS, PLEASE CALL FOR A QUOTE ON CURRENT SHIPPING RATES.

Payment Method:

☐ CHECK   ☐ MONEY ORDER
☐ AMERICAN EXPRESS   ☐ DISCOVER
☐ MASTERCARD   ☐ VISA

CREDIT CARD NUMBER

EXPIRATION (MM/YY)   NAME ON CARD (PLEASE PRINT)

SIGNATURE OF CARDHOLDER (REQUIRED)

Fax this order form to: (541) 476-1479 or mail it to: P.O. Box 3727, Central Point, Oregon 97502
For more information about our products or to order online, visit http://www.psi-research.com

OASIS PRESS
BOOKS & SOFTWARE